Distributed in the United States of America by
Sterling Publishing Co., Inc.
387 Park Avenue South
New York
NY 10016-8810

ISBN 0-304-35903-3

Translated by Jane Moseley
Proofread by Nikki Sims

Cassell & Co
Orion House
5 Upper Saint Martin's Lane
London WC2H 9EA

THE DREAM CATALOG

A revolutionary, new, illustrated directory of the most beautiful, stylish and amazing objects available on the Internet

CASSELL&CO

South Africa

Germany

Argentina

Australia

Austria

Belgium

Brazil

Canada

China

Korea

Denmark

United Arab Emirates

Spain

USA

Finland

France

Great Britain

Greece

India

Indonesia

Ireland

The Dream Catalog: its concept and realisation

The twenty-first century is upon us, having brought with it new ways of consumer thinking and practices. It heralds enormous enthusiasm for designer items, and in particular for design magazines and books that act as showcases of international products. We now put art forms on our shopping (and wish) lists, disguised as everyday objects. It seems we are unable to resist today's unusual items, such as crocodile-shaped pegs or camera watches, falling in the same way as their creators did for colours and shapes, new materials or the latest technology. Our dreams have turned into realities. There is also a sense of frivolity in the air, with polka-dot iMacs and CD-holders in the form of the Empire State Building no longer reserved for children.

shopping for dreams...

A gap in the world of contemporary design and shopping appeared to open up. The concept was born of a catalog that could act as an inventory of thousands of dream objects for sale throughout the world. Each item would be accompanied by its relevant website, allowing direct contact with the designers and manufacturers and the galaxy of other dream items on offer. Consumer browsing is no longer an activity limited to shops or catalogs – it has also become a virtual experience and one that we embrace more and more enthusiastically. *The Dream Catalog* succeeds in combining all these possibilities by offering a world of design classics and innovations that can be admired, explored and put in a virtual or real shopping basket. The question is how to define a 'dream object'? The answer comes in four parts:

THE MYTH – Jacuzzi, Zippo, Alessi and Conran – names so famous, they are almost commonplace. You'll find them in the selection alongside more unexpected designers and objects, including tree houses, submarines, trampolines, night vision binoculars and huge screens. Such items are at the frontier of collective imagination and economic reality, having successfully combined conceptual skill with solid commercial application. It is the aim of this book to reveal both the concept behind the design object and the world of which it forms a part. To use a visual metaphor, *The Dream Catalog* makes public the secret location of the hidden treasure on the designer island.

THE SELECTION AND THE DESIGN – *The Dream Catalog* highlights those practitioners who work their extraordinary magic on such daily items as sponges, lampshades, toothbrushes or soap holders. Philippe Starck, Marc Newson and others are engaged in the visual war against the banal and the ordinary. Key to the selection are the humorous, sensual, unexpected objects that are expressive and bold in both their concept and execution and their exploration of the boundaries, pushing back the envelope of design.

THE TECHNOLOGY – The focus is often on the latest materials used in the 21st-century design of such varied items as hi-fis, golf clubs, fishing equipment or aviation and car construction. Investigative research was conducted in hot-off-the-press technology to whet the appetite for futuristic and high-tech dreams. Even prototypes are included, in order to make embryonic dreaming part of the book's function. Most of the items are dreams you can realise today.

THE UNEXPECTED – We have gone in search of the unusual so that dreams can be expanded into unanticipated areas. The surprises in store include an eight-person tandem, a lie-detecting telephone, fancy dress for fridges and a garden chair over which your garden grows. However, the selection is based firmly around those items that have travelled the long road to bring together successfully both imaginative genius and commercial reality.

...on the Internet

The Internet is integral to the concept and function of *The Dream Catalog* , a global public platform on which you can encounter talent and exchange information. Over 50,000 website pages were visited in the research, more than 5,000 sites investigated and nearly 3,000 finally selected (with thousands more to come in future volumes). Researchers enjoyed being web-surfers, making unanticipated but logical connections that uncovered windsurfs during a search for torches. They played web detectives by following the tracks left by a manufacturer at the other end of the world with just a reference or name. They indulged in a strategy of web-exploring by exhaustive use of links and web-Russian-Roulette, using search engines to key in unusual combinations in various languages (with fingers crossed on the keyboard). 'Inflatable guitar' and 'floating city' seemed unlikely combinations but revealed wonderful results. In the real world shops and magazines were scoured, professionals interviewed and trade fairs visited. It took a year to check out all the latest, most fashionable designer items.

Designers, architects, engineers and craftspeople were united by a deep and incontrovertible faith in their products, often the result of long years of research. Their enthusiasm was infectious and integral to the execution of the aim of *The Dream Catalog* – to touch and communicate a passion for design dreams. Prices have not been included. They are available on most of the websites but their omission is deliberate since *The Dream Catalog* is not strictly a consumer guide, but rather a catalog of temptation that flirts with the readers' imagination and their wish lists.

The dream exists. It's here, just a mouse click away...

RAPHAËLE VIDALING

Warning: any changes to website addresses are not the responsibility of the publisher or the manufacturers. No guarantee is made of the availability of any products shown in *The Dream Catalog*. Not all websites contain products that you can purchase on-line – some websites are showcases only.

 Iceland

 Israel

 Italy

 Japan

 Lebanon

 Morocco

 Norway

 New Zealand

 The Netherlands

 Portugal

 Czech Republic

 Russian Federation

 Singapore

 Slovenia

 Sweden

 Switzerland

 Syria

 Taiwan

 Thailand

 Tunisia

 Ukraine

 Vietnam

in the home

contents

kitchen equipment

in the bathroom

fashion & beauty

sports &

sporting activities

high-tech

leisure

transport

holidays & hobbies

❶

www.bartprince.com

BART PRINCE: is an unpredictable architect, willing to execute even the most extravagant commissions from his clients on the condition they are in harmony with their environment. This house is an interplay of curves and levels.

❷

www.architecteurs.com

FLAGSHIP: one of the innovative concepts proposed by Architecteurs, a group of architects and builders whose private commissions let the imagination run free.

❸

www.zdomes.com

Z DOMES: a round house designed by Jonathan Zimmerman, based on an inflatable structure covered in concrete.

❹

chrhabitat@wanadoo.fr

ANTTI LOVAG is an innovative architect who designs circular homes perfect for meditation. These are the headquarters of Homme et Habitat, made with a veil of concrete. The dining room is semi-circular and opens on to the terrace.

❺

www.oshatz.com

ROBERT OSHATZ'S mission is 'to capture the spirit of a place and translate it into architectural poetry.' His commissioned homes hover between dream and reality.
• MOUNT CRESTED BUTTE (USA)
• MIYASAKA RESIDENCE (JAPAN)

❶
www.nextgenreforestation.com/
freespiritspheres

FREE SPIRIT SPHERES: wooden spheres, 2.7m in diameter, make perfect 'tree bedrooms'. A spiral staircase takes you to your dreams.

❷
www.treehouseworkshop.com

TREEHOUSE WORKSHOP: this team of carpenters specialises in tree-houses. After seeing the environment, they design the project and deliver the house in kit form or already constructed.

❸
www.hometown.aol.com/
sunsenergy

SOLAR POWERED: north-facing it's an ordinary house. South-facing, its roof is made entirely of solar panels, generating enough electricity to heat and power the whole house.

❹
www.darblaywood.com

JÉRÔME DARBLAY is a French architect specialising in commissions for wooden homes in American or Asian styles in harmony with the environment.

❺
www.oshatz.com

GIBSON BOATHOUSE: a waterside home, complete with boathouse, built into the side of the hill under the road.

❻
www.peartreehouse.com

PEAR TREE: this Scottish company builds treehouses that make great huts for children and homes for adults, complete with hot water, electricity and creature comforts. The high life for tree dwellers.

www.kingdomes.com

HELLA DOME: a glass dome (7m in diameter) that covers the house like an enormous verandah with an indoor garden. It originates in Iceland and ensures that the house is kept warm for eight months of the year. Insulation on the outside.

www.skypadtech.com

NEW MILLENIUM SKY HOME: this is a new concept in family-size private skyscrapers, with between three and eight storeys. It has a panoramic view, circular terraces, roof pool or helicopter pad and a fully automated interior.

🇺🇸 www.domespace.com

DOMESPACE: this revolving home, in the shape of a flying saucer, can be moved around according to the seasons by just two adults. Made entirely of wood, it's a warm, peaceful and spacious environment.

🇺🇸 www.ussubs.com

SEAROOM RESIDENCE: floating house and hotel designed by a submarine architect. The bedroom and bathroom are below sea level and surrounded by fish, drawn to the panoramic windows by automatic feeders.

🇺🇸 www.freedomship.com

FREEDOM SHIP: this is the world's longest vessel (1.5km). Destined to travel constantly, taking two years to sail around the world and spending 70 per cent of the time in ports of call en route. It's a floating city, complete with school, tram, hospital, library, airport, green spaces, cinemas and theatres. It contains 70,000 apartments of various sizes and 4,000 businesses. Where do you call home?

www.neotu.com

CORBEILLE by Garouste and Bonetti: curl up and dream in luxury.

www.cassina.it

LC2: Le Corbusier's famous chair, first produced in 1928, remains one of the most successful designer chairs ever.

www.n-udesign.com

AIR: part chair, part sculpture by Nathalie Auzépy.

www.chairs-designs.co.uk

MEZMER: a very feminine and frilly chair designed by a firm that specialises in creative seating.

www.edra.com

TATLIN: inspired by the tower in Ukraine by the same name, this spiral sofa is causing red revolutions of its own.

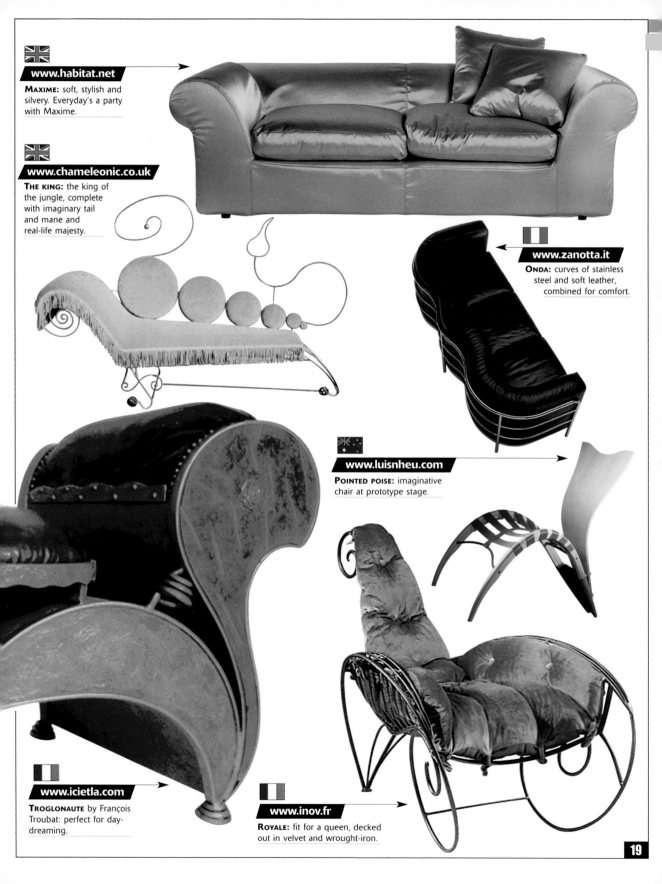

🇬🇧 **www.habitat.net**

MAXIME: soft, stylish and silvery. Everyday's a party with Maxime.

🇬🇧 **www.chameleonic.co.uk**

THE KING: the king of the jungle, complete with imaginary tail and mane and real-life majesty.

🇮🇹 **www.zanotta.it**

ONDA: curves of stainless steel and soft leather, combined for comfort.

🇦🇺 **www.luisnheu.com**

POINTED POISE: imaginative chair at prototype stage.

🇫🇷 **www.icietla.com**

TROGLONAUTE by François Troubat: perfect for day-dreaming.

🇫🇷 **www.inov.fr**

ROYALE: fit for a queen, decked out in velvet and wrought-iron.

19

www.edra.com

FLAP: a flexible sofa with six different ways to recline.

www.leijn.com

COCOON: a one-piece prototype couch.

www.antidiva.it

MICAMA: a string of cushions to unfold or fold at leisure.

www.giovannetti-collezioni.it

VIRAGES: enjoy sitting on a cloud.

www.leolux.com

BALOU: with adjustable seat back operated by its 'tail'.

www.desede.ch

BOXING GLOVE: a great way to relax after taking life on the chin.

www.studio65.com

MIKEY: a sofa that reminds you of a mushroom, manufactured since 1972.

www.studio65.com

ENDLESS SOFA: straight, concave or convex, Chiocciola, Chiocciolin or Chiocciolout, make up the three elements of this kit couch.

www.neotu.com

MASSAÏ: a low chair in which to curl up, designed by Kristian Gavoille.

www.neotu.com

ZOID by Dan Friedman: a comfortable island that can float in the middle of a room.

www.ennemlaghi.com

X-RAY CHAIR: 224 springs assembled by hand are revealed through the translucent cover.

www.cinna.fr

CÂLIN: as cuddly as a pillow, the creation of Pascal Mourgue.

www.roombywellis.com

KORA: meridienne disguised as a bed with the help of a giant pillow, designed by TEAM at WelliS.

www.norellmobel.se

PILOT: designed for spacious comfort in soft leather.

www.le-webstore.com

MOBY CHAIR: the chair took over the mind of its designer, Ashley Hall, just as Moby Dick took over the captain's psyche - hence its name.

www.styling.it

NEW YORK: a seat designed by K.L. Heitlinger in the style of its namesake – in blocks and strategic lines.

www.roombywellis.com

DEA: a revolving chair with relaxing headrest from TEAM by WelliS.

www.promemoria.com

MARELLA: the difference is in the detail – a handle made smooth by a million caresses.

www.artifort.com

CHAISE LONGUE: a restful sculpture by Pierre Paulin and Geoffrey Harcourt, covered in a stretch wool fabric.

www.livingdivani.it

BALESTRO: straight-talking seats with cushions.

www.ap-art.fr

CARDBOARD CHAIR: designed in a light yet robust (and biodegradable) material.

www.cappellini.it

WOOD CHAIR: designed by Marc Newson for Cappellini.

www.glamorous-co.jp

OZABU: Chinese tradition revisited by two young Japanese designers.

www.twentytwentyone.com

KEEP AFLOAT on this raft-sofa with six leather tubes by William Plunkett.

www.kallemo.se

LEATHER WAVE: lined and studded, this undulating chaise longue is just perfect for laid-back meditative moments.

www.jlgott.co.uk

PERFECT POISE: James Gott's chair adapts to the weight of your body.

steel_fbdesign@hotmail.com

STEELY SLUMBER: Frédéric Butz's designs all have a feel of 1960s science-fiction about them. This steel chaise longue is no exception.

www.rondel.co.nz

SENSUAL AND SLENDER: this design stretches the concept of the chaise longue to its limits.

www.lloydloom.com

THE LOOM CHAIR is unmistakable with its delicate texture and sil-houette. A classic design in twisted paper.

www.porada.it

MADE OF WOOD: designed by T. Colzani, this daybed can massage your back when uncovered or soothe it when equipped with a small mattress.

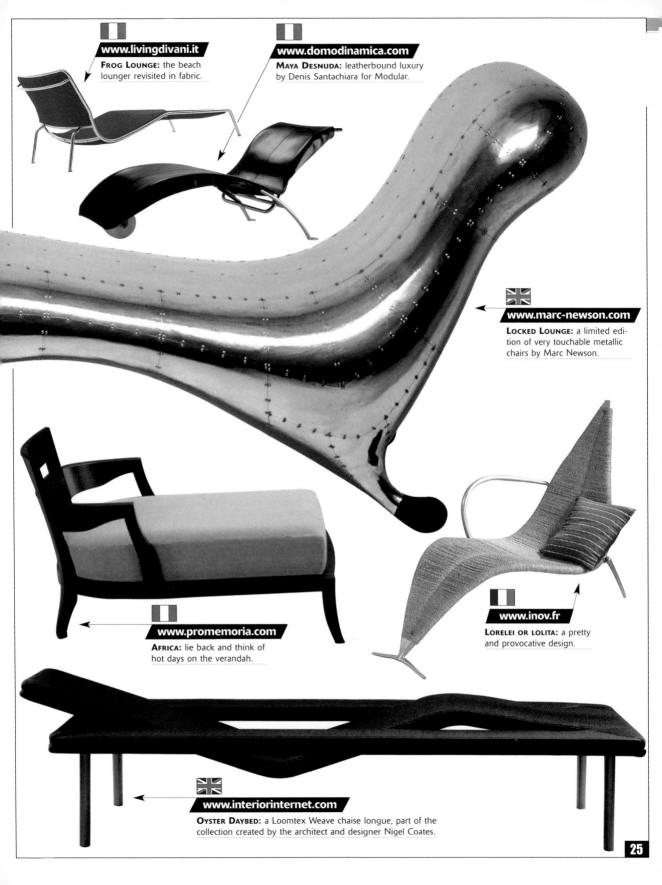

www.livingdivani.it

FROG LOUNGE: the beach lounger revisited in fabric.

www.domodinamica.com

MAYA DESNUDA: leatherbound luxury by Denis Santachiara for Modular.

www.marc-newson.com

LOCKED LOUNGE: a limited edition of very touchable metallic chairs by Marc Newson.

www.promemoria.com

AFRICA: lie back and think of hot days on the verandah.

www.inov.fr

LORELEI OR LOLITA: a pretty and provocative design.

www.interiorinternet.com

OYSTER DAYBED: a Loomtex Weave chaise longue, part of the collection created by the architect and designer Nigel Coates.

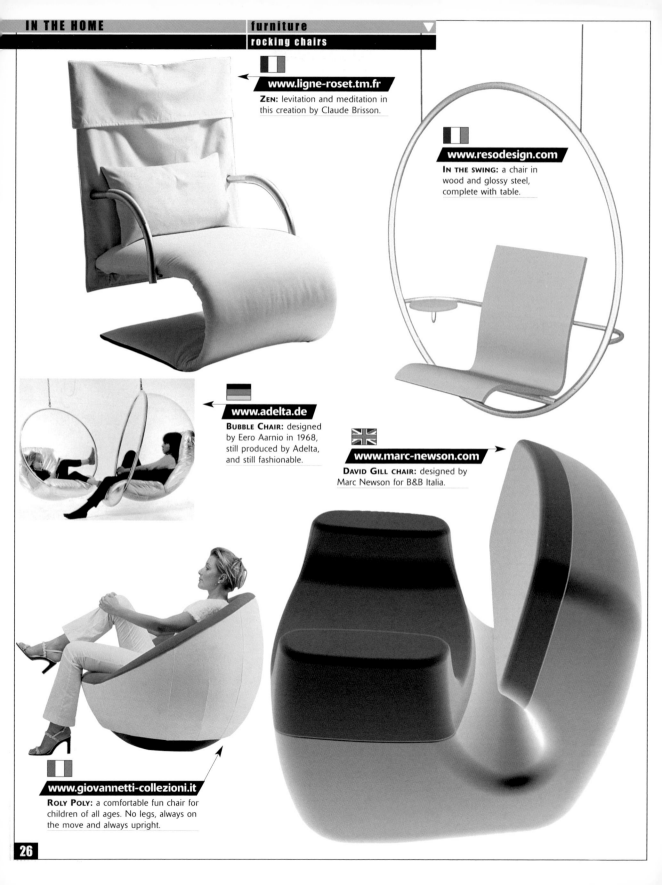

www.ligne-roset.tm.fr

ZEN: levitation and meditation in this creation by Claude Brisson.

www.resodesign.com

IN THE SWING: a chair in wood and glossy steel, complete with table.

www.adelta.de

BUBBLE CHAIR: designed by Eero Aarnio in 1968, still produced by Adelta, and still fashionable.

www.marc-newson.com

DAVID GILL CHAIR: designed by Marc Newson for B&B Italia.

www.giovannetti-collezioni.it

ROLY POLY: a comfortable fun chair for children of all ages. No legs, always on the move and always upright.

www.yamakado.com

YAM: a union of French and Japanese design and of yin and yang. One of the first creations by the Yamakados.

www.adelta.de

FORMULA: the creation of Eero Aarnio, who was inspired by racing car design.

www.formforu.com

ERO: Boris Marton's chair contains a metal rod that maintains its balance and its shape. Furniture with functionality.

www.stokke.com

GRAVITY: a stylish recliner in maple wood, from the selection of chairs designed by Stokke, a company founded in 1932.

www.rolf-benz.de

SWIVEL IN STYLE: recline, revolve and relax in this chair, complete with matching pouffe.

www.interprofil.de

SHAKE: designed by Wolfgang Mezger, this chair can turn 180 degrees due to its system of ball bearings.

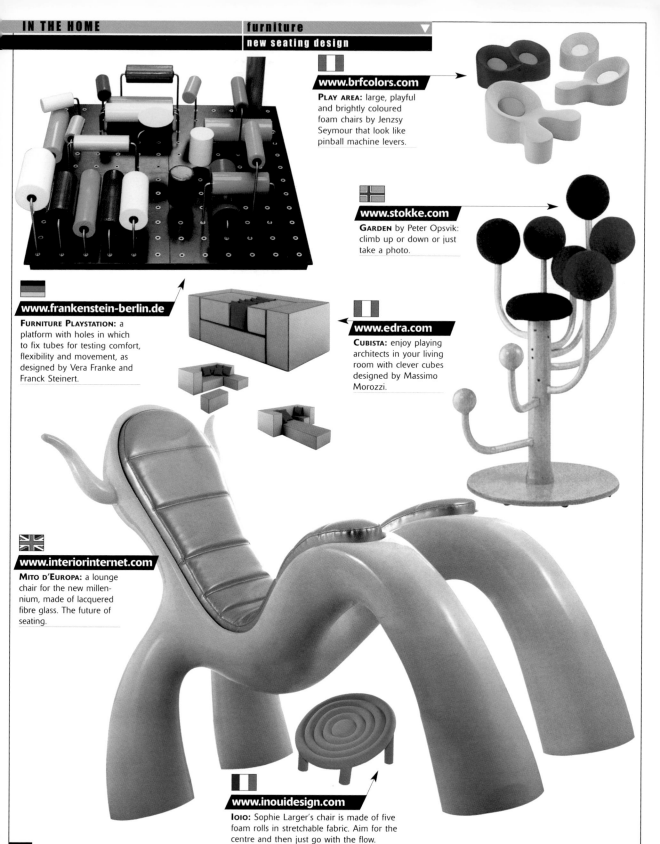

www.brfcolors.com

PLAY AREA: large, playful and brightly coloured foam chairs by Jenzsy Seymour that look like pinball machine levers.

www.stokke.com

GARDEN by Peter Opsvik: climb up or down or just take a photo.

www.frankenstein-berlin.de

FURNITURE PLAYSTATION: a platform with holes in which to fix tubes for testing comfort, flexibility and movement, as designed by Vera Franke and Franck Steinert.

www.edra.com

CUBISTA: enjoy playing architects in your living room with clever cubes designed by Massimo Morozzi.

www.interiorinternet.com

MITO D'EUROPA: a lounge chair for the new millennium, made of lacquered fibre glass. The future of seating.

www.inouidesign.com

IOIO: Sophie Larger's chair is made of five foam rolls in stretchable fabric. Aim for the centre and then just go with the flow.

www.stokke.com

EKSTREM: an accomplished sculpture but also a great chair, loved by all the kids. Designed by Terje Ekstrom.

www.multimania.com/gabuzo

KNOT OF MŒBIUS: two slabs of stainless steel anchor this foam rubber arabesque, the inspiration of the young designer Manon Legros.

www.edra.com

PASSEPARTOUT: mounted on wheels, this chaise longue has a metallic structure and polyurethane padding. It is a vertical rather than horizontal seating area. Change the way you sit and think.

www.edra.com

MONSTER: a moulded fibre-glass structure with padded cushions that looks like a creature from science-fiction. Designed for the 21st-century home.

www.n-udesign.com

'M' IS FOR MAGNET: position the magnetic cushions in exactly the right place for you on this design by Nathalie Auzepy and François Leduc.

www.edra.com

HEIMWEH: Sven-Anvar Bibi, Mark Gutjahr and Jörg Zimmermann drew inspiration from the seventies in the design of this retro and relaxing polyurethane and rosewood cube.

www.studioball.co.uk

DE RARUM NATURA: bring the Garden of Eden home.

www.cattelanitalia.com

FIORDALISO: four frosted-glass petals cluster around a bowl of fruit – a floral composition from the Kronos studio.

www.antidiva.it

MARGY: hover like a butterfly in Marco Minotti's white petals.

www.aquagallery.com

MINIPURPLE: a pouffe made of a bouquet of velvet flowers.

www.edra.com

SOSHUN, FORTUNA, GETSUEN AND ANTHURIUM: three seats and a small table inspired by Nature's own designs.

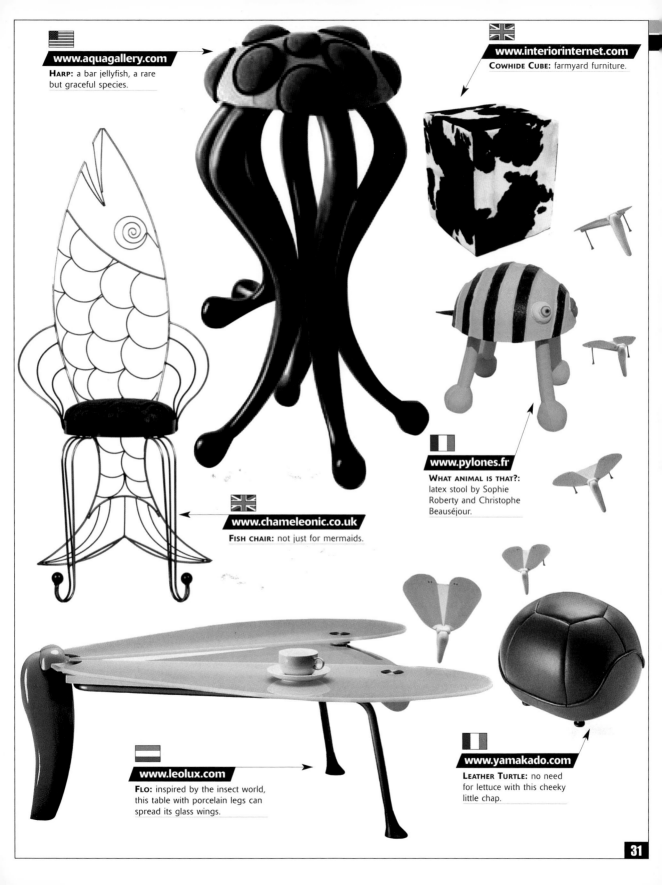

www.aquagallery.com

HARP: a bar jellyfish, a rare but graceful species.

www.interiorinternet.com

COWHIDE CUBE: farmyard furniture.

www.chameleonic.co.uk

FISH CHAIR: not just for mermaids.

www.pylones.fr

WHAT ANIMAL IS THAT?: latex stool by Sophie Roberty and Christophe Beauséjour.

www.leolux.com

FLO: inspired by the insect world, this table with porcelain legs can spread its glass wings.

www.yamakado.com

LEATHER TURTLE: no need for lettuce with this cheeky little chap.

www.spacespice.com

SPACE POUFFES: small seats for small people or a low table for their larger parents. This collection comes from a new company inspired by the seventies.

www.soca.fr

DÉDÉ CAÏXO: make an impression on Kristian Gavoille's bar stool.

www.squeezedesign.com

ON THE REBOUND: a design that makes an interesting centrepiece as a table or pouffe.

www.interiorinternet.com

AN ELEGANT FOOTREST that draws inspiration for its design from Italianate theatre furniture.

www.planetdesign.nl

B-HOME: a pastel-coloured chrome stool that makes a perfect hiding place for those secret treasures.

www.zanotta.it

PRIMATE: Achille Castiglioni's kneeling stool, designed in 1970, can still hold its own in contemporary interiors.

www.studiofusion.co.uk

FLIP: a soft pouffe with a hard centre on which to work, eat or play. Enjoy a spot of low living.

www.allermuir.co.uk

WAVE by Carsten Schmidt and Jens Bredsdorff: three wooden waves on a metal base.

www.leolux.com

VOLARE: a curvaceous foo-trest designed by Jan Armgardt for real relaxation.

www.dmd-products.com

TABLE + STOOL = armchair. An equation put together by Richard Hutten for Droog Design.

www.creativando.nu

POPDISC: a pouffe/coffee table covered in plastic and decorated with Keith Haring's celebrated motifs.

www.heribrauner.de

HOCKER: designed for those people who hanker for the days when porters took the load off their feet.

www.ligne-roset.com

GLÜP by Sophie Larger: pouffes filled with polystyrene balls and topped with a stretch fabric that moulds itself to every inch of your body while remaining firm and supportive.

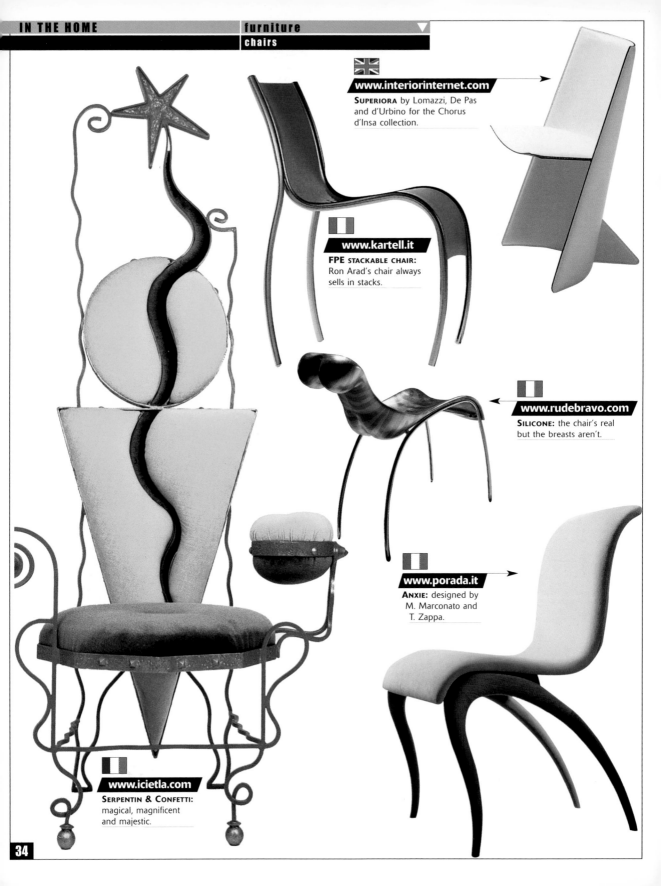

www.interiorinternet.com

SUPERIORA by Lomazzi, De Pas and d'Urbino for the Chorus d'Insa collection.

www.kartell.it

FPE STACKABLE CHAIR: Ron Arad's chair always sells in stacks.

www.rudebravo.com

SILICONE: the chair's real but the breasts aren't.

www.porada.it

ANXIE: designed by M. Marconato and T. Zappa.

www.icietla.com

SERPENTIN & CONFETTI: magical, magnificent and majestic.

www.marc-newson.com

COAST CHAIR: designed by Marc Newson for Magis.

www.edra.com

AZUL by Fernando and Humberto Campana: a steel structure, covered in a maze of intertwined green ropes.

www.interiorinternet.com

MUSICAL CHAIR: make a note of this silver beech design.

www.rondel.co.nz

PEANUT: attractive aluminium filigree .

www.pwlimited.co.uk

SPINAL CHAIR: the backbone of Johnny Hawkes's design.

www.kartell.it

LA MARIE: Philippe Starck's celebrated transparent chair.

www.studio65.com

REMINISCENCE: one of four chairs in a collection based on the work of Miró (prototype).

Ese: integral table legs with an unusual twist.

www.bebitalia.it

Io: Marc Newson's design focuses on the cable running around the table's outer edge. The interchangeable components are held together and in place by tensioned cord.

www.protis.fr

Manon: a glass top and aluminium support in the shape of a butterfly, designed by Bernard Dequet.

www.kreo.fr

Bleu: Dominique Mathieu's clever concept for Kréo incorporates a stool in its lacquered steel table design.

www.loydloom.com

Loom table: the traditional loom weave is combined with a stylish design by Ross Lovegrove.

www.promemoria.com

Battista: a leather-covered folding table.

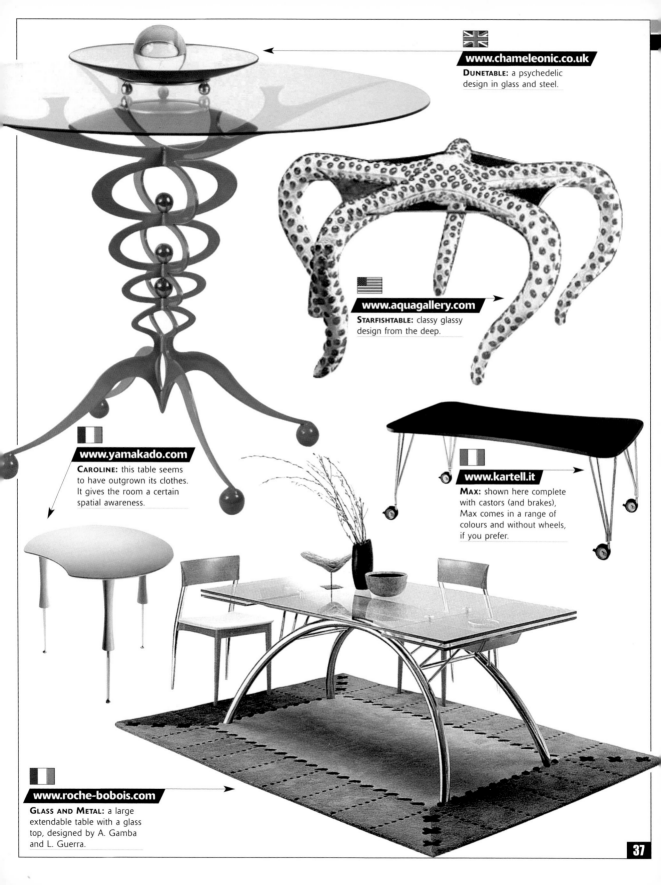

www.chameleonic.co.uk

DUNETABLE: a psychedelic design in glass and steel.

www.aquagallery.com

STARFISHTABLE: classy glassy design from the deep.

www.yamakado.com

CAROLINE: this table seems to have outgrown its clothes. It gives the room a certain spatial awareness.

www.kartell.it

MAX: shown here complete with castors (and brakes), Max comes in a range of colours and without wheels, if you prefer.

www.roche-bobois.com

GLASS AND METAL: a large extendable table with a glass top, designed by A. Gamba and L. Guerra.

37

www.cinna.fr

MÉDUSA: three tables intertwined.

www.interiorinternet.com

VENTOGLIO: a revolving double oval table covered in goatskin.

www.rondel.co.nz

TABLE CLOTH: a metal cloth turned table.

www.studiofusion.co.uk

LUCATAB: table complete with lamp and magazine rack. The 12-volt current runs through the table.

www.roche-bobois.com

IDEOGRAM: a single piece of wood that forms a table and shelves in a calligraphic shape.

www.pagedeco.com

MEMORY OF THE BEACH: Bleu Nature specialises in driftwood designs.

www.porada.it

POLIPHILO: a pedestal table with lamp designed by G. Mapelli and P. Pasassarino.

www.tohubohu.com

TIDY TABLE: an occasional table in steel and rattan, with a selection of useful pockets.

www.porada.it

ROMÉO AND JULIETTE: T. Colzani's design is intimate and inseparable.

www.artistavisitatore.it

DILETTO: this reading table has practical bicycle paniers.

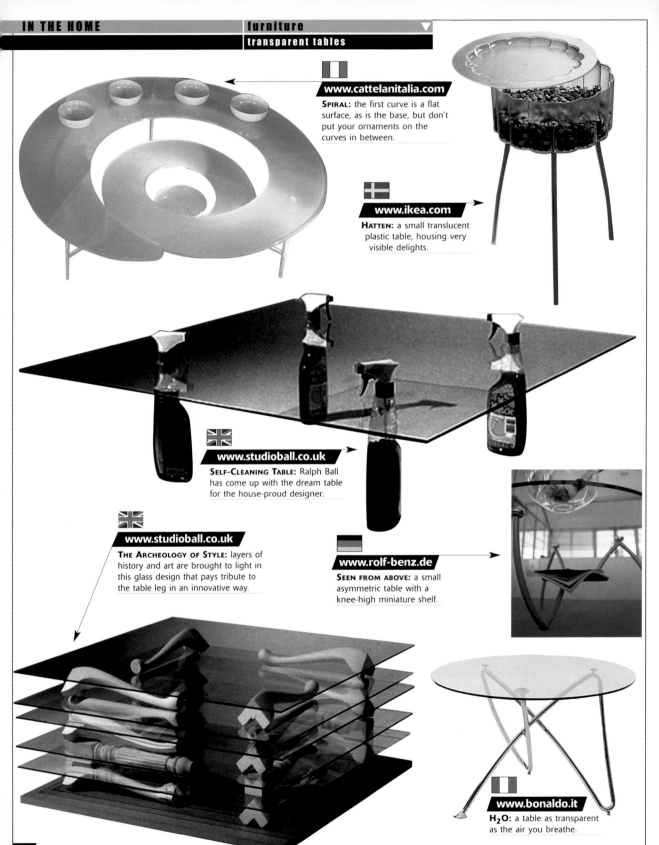

www.cattelanitalia.com

SPIRAL: the first curve is a flat surface, as is the base, but don't put your ornaments on the curves in between.

www.ikea.com

HATTEN: a small translucent plastic table, housing very visible delights.

www.studioball.co.uk

SELF-CLEANING TABLE: Ralph Ball has come up with the dream table for the house-proud designer.

www.studioball.co.uk

THE ARCHEOLOGY OF STYLE: layers of history and art are brought to light in this glass design that pays tribute to the table leg in an innovative way.

www.rolf-benz.de

SEEN FROM ABOVE: a small asymmetric table with a knee-high miniature shelf.

www.bonaldo.it

H$_2$O: a table as transparent as the air you breathe.

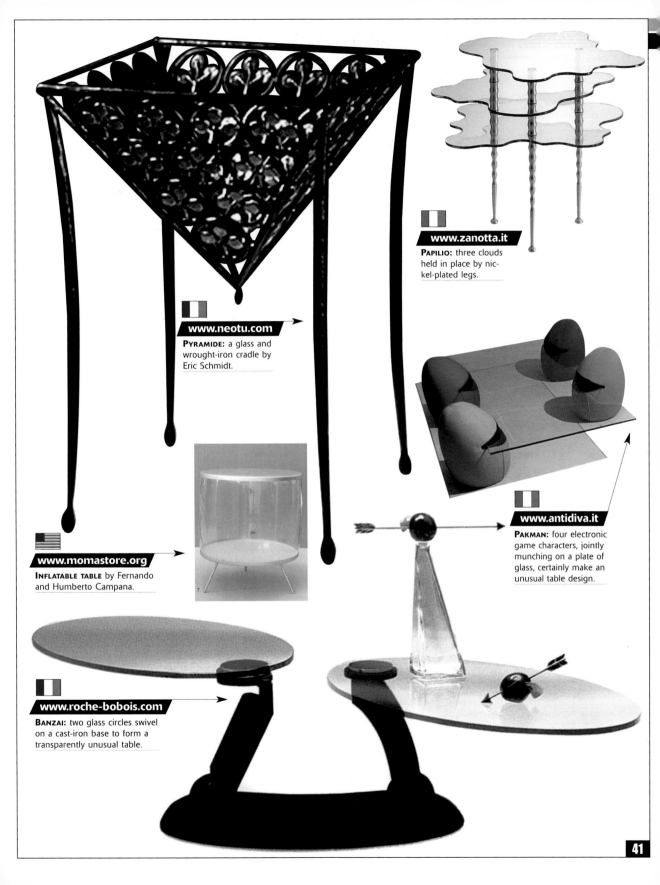

www.zanotta.it

PAPILIO: three clouds held in place by nickel-plated legs.

www.neotu.com

PYRAMIDE: a glass and wrought-iron cradle by Eric Schmidt.

www.antidiva.it

PAKMAN: four electronic game characters, jointly munching on a plate of glass, certainly make an unusual table design.

www.momastore.org

INFLATABLE TABLE by Fernando and Humberto Campana.

www.roche-bobois.com

BANZAI: two glass circles swivel on a cast-iron base to form a transparently unusual table.

41

www.interiorinternet.com

ALUMINIUM TALL BOY: gloss, height and capacity – all the attributes its name suggests.

www.rolf-benz.de

VITRINE: nine small windows of frosted glass, each with its own compartment in which to display or store trinkets.

www.bernini.it

COMBI-CENTER: a tower that combines several different storage options. The height of design.

www.brfcolors.com

BANG-BANG: a hanging wardrobe topped with a convex mirror, designed by Massimo Iosa Ghini.

www.neotu.com

SILVER CABINET by Garouste and Bonetti.

www.alsi-design.com

RODINAH JOY: you'll find this and more on the website for e-tail designers.

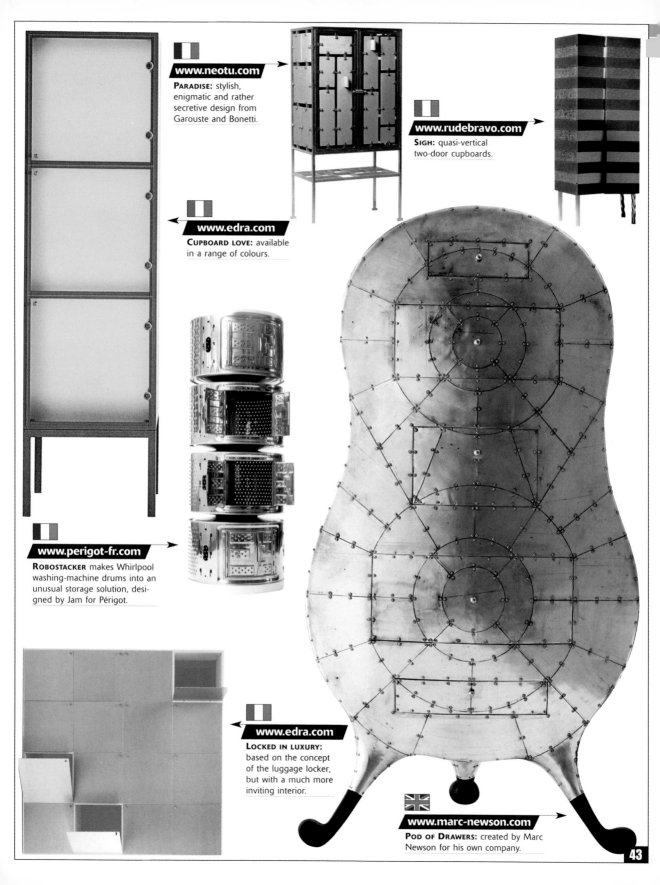

www.neotu.com

PARADISE: stylish, enigmatic and rather secretive design from Garouste and Bonetti.

www.rudebravo.com

SIGH: quasi-vertical two-door cupboards.

www.edra.com

CUPBOARD LOVE: available in a range of colours.

www.perigot-fr.com

ROBOSTACKER makes Whirlpool washing-machine drums into an unusual storage solution, designed by Jam for Périgot.

www.edra.com

LOCKED IN LUXURY: based on the concept of the luggage locker, but with a much more inviting interior.

www.marc-newson.com

POD OF DRAWERS: created by Marc Newson for his own company.

43

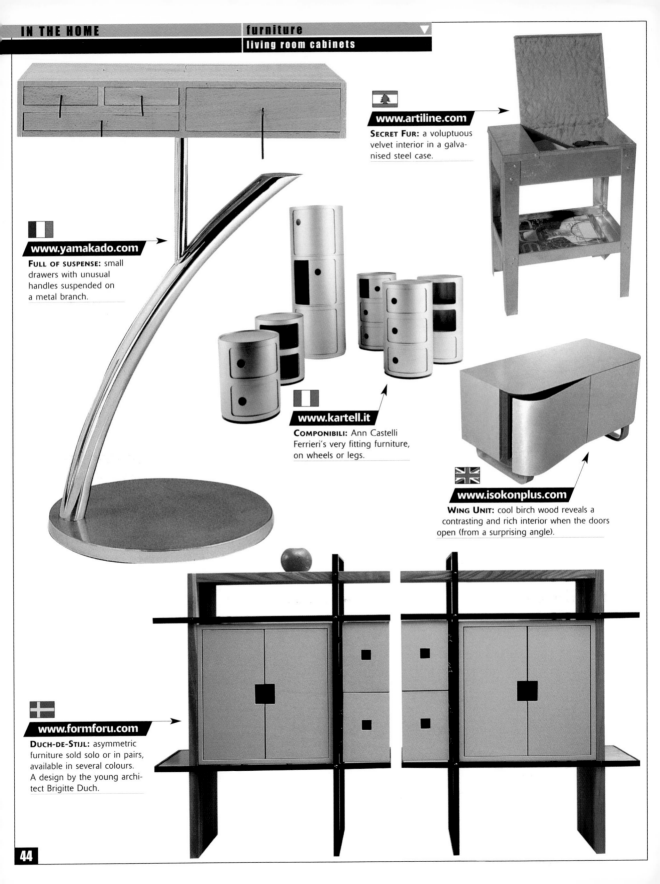

www.artiline.com

SECRET FUR: a voluptuous velvet interior in a galvanised steel case.

www.yamakado.com

FULL OF SUSPENSE: small drawers with unusual handles suspended on a metal branch.

www.kartell.it

COMPONIBILI: Ann Castelli Ferrieri's very fitting furniture, on wheels or legs.

www.isokonplus.com

WING UNIT: cool birch wood reveals a contrasting and rich interior when the doors open (from a surprising angle).

www.formforu.com

DUCH-DE-STIJL: asymmetric furniture sold solo or in pairs, available in several colours. A design by the young architect Brigitte Duch.

michaelnoah@hotmail.com

WAVE CONTROL: easy to get a handle on this design.

http://perso.wanadoo.fr/lachipote

RUSTIC: traditional Savoyard furniture reproduced with salvaged wood in the studios of La Chipote.

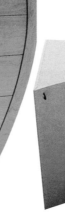

www.roombywellis.com

TRIANGOLO from TEAM by WelliS. Concave containment.

www.porada.it

FILOU: shapely cherry wood cabinet with a crystal top as smooth as satin.

www.neotu.com

PALERME: by Garouste and Bonetti.

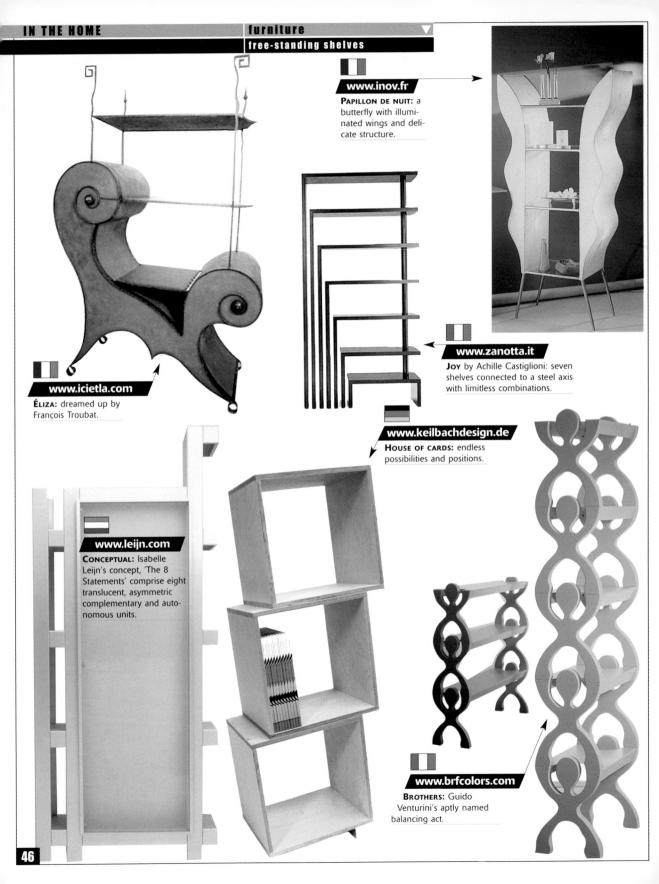

www.inov.fr

PAPILLON DE NUIT: a butterfly with illuminated wings and delicate structure.

www.icietla.com

ÉLIZA: dreamed up by François Troubat.

www.zanotta.it

JOY by Achille Castiglioni: seven shelves connected to a steel axis with limitless combinations.

www.keilbachdesign.de

HOUSE OF CARDS: endless possibilities and positions.

www.leijn.com

CONCEPTUAL: Isabelle Leijn's concept, 'The 8 Statements' comprise eight translucent, asymmetric complementary and autonomous units.

www.brfcolors.com

BROTHERS: Guido Venturini's aptly named balancing act.

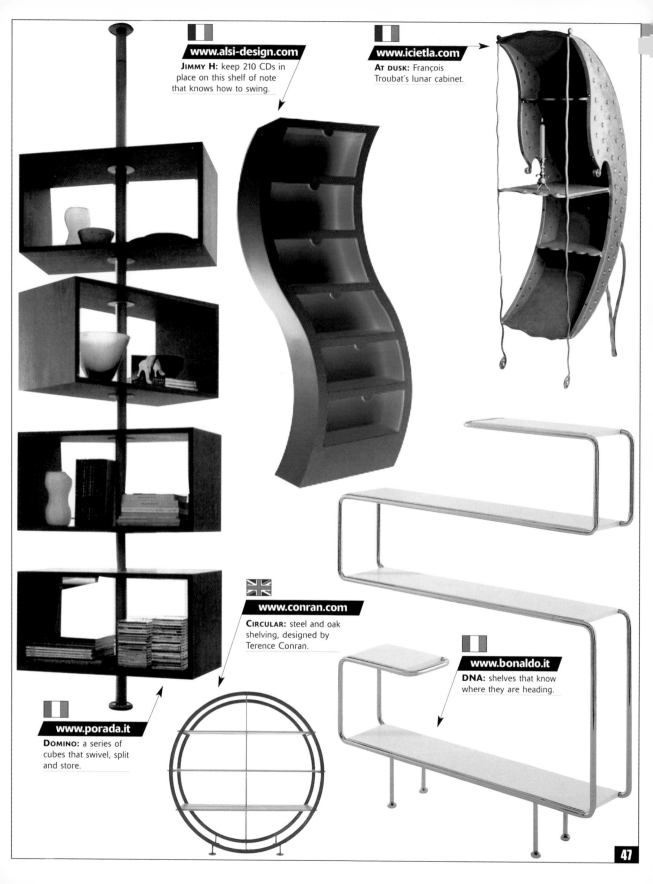

www.alsi-design.com

JIMMY H: keep 210 CDs in place on this shelf of note that knows how to swing.

www.icietla.com

AT DUSK: François Troubat's lunar cabinet.

www.conran.com

CIRCULAR: steel and oak shelving, designed by Terence Conran.

www.bonaldo.it

DNA: shelves that know where they are heading.

www.porada.it

DOMINO: a series of cubes that swivel, split and store.

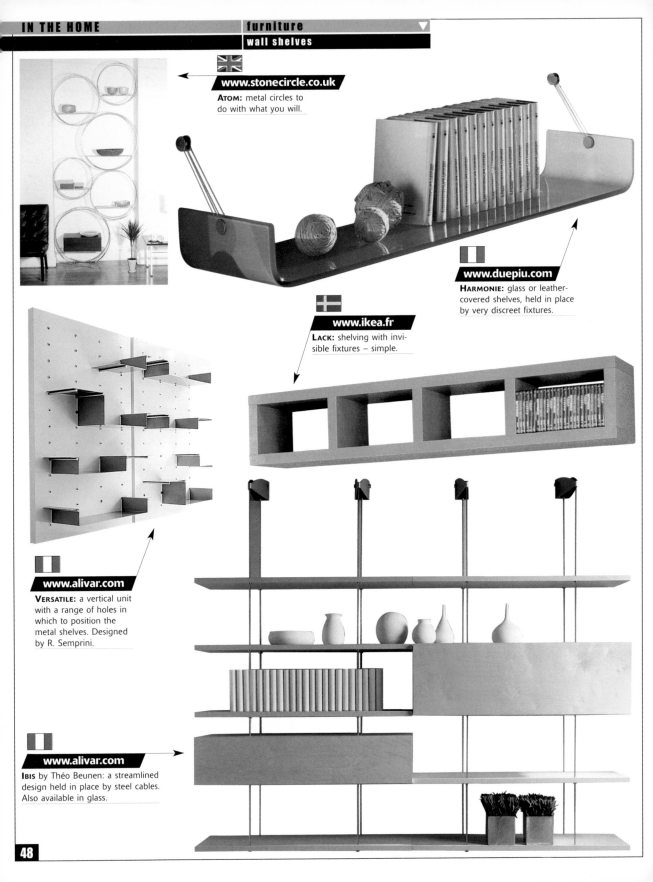

www.stonecircle.co.uk

ATOM: metal circles to do with what you will.

www.duepiu.com

HARMONIE: glass or leather-covered shelves, held in place by very discreet fixtures.

www.ikea.fr

LACK: shelving with invisible fixtures – simple.

www.alivar.com

VERSATILE: a vertical unit with a range of holes in which to position the metal shelves. Designed by R. Semprini.

www.alivar.com

IBIS by Théo Beunen: a streamlined design held in place by steel cables. Also available in glass.

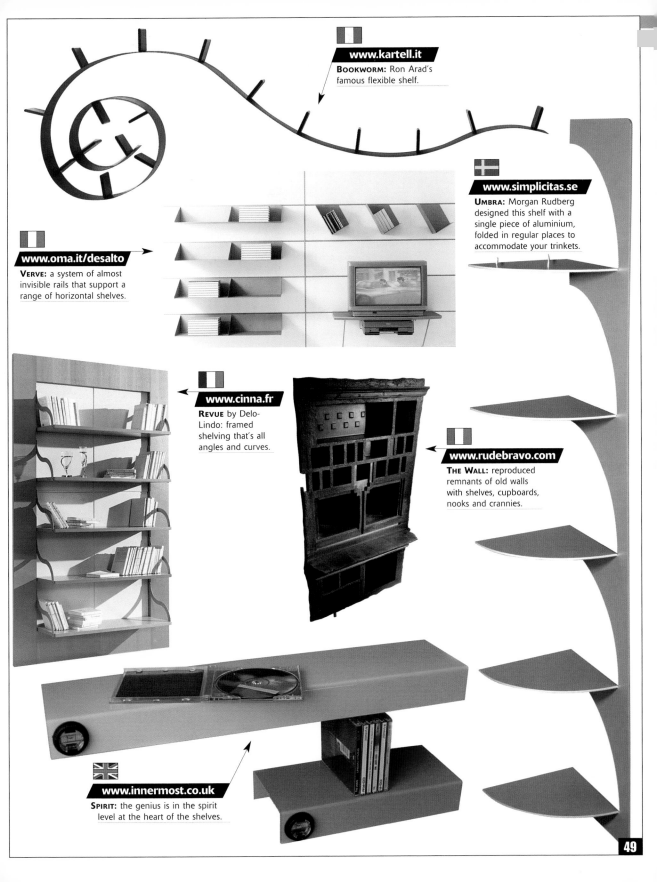

www.kartell.it

BOOKWORM: Ron Arad's famous flexible shelf.

www.simplicitas.se

UMBRA: Morgan Rudberg designed this shelf with a single piece of aluminium, folded in regular places to accommodate your trinkets.

www.oma.it/desalto

VERVE: a system of almost invisible rails that support a range of horizontal shelves.

www.cinna.fr

REVUE by Delo-Lindo: framed shelving that's all angles and curves.

www.rudebravo.com

THE WALL: reproduced remnants of old walls with shelves, cupboards, nooks and crannies.

www.innermost.co.uk

SPIRIT: the genius is in the spirit level at the heart of the shelves.

49

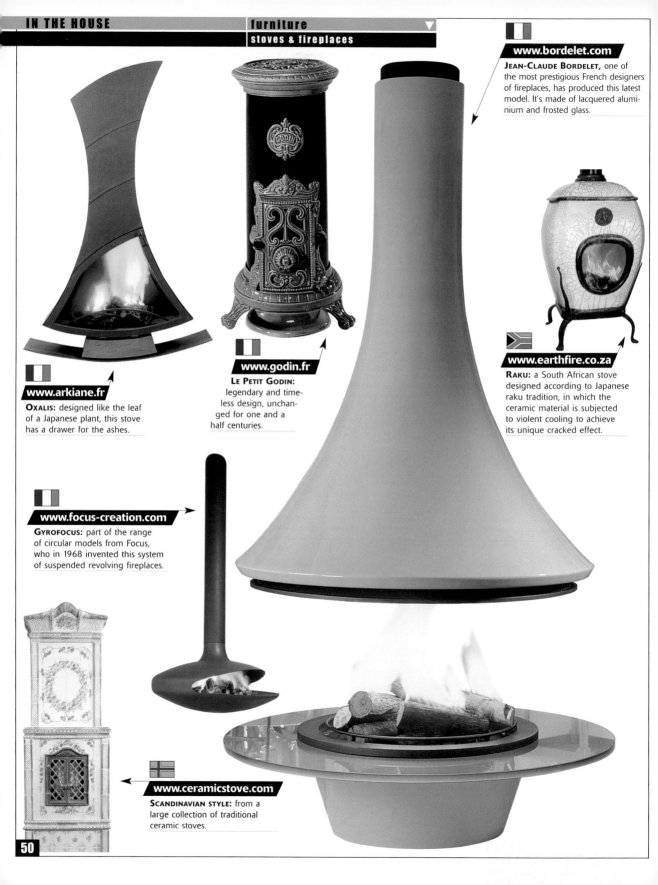

www.bordelet.com

JEAN-CLAUDE BORDELET, one of the most prestigious French designers of fireplaces, has produced this latest model. It's made of lacquered aluminium and frosted glass.

www.arkiane.fr

OXALIS: designed like the leaf of a Japanese plant, this stove has a drawer for the ashes.

www.godin.fr

LE PETIT GODIN: legendary and time-less design, unchanged for one and a half centuries.

www.earthfire.co.za

RAKU: a South African stove designed according to Japanese raku tradition, in which the ceramic material is subjected to violent cooling to achieve its unique cracked effect.

www.focus-creation.com

GYROFOCUS: part of the range of circular models from Focus, who in 1968 invented this system of suspended revolving fireplaces.

www.ceramicstove.com

SCANDINAVIAN STYLE: from a large collection of traditional ceramic stoves.

www.morsoe.com

SQUIRREL: designed in Scandinavia and sold throughout Europe and America, this Morso model is Britain's most popular cast-iron stove.

www.dovre.co.uk

STOVE FIREPLACE: reduces heat less dramatically and efficiently.

www.wonderfire.co.uk.

ADAM: rustic style combined with modern technology (i.e. a gas fire).

medusan@t-online.de

OLIX: one of many unconventional designs from Matten.

www.kreo.fr

SLEEPING CAT: the Radi designers came up with this stylish illusion, of a pure wool carpet with built-in cat motif and silk flames, operated by a silent mechanism.

www.bisque.co.uk

HOT SPRING: Priestman Goode's impressive coil radiator that springs into action when things get too cool for comfort.

www.stadlerform.ch

MAX: a space creature that keeps you cosy or cool according to the season. Designed by Matti Walker.

www.lassco.co.uk

OLD-STYLE: Lassco restores furniture and sells radiators from bygone days.

www.focus-creations.com

RISING SUN: a circular radiator that follows the style of fireplaces designed by Focus since the sixties. All-round warmth.

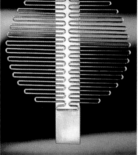

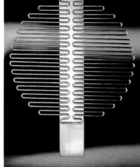

www.hudevad.dk

RADIUS (60cm x 2m) has won two prizes for its innovative design. Long, spherical and effective.

www.bisque.co.uk

MURAL: X-stream is nearly two metres in height and gives out X-cellent heat.

www.bisque.co.uk

MULTICOLOURED: Flow Form bids farewell to discreet heat.

www.radiatingstyle.co.uk

SENSUOUS SCULPTURE: steely Sima keeps towels warm and rooms interesting.

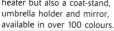

www.acova.fr

AT YOUR SERVICE: not just a wall heater but also a coat-stand, umbrella holder and mirror, available in over 100 colours.

www.bisque.co.uk

CORNICHE: perfect in the bathroom for keeping towels warm.

www.radiatingstyle.co.uk

COLUMN OF HEAT: Zeta the heater (160cm x 240cm) makes an attractive feature in any room.

www.radiatingstyle.co.uk

TWO IN ONE: Paramount combines heating with wooden shelving for hallways, living rooms and bathrooms.

www.bernini.it

ALA: a wooden writing desk with a sliding compartment, designed by Giotto Stoppino.

www.interluebke.de

INFORMATION TECHNOLOGY: capable of swivelling 270 degrees, this office is part information centre, part bar.

www.quartdepoil.com

ISABELLE: Essaime's pyramid-shaped desk is in maple and ash. A design in which yesterday meets tomorrow.

www.ladenbau.de

CAP 21: mobile and flexible, this information centre is perfect for those working on their feet or on their seat.

www.ligne-roset.tm.fr

SAINT-JAMES: Jean Nouvel's design incorporates a touch-sensitive control for the integrated lamp. Increase the brightness with a brush of the hand.

www.studiofusion.co.uk

PUSH ME, PULL ME: a prototype design for an office cum kitchen table. It folds up and can be easily moved around the kitchen.

www.promemoria.com

NATALIE: a wooden desk covered with topstitched leather.

www.codutti.it

MASTER POINT: this office workstation is available in frosted glass or wood.

www.porada.it

SCRIBA: an elegant writing desk in cherry wood that takes up just the right amount of space.

www.roche-bobois.com

OPEN SESAME: when closed it looks like a cupboard. Open its doors and behold an office!

www.lexon-design.com

CAPTAIN HOOK: fold this chair and hang it up on its hook. Now you see it, now you don't.

www.kartell.it

GASTONE: a foldable trolley designed by Antonio Citterio, with plastic top and chrome steel structure.

www.domeau-peres.fr

GUESS WHO'S COMING TO STAY: this spare bed, designed by Matali Crasset, unfolds from an upright structure complete with lamp and alarm clock.

www.habitat.net

BEDINABOX: a seat composed of a three-part mattress with two side cupboards for storing the bedlinen.

www.vuitton.com

FOLDING TABLE by Louis Vuitton that fits snugly in a bag. Made to order.

www.vibel.com

MURAL MATTRESS: hidden vertically behind shelving, the mattress unfolds to become a reading table or spare bed.

www.raumgestalt-en.de

FELT MATTRESS: easy to roll up or out for no-frills comfort.

www.inflate.co.uk

SNOOZY: made of five stackable sections, this bed is easy to store away.

www.le-webstore.com

ANDROS: a folding chair in the form of a human, allowed standing room only when upright.

www.kreo.com

SLICE: a chair cum bed, designed in slices by Pierre Charpin.

www.poltronafrau.it

DONALD CHAIR: this folding chair has a duck-like profile.

www.giovanetti-collezioni.it

NARCISA: a reflective storage opportunity with an eye-level mirror.

www.tohubohu.fr

TRADITIONAL WARMTH: a jersey-wool hot-water bottle cover to remind you of cosy nights in your childhood.

www.giorgetti-spa.it

TALO: handmade in maple wood, an elegant table with a swivel drawer and a built-in lamp.

www.inov.fr

AUDREY: modelling shades takes on a completely new dimension for a former mannequin worth her metal.

www.brfcolors.com

TROLLEY: a bedside table on castors, perfect for breakfast in bed on lazy Sunday mornings.

www.giorgetti-spa.it

TÉMÉNOS: spend picturesque and romantic nights under floating curtains and sculpted wooden columns.

www.alivar.com

BOSS: modern design, timeless slumber, endless dreams.

www.bonaldo.it

CRIO: a bedside vanity table for those midnight make-overs.

www.porada.it

SIRBIS: this valet has designs on your tidiness.

www.mayhemuk.com

TIME ON YOUR WALLS: this clock doesn't just tell the time, it projects it.

www.palluccobellato.it

LOVE CAGE: it doesn't get much more minimalist than this bed design.

www.cinna.com

GRAPHIC SOLUTION: an imaginative doodle becomes a coat-hanger.

www.edra.com

SQUARE 2: Massimo Morozzi has created a haven of peace with this jigsaw bed on castors. Lots of ways to make your bed and lie in it.

www.interluebke.de

CAMPA: a combined bedside table and lamp.

www.rolfbenz.de

TROLLEY DOLLY: simply slide this table over the duvet and breakfast is served, madam.

www.lexon-design.com

CLOCK IT AND RECORD IT: Lexon's mission to design clever and stylish objects is accomplished once more with a wall clock that records a ten-second message.

www.stilic-force.com

SOCK IT TO YOU: say farewell to lonely socks for ever.

www.perigot-fr.com

HANGING HONEYCOMB in which to keep socks, gloves and small items neatly together in your wardrobe.

www.ligne-roset.tm.fr

MALY: make your bed a complete living space in this beechwood frame that comes complete with movable features and versatile cushions.

www.leonardo.de

LEONARDEAU helps you stay cool and fresh on long hot nights.

www.bebitalia.it

ALETTO: soft and sheer, this elegant bedhead is made of a fabric net stretched between two metal wings to form an attractive arch.

61

www.chameleonic.co.uk

FLOWER: wrought-iron flowers give this bucolic bed a 'flower power' feel from head to toe.

www.authenticmodels.com

PORTHOLE MIRROR: a resinous replica of a cargo ship porthole. Can you see the sea?

www.horm.it

NOS: stylish slumber with this curvaceous and voluptuous bedhead.

www.talisman-trading.co.uk

ART IN MINIATURE: a Moroccan camel-bone jewellery box.

www.pylones.fr

LOLO'S HOT IN BED: someone to keep you warm at night.

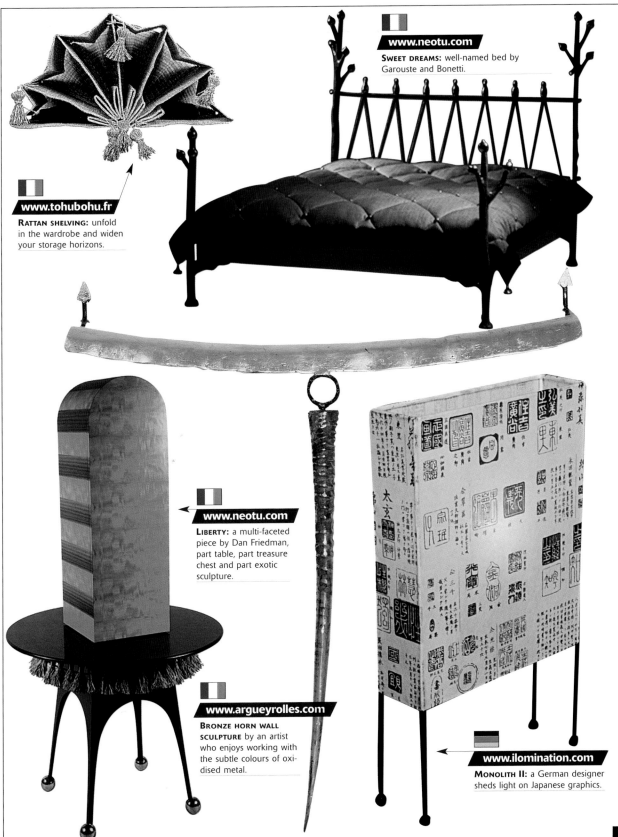

www.neotu.com

SWEET DREAMS: well-named bed by Garouste and Bonetti.

www.tohubohu.fr

RATTAN SHELVING: unfold in the wardrobe and widen your storage horizons.

www.neotu.com

LIBERTY: a multi-faceted piece by Dan Friedman, part table, part treasure chest and part exotic sculpture.

www.argueyrolles.com

BRONZE HORN WALL SCULPTURE by an artist who enjoys working with the subtle colours of oxidised metal.

www.ilomination.com

MONOLITH II: a German designer sheds light on Japanese graphics.

EAU DE TEDDY: a cedar wood bear in a cosy felt case that keeps your clothes smelling fresh and lovely.

www.tohubohu.fr

CHIC SHEETS: silk sheets in grey, yellow and brown. Compact, cool style.

www.inov.fr

TWEED: a dressing table complete with shelf and coat rack.

www.o-to-o.com

CRINOLINE: stylish storage in silk and bamboo by Tungstène.

www.inov.fr

CURLS AND SCROLLS: an ornate clock to fill the night with the sun's rays.

www.defyinterior.com

SCROLL: a canopy bed with metal flourishes.

www.icietla.com

LIBERTINE: an ornamental writing desk perfect for composing love poems, designed by François Troubat.

www.chichesterdesigns.com

FIT FOR A KING: four columns covered in silver leaf and a mirror-effect bedhead help you dream of the 18th century.

www.ritzenhoff.de

SIMSALABIM: Damien Ligier's bedspread keeps you safe at night with its guardian angels.

www.moonfirework.de

SNOW WHITE'S DRESSING TABLE: all in wood for a mirror fit for a princess and a drawer for her royal secrets.

www.atypyk.com

FIFTY FIFTY: a luminous line on the quilt cover keeps everything fair by splitting it right down the middle.

www.leitmotiv.nl

NEST: no need to make your own nest, just nestle in this design.

www.thebodyshop.com

PILLOW SPRAY: a blend of essential oils and natural plants to make sleep beneficial.

www.ritzenhoff.de

BEAUTY SLEEP: Wake up with the sun in your face with a pillow designed by Maria Christina Hamel.

www.muji.co.jp

SWEET DREAMS ensured when you put these sachets under your pillow. Enjoy up to three months of sweet-scented slumber.

www.mathy-by-bols.be

CANOPY BED: a house-bed for those who like their own space.

www.outsidein.co.uk

GENTLE WAKE-UP: the lamp gets brighter by the minute and wakes you like the gently rising sun. Much less stressful than an alarm clock.

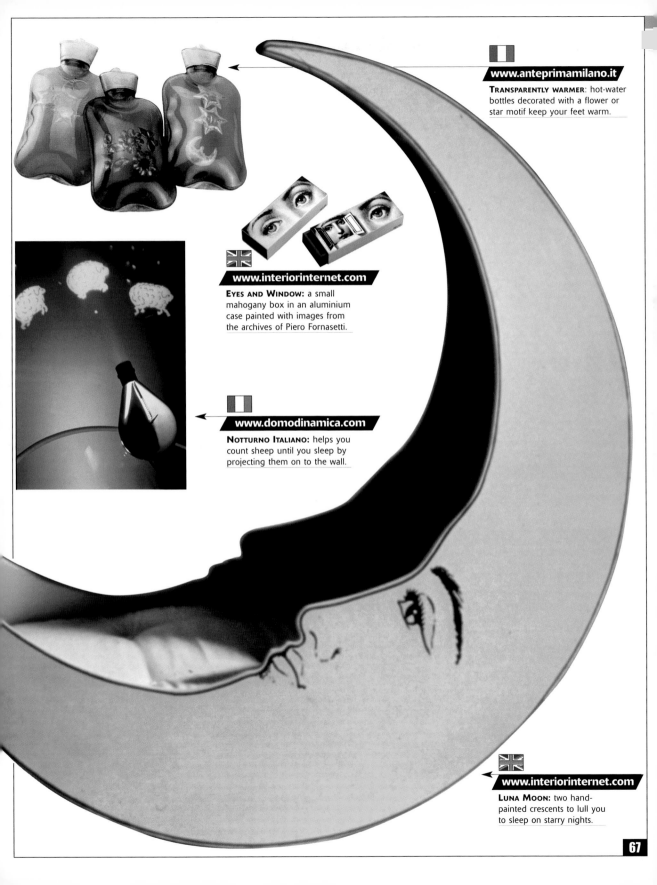

1

www.annacharlotte.se

WAFFLE COVERS: bedding in natural fibres, in true Swedish tradition.

 2

www.designersguild.com

THE DESIGNERS GUILD: created by Tricia Guild in 1970, this company has over 2,000 top-quality fabrics.

 3

www.jab.de

JAB ANSTOETZ: manufacturers of luxury fabrics since 1946, this company has an interactive website.

 4

www.frette.it

ALHAMBRA: even Frette's catalogue is a sensuous object. This is just one of their magical designs.

 5

www.mastroraphael.com

NATURAL LOOK sheets in pastel shades, designed by the Italian master of bedlinen.

 6

www.descamps.fr

BEDLINEN BY ANY OTHER NAME: the Descamps collection has poetic names and comes in nostalgic pastel shades.

 7

www.simmons.fr

BED FRAME COMPLETE WITH DRAWERS: designed by Simmons, inventors of the sprung mattress in 1870.

 8

www.swissflex.ch

FLEXIBLE: perfectly adjustable comfort with remote control commands.

 **1**

 **2**

 **3**

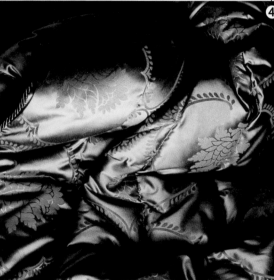 **4**

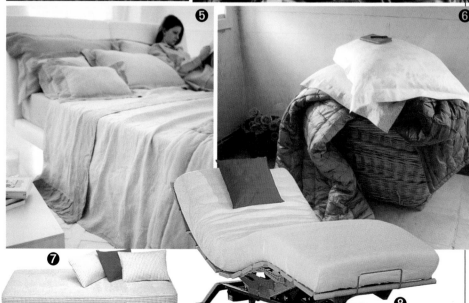 **5** **6**

7 **8**

www.merinos.fr

AXEL: the mattress is covered on one side with wool for winter, the other with linen for summer. It has specially reinforced zones for body support.

www.epeda.fr

CHROMATIC: four different areas of support focus on the key movements of the body to give perfect support while you sleep.

www.fly-meubles.tm.fr

CYBER BED: for those on the move – a bed on wheels and a sporty bedhead.

www.ikea.com

TRONSÖ: Ikea's space-saving mezzanine bed in stainless steel.

www.mathy-by-bols.be

WORKER: pine and sheet metal furniture with an integrated lamp, magnetic panels and even slots for skates.

www.tigertoys.com

STAR WARS: fanatics of Star Wars will love this telephone.

www.oregonscientific.com

TIME TO SURFACE: time to get up is writ large on the wall.

www.alma.nl

SPOT THE CLOCK: time is projected onto the wall and captured there for a moment.

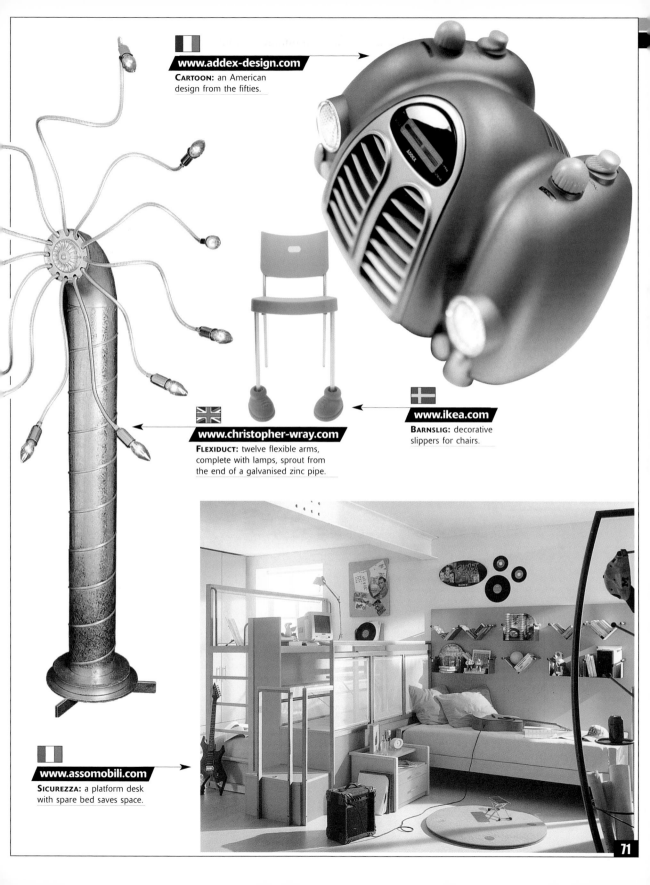

www.addex-design.com

CARTOON: an American design from the fifties.

www.christopher-wray.com

FLEXIDUCT: twelve flexible arms, complete with lamps, sprout from the end of a galvanised zinc pipe.

www.ikea.com

BARNSLIG: decorative slippers for chairs.

www.assomobili.com

SICUREZZA: a platform desk with spare bed saves space.

www.moonfirework.de

EGG AND SPOON: an unusual storage concept, complete with spoons to open the drawers.

www.vibel.com

MADE TO MEASURE: each Vibel room is the unique result of close collaboration between the architect and parents, according to the personality and tastes of each individual child.

www.radiatingstyle.co.uk

BEAR: this furry creature hides a radiator. His friends include an elephant and a dolphin.

www.atelier-sommer.de

NIGHT TIME: are they real beds or foam rubber boats on wheels?

www.authenticmodels.com

INDOOR TRAVEL: a boat converted into a set of shelves, with antique hinges and a crackled paint effect.

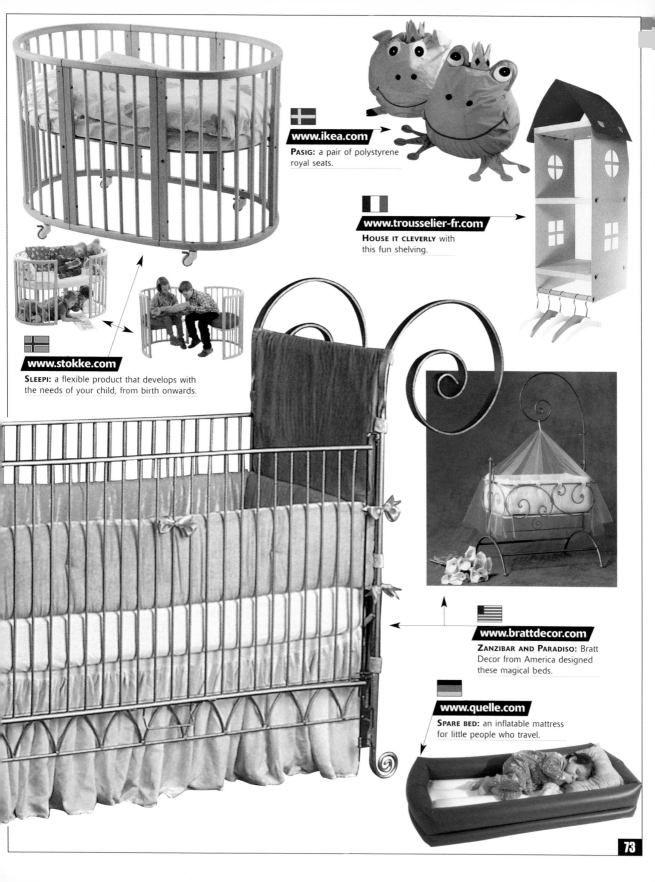

www.ikea.com

PASIG: a pair of polystyrene royal seats.

www.trousselier-fr.com

HOUSE IT CLEVERLY with this fun shelving.

www.stokke.com

SLEEPI: a flexible product that develops with the needs of your child, from birth onwards.

www.brattdecor.com

ZANZIBAR AND PARADISO: Bratt Decor from America designed these magical beds.

www.quelle.com

SPARE BED: an inflatable mattress for little people who travel.

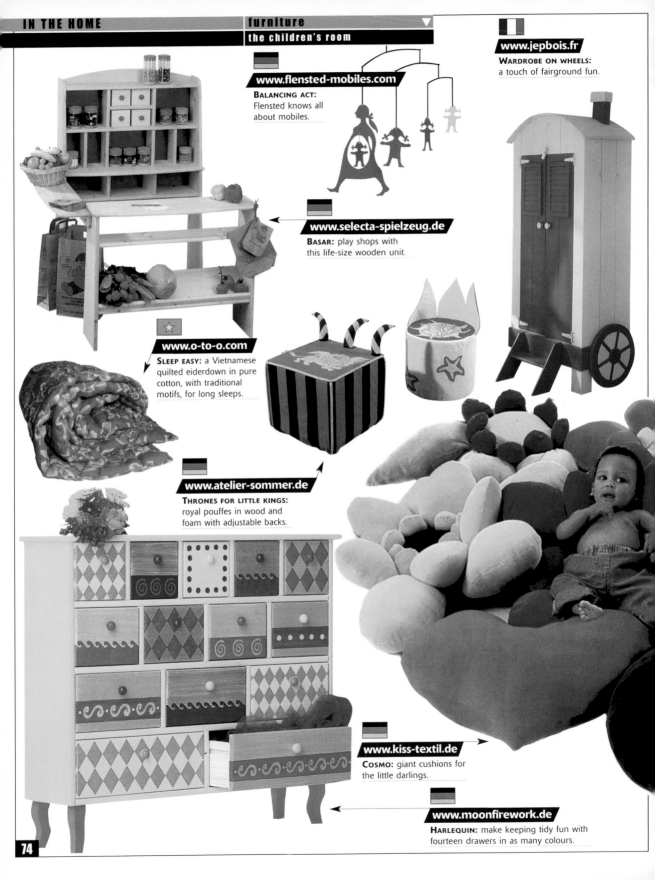

www.jepbois.fr

WARDROBE ON WHEELS: a touch of fairground fun.

www.flensted-mobiles.com

BALANCING ACT: Flensted knows all about mobiles.

www.selecta-spielzeug.de

BASAR: play shops with this life-size wooden unit.

www.o-to-o.com

SLEEP EASY: a Vietnamese quilted eiderdown in pure cotton, with traditional motifs, for long sleeps.

www.atelier-sommer.de

THRONES FOR LITTLE KINGS: royal pouffes in wood and foam with adjustable backs.

www.kiss-textil.de

COSMO: giant cushions for the little darlings.

www.moonfirework.de

HARLEQUIN: make keeping tidy fun with fourteen drawers in as many colours.

www.quandt-gmbh.de

FELINE FRIEZE: luminous tomcats strut their stuff at nightfall.

www.kinder-spielmoebel.de

TWO IN ONE: high chair or seat and table – a flexible friend.

www.evoluzione-srl.it

REVOLUTION: a cupboard on wheels with a selection of drawers covered in lightweight felt.

www.merrythought.co.uk

LADYBIRD: a rocking chair that is truly comfortable.

www.pintoys.com

FROG: a high chair for little people aged between eight months and three years.

www.flexa.dk

FORTIFIED CASTLE: Flexa offers a choice of four themes for the children's room – Far West, Space, Underwater, and Knights and Castles. Fire their imagination.

www.sedap.com

UNDULATING, unusual and unexpected, designed in plaster by Philippe Curry.

www.1912.co.kr

SATURN: traditional paper held in place by a metal ring. Designed by Ki Joo Park from the Korean artist collective known as 'Objet d'art 1912', all of whom work in the same paper.

www.christopher-wray.com

TILOS: sensual design.

www.waterfordcrystal.com

LIGHT UP: a crystal ceiling light by John Rocha.

www.bagues-france.com

PEACEFUL PARROT: a tower of crystals and gilded iron, almost two metres in height, by Garouste and Bonetti.

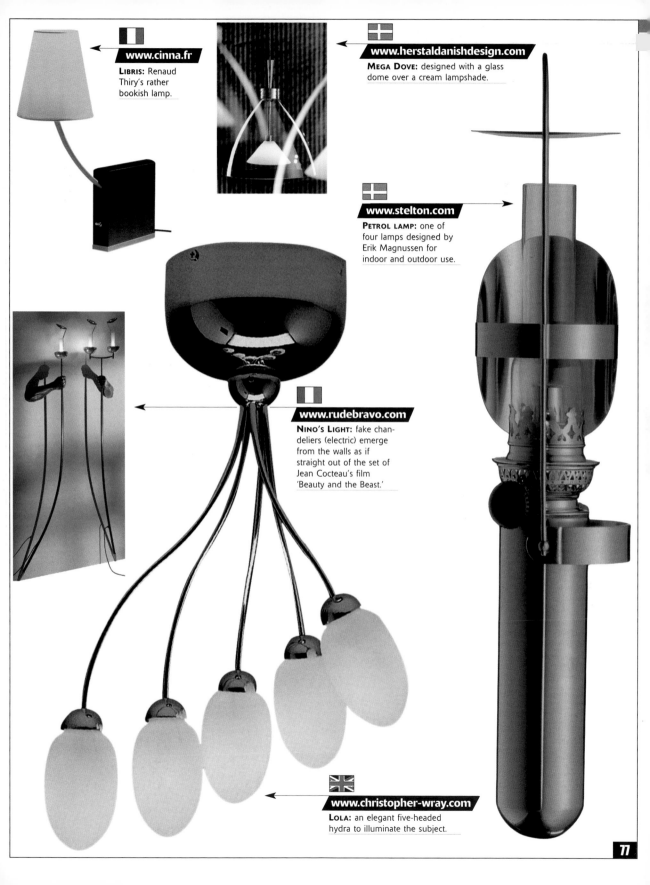

www.cinna.fr

LIBRIS: Renaud Thiry's rather bookish lamp.

www.herstaldanishdesign.com

MEGA DOVE: designed with a glass dome over a cream lampshade.

www.stelton.com

PETROL LAMP: one of four lamps designed by Erik Magnussen for indoor and outdoor use.

www.rudebravo.com

NINO'S LIGHT: fake chandeliers (electric) emerge from the walls as if straight out of the set of Jean Cocteau's film 'Beauty and the Beast.'

www.christopher-wray.com

LOLA: an elegant five-headed hydra to illuminate the subject.

❶

www.ingo-maurer.com

ZETTEL'S: both light and mobile, made of small pieces of paper.

 ❷

www.venini.it

MURANO GLASS: designed in 1946 by Gio Ponti, this light has been popular ever since.

 ❸

www.christopher-wray.com

LUCCIOLE: a swarm of electric candles (thirty-six in all).

 ❹

www.flos.net

FUCSIA: a famous light designed in 1996 by Achille Castiglioni, joint founder with his brother Piergiacomo, of Flos in 1962.

 ❺

www.harcoloor.nl

STRAWBERRY: a swirl of complementary colour, as pretty as a necklace.

 ❻

www.flos.net

TARAXACUM: an illuminating concept.

 ❼

www.ligne-roset.tm.fr

LIGHT POCKET: designed by Arik Levy, this steel pouch contains bulbs that emit a mysterious light.

 ❽

www.chameleonic.co.uk

CELSIUS: asymmetric style, bluish emission.

 ❾

www.leitmotiv.nl

BOTTLE CHANDELIER: a transparently innovative design from Duchamp, high priest of ready-made items.

 ❿

www.anthologiequartett.de

CELLULA: a magnificent curtain of pearls.

6

7

8

9

10

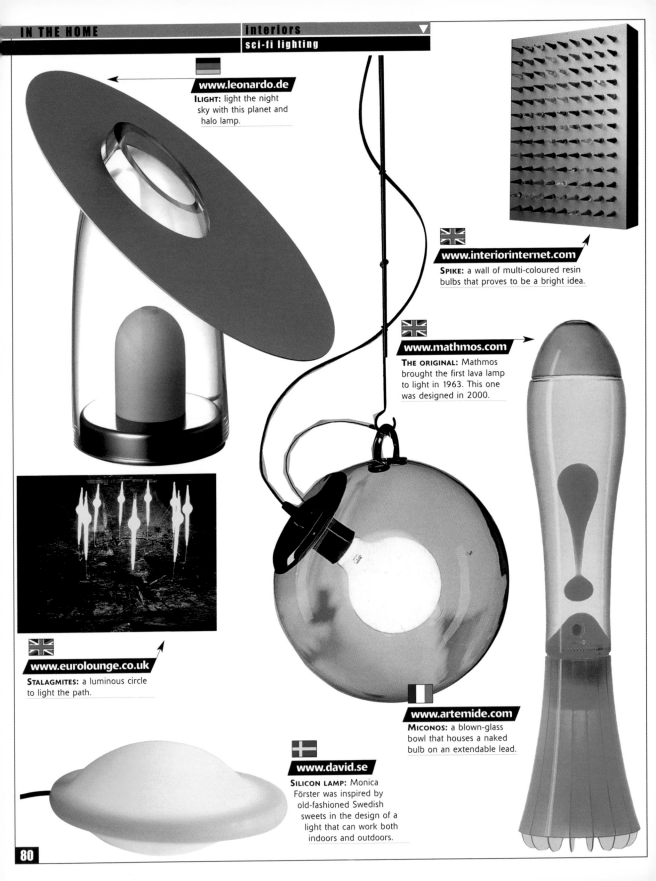

www.leonardo.de

ILIGHT: light the night sky with this planet and halo lamp.

www.interiorinternet.com

SPIKE: a wall of multi-coloured resin bulbs that proves to be a bright idea.

www.mathmos.com

THE ORIGINAL: Mathmos brought the first lava lamp to light in 1963. This one was designed in 2000.

www.eurolounge.co.uk

STALAGMITES: a luminous circle to light the path.

www.artemide.com

MICONOS: a blown-glass bowl that houses a naked bulb on an extendable lead.

www.david.se

SILICON LAMP: Monica Förster was inspired by old-fashioned Swedish sweets in the design of a light that can work both indoors and outdoors.

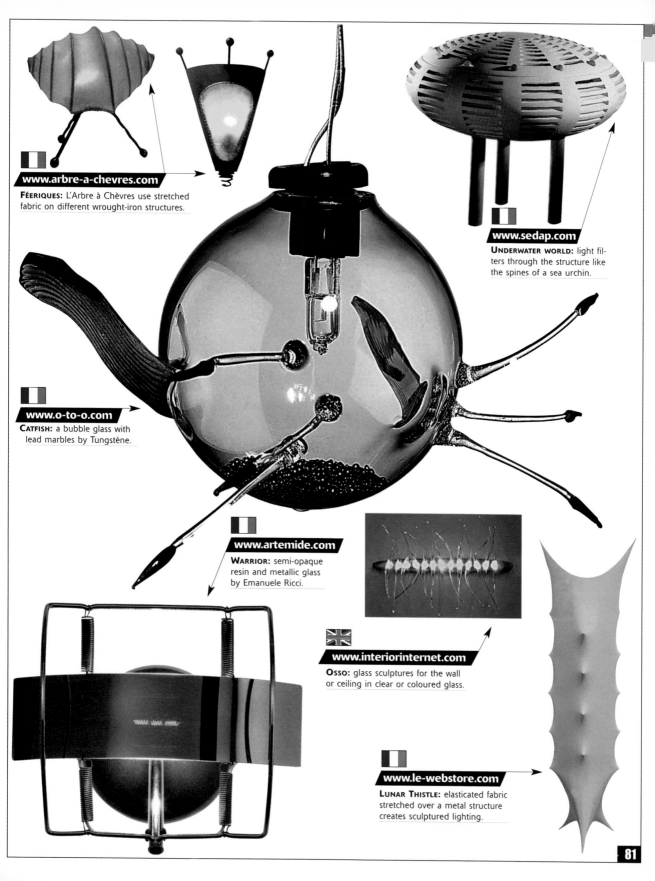

www.arbre-a-chevres.com

FÉERIQUES: L'Arbre à Chèvres use stretched
fabric on different wrought-iron structures.

www.sedap.com

UNDERWATER WORLD: light filters through the structure like
the spines of a sea urchin.

www.o-to-o.com

CATFISH: a bubble glass with
lead marbles by Tungstène.

www.artemide.com

WARRIOR: semi-opaque
resin and metallic glass
by Emanuele Ricci.

www.interiorinternet.com

OSSO: glass sculptures for the wall
or ceiling in clear or coloured glass.

www.le-webstore.com

LUNAR THISTLE: elasticated fabric
stretched over a metal structure
creates sculptured lighting.

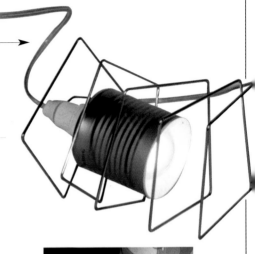

www.o-to-o.com

DON'T BE KEPT IN THE DARK: this string of lights can be suspended or placed on a surface, thanks to the spiral support. Designed by Didou and Véro.

www.domodinamica.com

CROMATICA: atmospheric lighting that varies with the colour of the pages in the book.

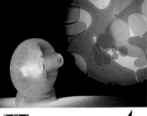

www.mathmos.com

SPACE PROJECTOR: projects on to the wall a kaleidoscopic image with a diameter of 1.5m.

www.domodinamica.com

OLYMPIONA: your very own Olympic flame.

www.ernst-berlin.de

DIASPURA: combines a selection of extraordinary lighting effects with images for a new concept in home decor. It even projects messages.

www.ikea.com

LAMPIS: a wall lamp with a bulb that's sculpted into the frame for a more dramatic optical illusion.

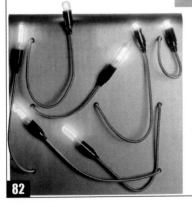

www.n-udesign.com

NO: these magnetic bulbs can be arranged imaginatively on a metal sheet.

www.petiteplanet.com

WATER, WATER EVERYWHERE: a steel basin with its water-effect surface lit from behind. Designed by Anne Chédeville.

🇬🇧 **www.inflate.co.uk**

OVNI: a blow-up ceiling light by Nick Crosbie and Marc Sodeau, experts in all things inflatable.

🇮🇹 **www.indarte.it**

BARTOLO: Paolo Ulian's creative way of pre-serving energy.

🇬🇧 **www.black-blum.com**

READING LIGHT: a bookish lampshade.

www.mawa-design.de

SSYMMANK: Günter Ssymmank designed this light in 1956, inspired by Hans Sharoun's concept. Its nylon petals open and close, changing the colour and brightness of the light.

83

www.emauxdelongwy.com

MERRY-GO-ROUND: vases made of genuine Longwy enamels, using an Italian technique imported in 1835 by Amédée de Craenza.

www.cinna.fr

GOUTTE: a glass vase with a ceramic interior in the shape of a drop of water.

www.egizia.it

CLYDE AND BOB, designed by Ettore Sottsass and James Irvine, respectively, for the celebrated Egizia firm.

www.zanotta.it

ULTIMO: blown-glass vase set in a drawn-glass base, bearing L'Anverre's signature.

www.venini.it

MEDUSA: there are only ninety-nine copies of Ettore Sottsass's transparent aquatic design.

www.scheurich.de

AMANO: asymmetric ceramic vases in a matt finish. Soothing to the eyes, gentle to the touch.

www.baccarat.fr

PARADOXICALLY, it's the hollow centre of the crystal vase that gives the single stem its definition.

www.bernardaud.fr

CROWN VASE: designed by Martin Szekely to give bouquets of flowers their rightful royal residence.

www.fuerstenberg-porzellan.com

SCULPTURES: designed by Werner Bünck and produced by the porcelain manufacturer Fürstenberg.

www.jgdurand.com

FLORA AND FAUNA: a collection of three crystal vases representing the seasons: Spring Roses, Indian Summer and Autumn Wind.

www.talisman-trading.co.uk

AUTHENTIC: Greco–Roman designs straight from the souks of Morocco.

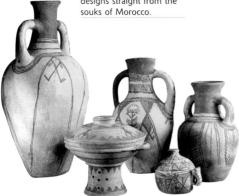

www.cinna.fr

LUMINOUS VASE: this blown-glass vase by Philippe Daney comes complete with a central lighting system.

www.ligne-roset.tm.fr

POMPONETTE: an enamelled ceramic vase designed by Catherine Bergeon.

www.eurolounge.co.uk.

BUBBLE: bubbles of water or air stay afloat in this reversible vase by Tom Dixon.

www.ilto.net

NEMO: a two-in-one design, in which one vase is contained and magnified inside the other.

www.cinna.fr

STEAMED FLOWERS OR VEGETABLES? Adrien Gardère has adapted the concept of the steamer to hold a bouquet or a single flower.

www.inov.fr

COCOON: exotic flowers flourish in a strangely appropriate environment.

www.chameleonic.co.uk

FIVE BOTTLES HANGING ON THE WALL: floral chemistry.

www.despots.nl

POTS: polyester pots by a Dutch designer, inspired by the homeland of flowers.

www.benzadesign.com

MUTANT VASE: malleable strips of metal allow you to create flexible floral forms.

www.ligne-roset.tm.fr

ÉCLIPSE: flutes with removable tubes resting on a beechwood base can be used as vases or candle holders.

www.pa-design.com

TLALOC: attach this vase to a window with small suction pads. A much copied idea from Assia Quétin.

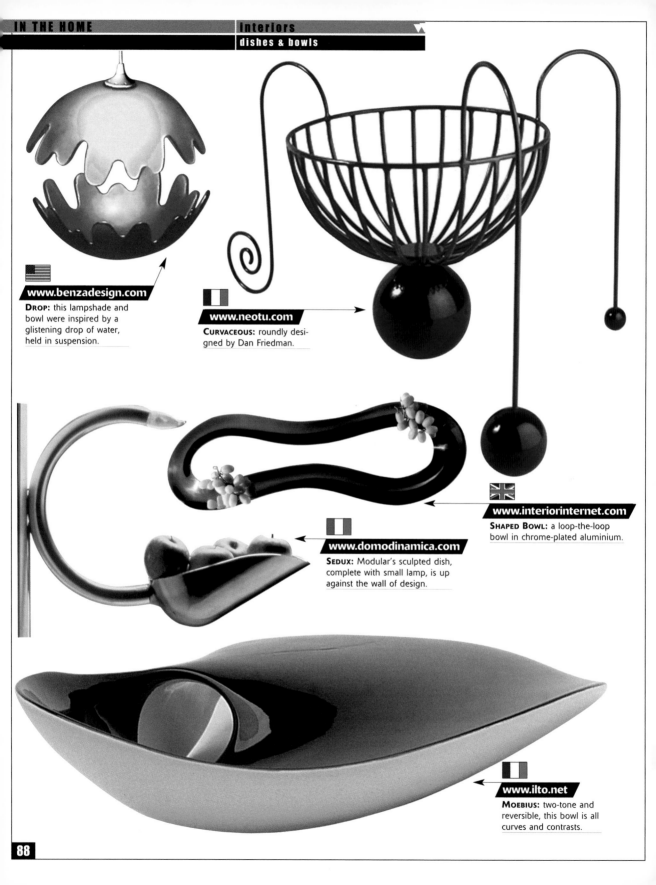

www.benzadesign.com

DROP: this lampshade and bowl were inspired by a glistening drop of water, held in suspension.

www.neotu.com

CURVACEOUS: roundly designed by Dan Friedman.

www.interiorinternet.com

SHAPED BOWL: a loop-the-loop bowl in chrome-plated aluminium.

www.domodinamica.com

SEDUX: Modular's sculpted dish, complete with small lamp, is up against the wall of design.

www.ilto.net

MOEBIUS: two-tone and reversible, this bowl is all curves and contrasts.

www.h1e.com

ZICKZACK: an unusual trompe-l'oeil container from Heinze.

www.leonardo.de

AMAZONAS adds another transparent dimension to bowl design.

www.jgdurand.com

SHANTUNG: this crystal bowl is shaped like an inverted asymmetrical pyramid.

www.designum.com

FRUIT ON WHEELS: designed by Arnout Wisser in 1993 and just as popular in 2001.

www.koerber-design.de

TROMPE-L'ŒIL: still life in aluminium.

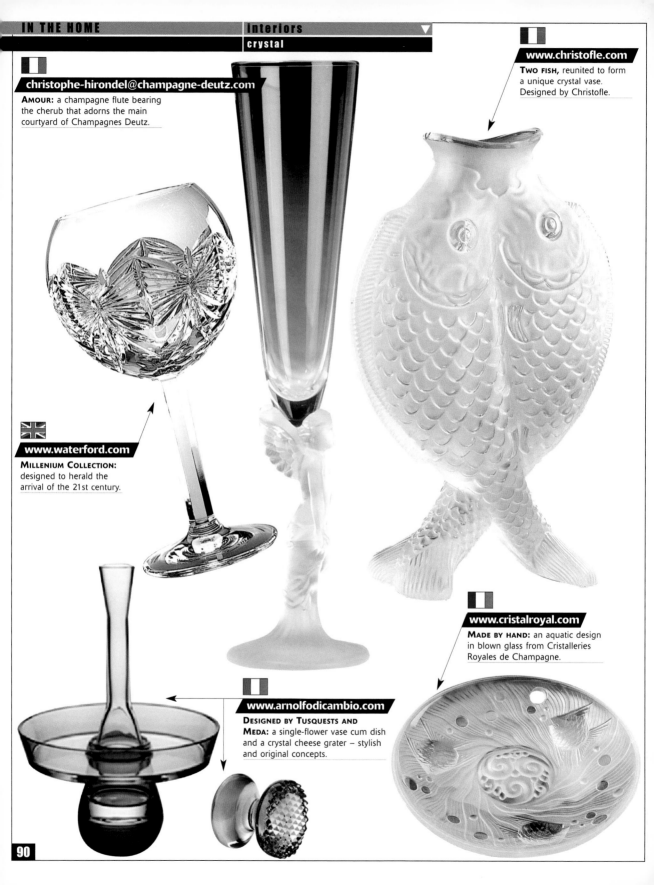

christophe-hirondel@champagne-deutz.com

AMOUR: a champagne flute bearing the cherub that adorns the main courtyard of Champagnes Deutz.

www.christofle.com

TWO FISH, reunited to form a unique crystal vase. Designed by Christofle.

www.waterford.com

MILLENIUM COLLECTION: designed to herald the arrival of the 21st century.

www.cristalroyal.com

MADE BY HAND: an aquatic design in blown glass from Cristalleries Royales de Champagne.

www.arnolfodicambio.com

DESIGNED BY TUSQUESTS AND MEDA: a single-flower vase cum dish and a crystal cheese grater – stylish and original concepts.

www.jgdurand.com

ORGANDI: a sophisticated collection of glasses and crystal that marries delicate curves and arabesque swirls.

www.baccarat.fr

BOTANICALS: this crystal vase is delicately decorated with motifs from the natural world.

www.lampeberger.com

GRANDE CATHERINE: designed by Régis Dho, the deep blue of this hand-cut crystal glass tiara is gilded with cabochons and bronze.

www.wedgwood.com

TRADITION MEETS INNOVATION: Jasper Conran's designs for Stuart Crystal (glass-makers for more than 200 years) are finely crafted.

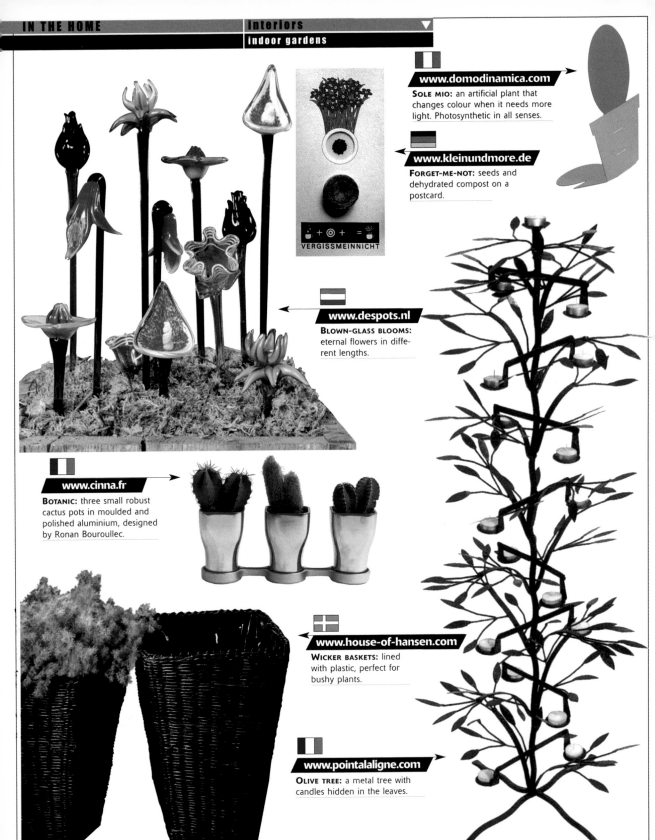

www.domodinamica.com

SOLE MIO: an artificial plant that changes colour when it needs more light. Photosynthetic in all senses.

www.kleinundmore.de

FORGET-ME-NOT: seeds and dehydrated compost on a postcard.

VERGISSMEINNICHT

www.despots.nl

BLOWN-GLASS BLOOMS: eternal flowers in different lengths.

www.cinna.fr

BOTANIC: three small robust cactus pots in moulded and polished aluminium, designed by Ronan Bouroullec.

www.house-of-hansen.com

WICKER BASKETS: lined with plastic, perfect for bushy plants.

www.pointalaligne.com

OLIVE TREE: a metal tree with candles hidden in the leaves.

www.cinna.fr

BLOOMING BOOKENDS: bookish blooms by Adrien Gardère.

www.zanotta.it

HORTUS: this metal and wooden tripod supports six clay flowerpots.

www.haws.co.uk

MINIATURE GARDEN TOOLS for indoor and bonsai plants.

www.o-to-o.com

BULB: three single-flower vases, in small, medium or large holders, create Tungstène's urban garden.

www.esteban.fr

PERFUMED GARDEN: ceramic flowers to plant in a glass bowl so that you can enjoy the scent of jasmine, patchouli, rosewood, benzoin and dried fruits.

www.smithandhawken.com

FLOWER PRESS: much more effective and aesthetic than a huge dictionary.

www.koziol.de

POWER FLOWER: fill with water and plant in the soil to protect your blooms from drying out.

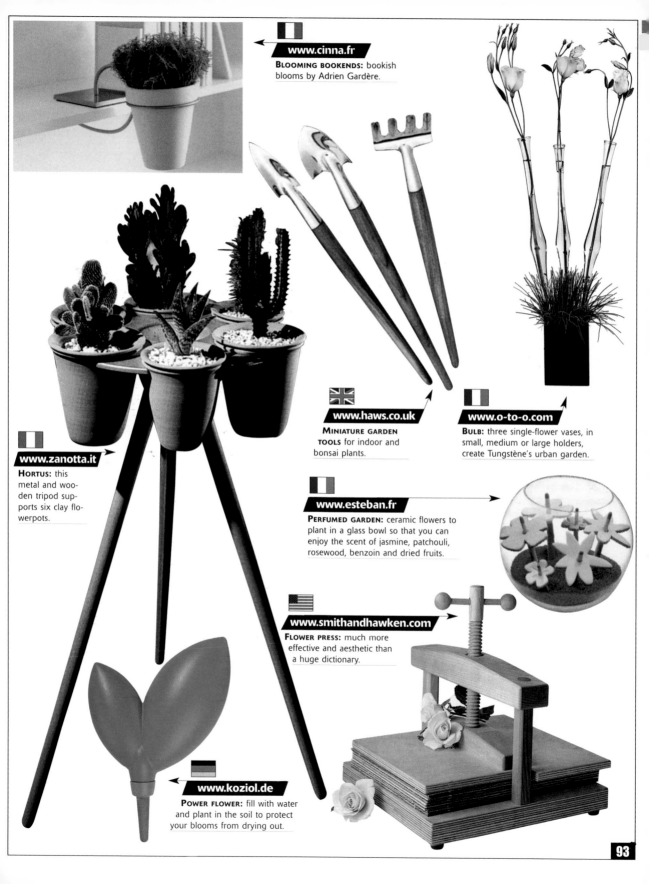

www.simplicitas.se

CANDELA: you have only one candle but, on reflection, two sources of light.

www.leonardo.de

FISH OR FLAME: a floating candle lights up this miniature world.

www.exemplaire.fr

THE MONKS OF CLUNY ABBEY used wax taper to monitor the transformation of their wine, by watching the colour of the flame. In this model a button ensures the candle is pushed up as it burns.

www.leonardo.de

INTERIOR DESIGN: sand, pebbles and marbles help to shed light on the subject.

www.stilic-force.com

TRANSPARENCY: Nicolas Trüb designed this ingenious system of casting light on images with a flickering flame.

www.talisman-trading.co.uk

LANTERN: the lamp may not be magical but the patterns and quality of light certainly are.

www.stallinga.nl

SOCKET TO THEM: the design of this flame is never short-circuited.

www.artistavisitatore.it

ALL IN A ROW: these designs are sold in pairs, threes, fives or sevens. Endlessly illuminating.

www.ikea.com

IS IT A VASE OR A CANDLE? Let its twisted spiral decide.

www.romanticglobe.de

PERFECTLY BALANCED: the wax doesn't surround the wick but melts when licked by the flame. A design that's literally on a roll.

www.raumgestalt-en.de

DECODER: the message isn't in the bottle but around the glass. Light the candle to see what the winged messenger has to say.

www.planetdesign.nl

RECTO-VERSO: candles, slender or chunky, fit in both ends of this holder. Turns your world upside down but keeps it alight just the same.

95

www.nobilis.fr

CONTEMPORARY ANTIQUE: Miller and Bertaux draw inspiration from the past for their modern design.

www.leijn.com

FRIED EGGS: rugs made of soft New Zealand wool complete with inflatable egg yolks, designed by Isabelle Leijn.

www.interiorinternet.com

KRENKERUP: an intriguing woollen maze carpet with different depths of pile. Children love it.

www.ligne-roset.tm.fr

STRIPE DIALOGUE: read questions and answers on this woollen rug by Jean-Charles de Castelbajac – a new interpretaton of 'lines of communication'.

www.sarahwels.com

FIGUEROS: Sarah Wels transfers photographic prints onto fabric.

Les figues aussi sont photogéniques

www.ritzenhoff.de

CARTOON CUSHIONS: François Gervais tells a story of romance in four parts.

www.interiorinternet.com

SNOWDRIFT: a trompe-l'œil rug for those keen to make early morning tracks in the snow.

www.cinna.fr

KLOC: this wool-covered felt rug by Kristian Gavoille comes complete with an enigmatic bump.

www.lachaiselongue.fr

HUNTING TROPHY: a fun fake-fur rug for animal lovers.

www.sergelesage.com

INFINITY: this yin and yang rug is 100 per cent wool and two metres in diameter.

www.tec-health

CUBE LEVITATOR: four images suspended in mid-air by magnetic forces.

www.h1e.de

FOTOCLIP: two magnetic metal curves keep photos firmly in place.

www.legnomagia.it

MAKING SHEEP'S EYES: a humorous frame made of felt and wood.

www.propagandaonline.com

BONE: an ingenious design that can be dismantled and positioned either vertically or horizontally.

www.efx.co.uk

ALUMINIUM ALBUM: each page is a metal frame in this professional portfolio.

www.ibride.fr

ANTI SCHOCK: a foam and aluminium photo frame from the hybrid 'Objenétique' collection.

www.outlookzelco.com

MIRA: a transparent photograph holder, complete with steel ball for stability.

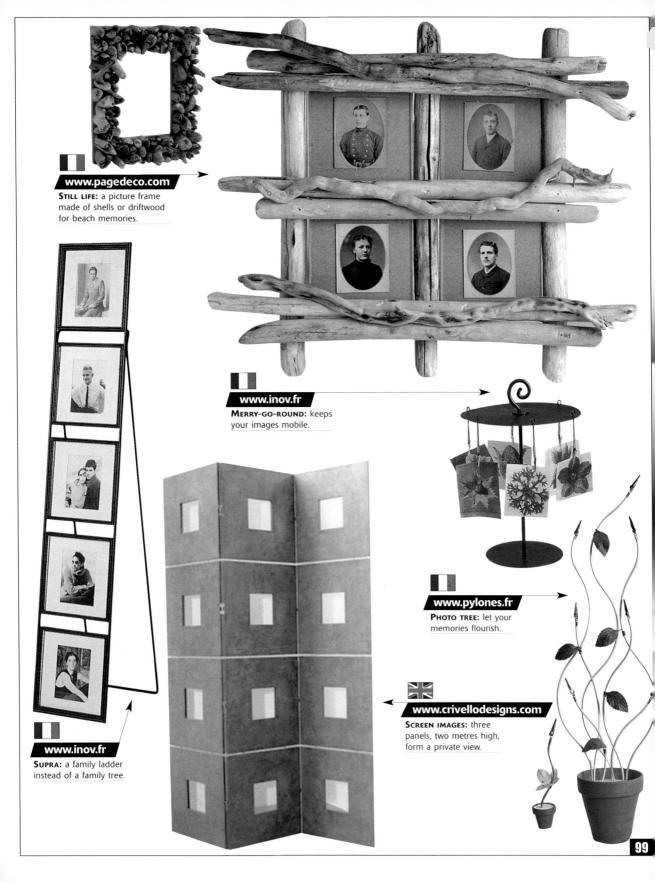

www.pagedeco.com

STILL LIFE: a picture frame made of shells or driftwood for beach memories.

www.inov.fr

MERRY-GO-ROUND: keeps your images mobile.

www.pylones.fr

PHOTO TREE: let your memories flourish.

www.crivellodesigns.com

SCREEN IMAGES: three panels, two metres high, form a private view.

www.inov.fr

SUPRA: a family ladder instead of a family tree.

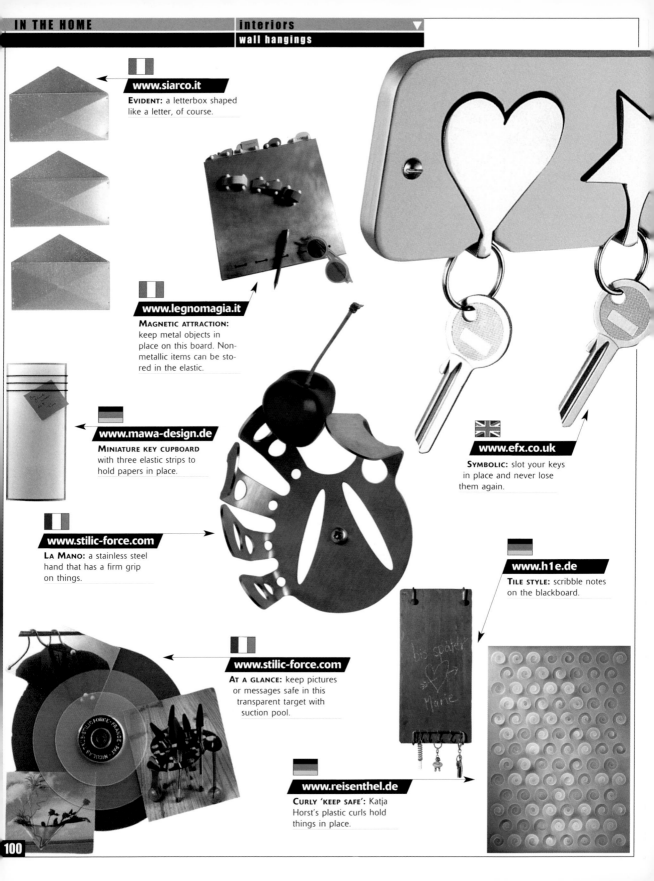

www.siarco.it

EVIDENT: a letterbox shaped like a letter, of course.

www.legnomagia.it

MAGNETIC ATTRACTION: keep metal objects in place on this board. Non-metallic items can be stored in the elastic.

www.mawa-design.de

MINIATURE KEY CUPBOARD with three elastic strips to hold papers in place.

www.stilic-force.com

LA MANO: a stainless steel hand that has a firm grip on things.

www.efx.co.uk

SYMBOLIC: slot your keys in place and never lose them again.

www.h1e.de

TILE STYLE: scribble notes on the blackboard.

www.stilic-force.com

AT A GLANCE: keep pictures or messages safe in this transparent target with suction pool.

www.reisenthel.de

CURLY 'KEEP SAFE': Katja Horst's plastic curls hold things in place.

www.kleinundmore.de

REMINDER: a magnetic exclamation mark designed by Akantus.

www.koziol.de

BILLY attaches himself to the wall with a suction pad ready to help hang things.

www.ardi.fr

CLIP: keep photos safe.

www.leitmotiv.nl

RE-USE: bath plugs get a second lease of life

www.ardi.fr

JAWS APPLAUSE: sharks get their teeth into anything.

RIFLESSO: no strict lines between reality and imagination.

www.duepiu.com

NARCISSUS: like Narcissus you can see your reflection in the undulating mirror.

www.inov-France.com

ON REFLECTION: framed by a scribble design.

www.koziol.de

LOOK: suction pads keep this mirror face in place by its ears.

www.rudebravo.com

GIUDITTA: a window through which to reflect.

www.porada.it

ELISO: elegant and versatile, this oval mirror is supported by a frame that becomes a shelf.

www.horm.it

HOPI: large, robust and very simple, this mirror is suspended by thick cord.

www.porada.it

NITEO: a clean and pretty break.

www.blomus.com

IRRÉSISTIBLE: an attractive wall mirror on a magnetic support.

www.talisman-trading.co.uk

SAHARA: a mirror inlaid with camel bone, imported from Morocco.

www.lamaconcept.nl

SELF-PORTRAIT: in a leather frame, this mirror sits on the desk like a picture frame.

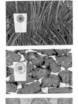

www.outlookzelco.com

Tico proves that time does not always move in straight lines.

www.x-form.de

Time Box: a foldable cardboard clock.

www.chaiselongue.fr

Submarine & sub-zero: tell the time on clocks that take you back 20,000 leagues under the sea.

www.artistavistatore.it

Tick tock: an aluminium pendulum with no frills.

www.benzadesign.com

Pin Up Clock: pin this fake-fur clock to the wall in twelve strategic places.

www.stallinga.nl

Strict minimum: keep time with no more than a pair of clock hands on your wall.

www.efx.co.uk

Zig-Zag: a triptych clock with photo frames for loved ones – keep tabs on the time and the timeless.

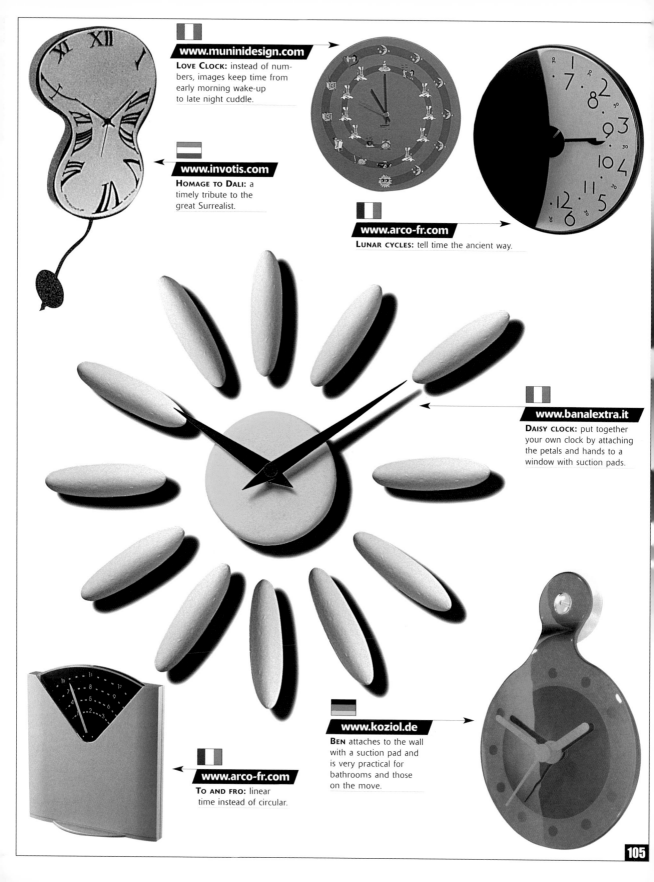

www.muninidesign.com

LOVE CLOCK: instead of numbers, images keep time from early morning wake-up to late night cuddle.

www.invotis.com

HOMAGE TO DALI: a timely tribute to the great Surrealist.

www.arco-fr.com

LUNAR CYCLES: tell time the ancient way.

www.banalextra.it

DAISY CLOCK: put together your own clock by attaching the petals and hands to a window with suction pads.

www.koziol.de

BEN attaches to the wall with a suction pad and is very practical for bathrooms and those on the move.

www.arco-fr.com

TO AND FRO: linear time instead of circular.

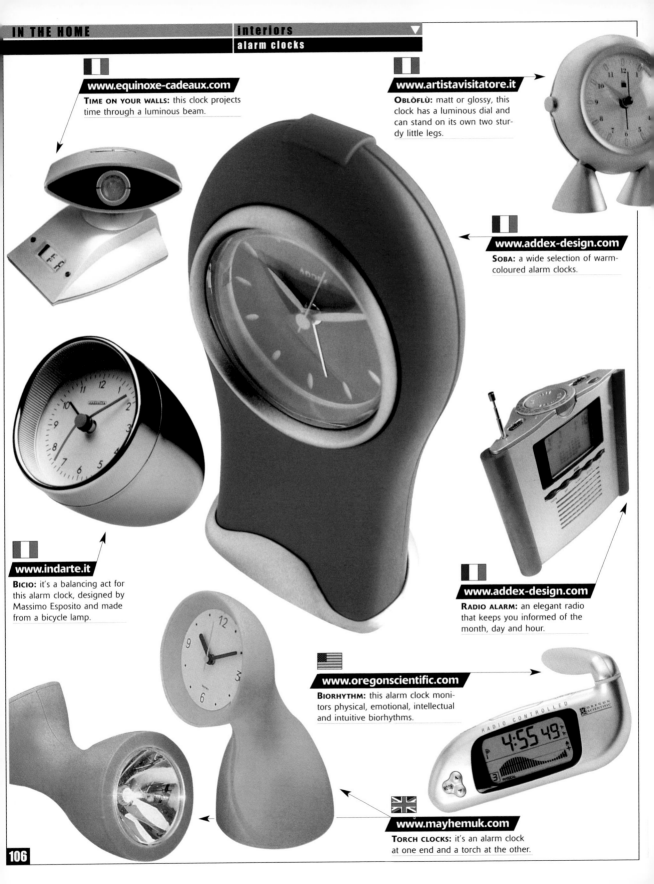

www.equinoxe-cadeaux.com

TIME ON YOUR WALLS: this clock projects time through a luminous beam.

www.artistavisitatore.it

OBLÒFLÙ: matt or glossy, this clock has a luminous dial and can stand on its own two sturdy little legs.

www.addex-design.com

SOBA: a wide selection of warm-coloured alarm clocks.

www.indarte.it

BICIO: it's a balancing act for this alarm clock, designed by Massimo Esposito and made from a bicycle lamp.

www.addex-design.com

RADIO ALARM: an elegant radio that keeps you informed of the month, day and hour.

www.oregonscientific.com

BIORHYTHM: this alarm clock monitors physical, emotional, intellectual and intuitive biorhythms.

www.mayhemuk.com

TORCH CLOCKS: it's an alarm clock at one end and a torch at the other.

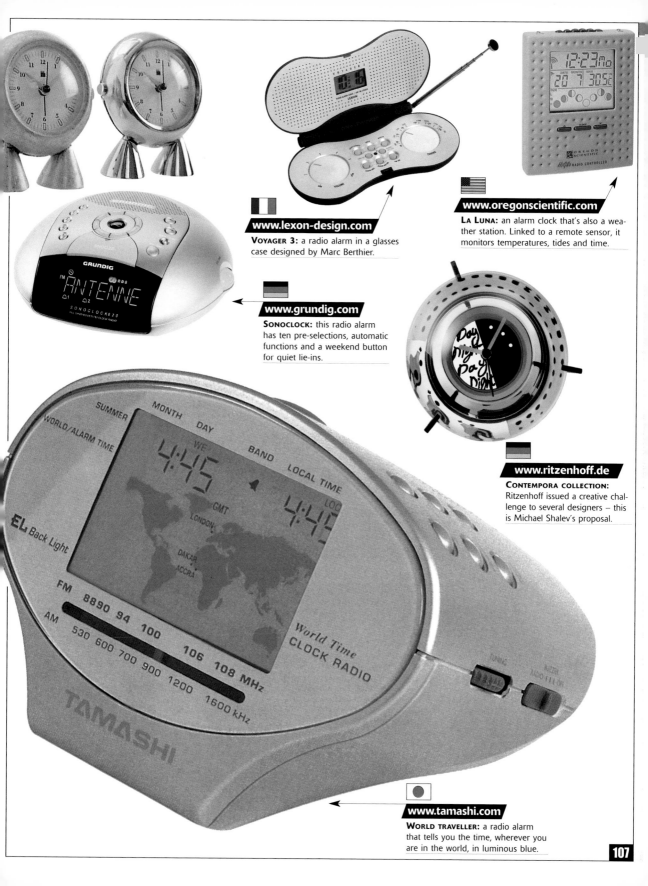

www.lexon-design.com

VOYAGER 3: a radio alarm in a glasses case designed by Marc Berthier.

www.oregonscientific.com

LA LUNA: an alarm clock that's also a weather station. Linked to a remote sensor, it monitors temperatures, tides and time.

www.grundig.com

SONOCLOCK: this radio alarm has ten pre-selections, automatic functions and a weekend button for quiet lie-ins.

www.ritzenhoff.de

CONTEMPORA COLLECTION: Ritzenhoff issued a creative challenge to several designers – this is Michael Shalev's proposal.

www.tamashi.com

WORLD TRAVELLER: a radio alarm that tells you the time, wherever you are in the world, in luminous blue.

www.dalvey.com

POCKET FLASKS: complete with telescopic cup encased in one side.

www.vuitton.fr

A CASE FOR LOUIS VUITTON: all you need for a high-class whisky tasting.

www.zippo.com

ZIPPO: since the invention of the famous windproof lighter in 1932, over 300 million have been sold worldwide. This is the gold version.

www.wedgwood.com

SPIRAL: an ashtray and ceramic lighter lighter by Nick Munro.

www.authenticmodels.com

HIDDEN SECRETS: originally invented by Prince Edward, son of Queen Victoria, the stick contains both a compass and a whisky flask.

www.lexon-design.com

PYROS: an electronic gas lighter in matt aluminium, designed by Marc Berthier.

www.ligne-roset.tm.fr

BY DESIGN: four ashtrays with individual style by Sophie Suchodolski.

www.banalextra.it

VIETATO: the ashtray with attitude.

www.ceramique.com

ELEPHANT PIPE: a traditional pipe from a collection by Compartment Fumeur.

www.stallinga.nl

PORTABLE STYLE: a fold-out metal ashtray.

www.adhoc-design.de

LIGHTER DESIGN: the orange colour in the reservoir responds to the lit flame.

www.mayhemuk.com

LIGHTER WATCH: all it takes is just one click. This analogue watch has a hidden cigarette lighter.

www.etainsducampanile.com

TRADITIONAL: made of pewter and distressed to look antique by a special technique.

www.rmn.fr

COMPAS: a reproduction 16th-century compass.

www.roche-bobois.com

PREFACE: a cherry wood bookcase with a flap that folds down to become a desktop.

www.fuerstenberg-porzellan.com

PAPERWEIGHT: just one of twelve zodiac designs in porcelain.

www.katespaperie.com

AT THE SHARP END: an authentic traditional sharpener, manually operated, with a small window through which to watch the mechanism at work.

www.zenith-watches.de

SHIPS CHRONOMETER: this prestigious precision instrument is also a coveted decorative piece with brass watchcase and protective mahogany box.

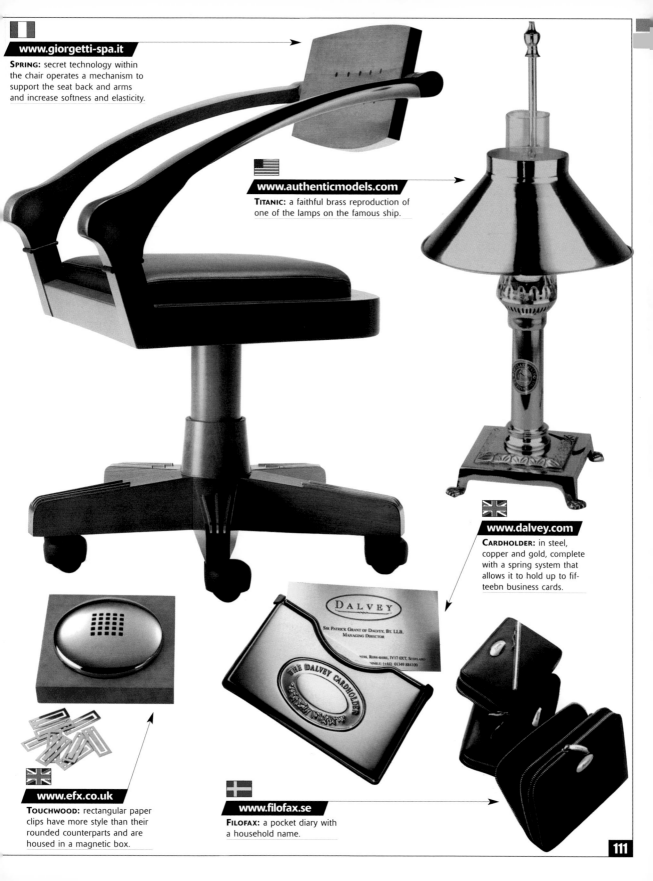

www.giorgetti-spa.it

SPRING: secret technology within the chair operates a mechanism to support the seat back and arms and increase softness and elasticity.

www.authenticmodels.com

TITANIC: a faithful brass reproduction of one of the lamps on the famous ship.

www.dalvey.com

CARDHOLDER: in steel, copper and gold, complete with a spring system that allows it to hold up to fifteebn business cards.

DALVEY

SIR PATRICK GRANT OF DALVEY, BT. LL.B.
MANAGING DIRECTOR

NESS, ROSS-SHIRE, IV17 0XT, SCOTLAND

MBLE: (+44) 01349 884100

THE DALVEY CARDHOLDER

www.efx.co.uk

TOUCHWOOD: rectangular paper clips have more style than their rounded counterparts and are housed in a magnetic box.

www.filofax.se

FILOFAX: a pocket diary with a household name.

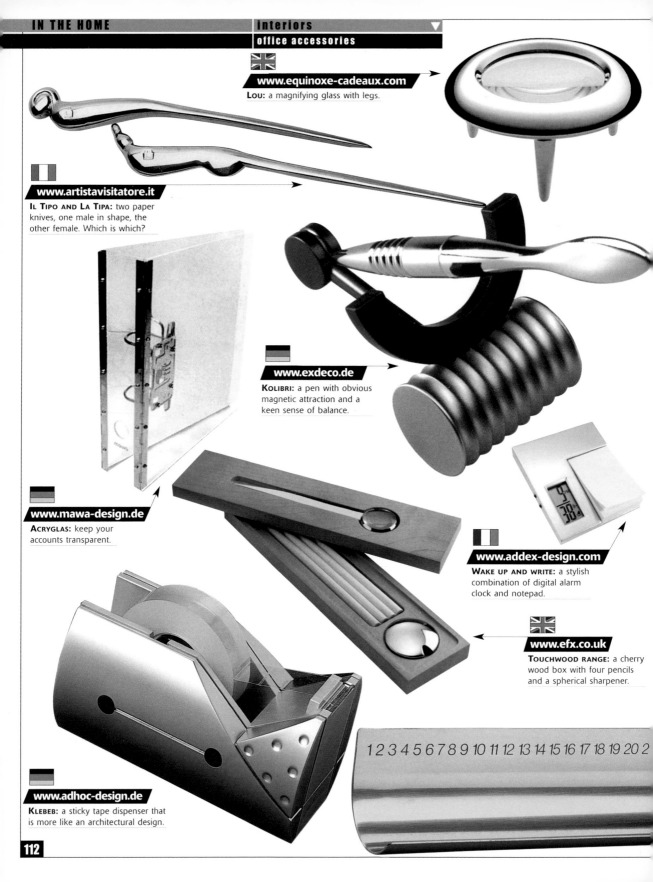

www.equinoxe-cadeaux.com

LOU: a magnifying glass with legs.

www.artistavisitatore.it

IL TIPO AND LA TIPA: two paper knives, one male in shape, the other female. Which is which?

www.exdeco.de

KOLIBRI: a pen with obvious magnetic attraction and a keen sense of balance.

www.mawa-design.de

ACRYGLAS: keep your accounts transparent.

www.addex-design.com

WAKE UP AND WRITE: a stylish combination of digital alarm clock and notepad.

www.efx.co.uk

TOUCHWOOD RANGE: a cherry wood box with four pencils and a spherical sharpener.

www.adhoc-design.de

KLEBEB: a sticky tape dispenser that is more like an architectural design.

1 2 3 4 5 6 7 8 9 10 11 12 13 14 15 16 17 18 19 20 2

www.adhoc-design.de

PAPER CLIP HOLDER: stylish and easy to use.

www.folle.dk

SELF-SERVICE ADHESIVE: the design and weight (1.2kg) of this dispenser mean you only need to use one hand.

www.bonaldo.it

WINNY IO: a cool spacious chair design from Bonaldo.

www.katespaperie.com

NO TEARS CROCODILE: a stapler with teeth and attitude.

www.folle.dk

THE WRITE DATE: a calendar and pen holder.

6 27 28 29 30 31

www.folle.dk

CURVACEOUS CARD HOLDER: Folmer Christensen's wonderful wave design.

113

www.addex-design.com

SUM IT UP IN STYLE: easy to handle and carry and available in a range of colours.

www.golla.fi

GRASSY DESK: even pens enjoy a patch of green in which to rest.

www.reisenthel.de

STYLE FILE: files with zip fasteners keep your documents safe.

www.kutsuma.co.jp

ADJUSTABLE PENCIL SHARPENERS: five degrees of sharp are possible with these sharpeners.

www.sabbah.fr

SHARK STAPLER: shows no mercy but lots of style.

www.kreo.com

BUREAU CABANE: Sylvie Filière and Jean Dingjian designed a limited edition of these humorous desks.

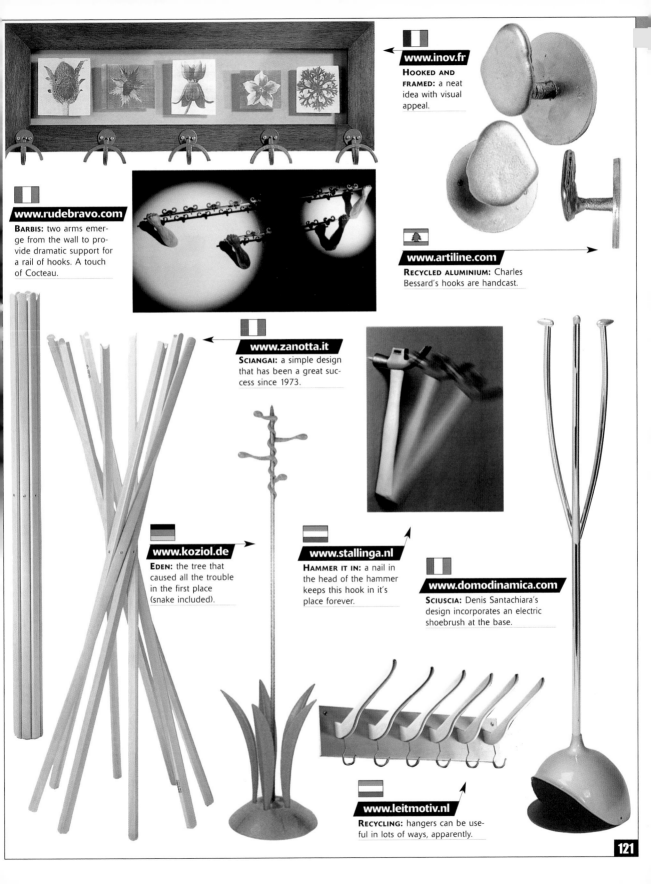

www.inov.fr
HOOKED AND FRAMED: a neat idea with visual appeal.

www.rudebravo.com
BARBIS: two arms emerge from the wall to provide dramatic support for a rail of hooks. A touch of Cocteau.

www.artiline.com
RECYCLED ALUMINIUM: Charles Bessard's hooks are handcast.

www.zanotta.it
SCIANGAI: a simple design that has been a great success since 1973.

www.koziol.de
EDEN: the tree that caused all the trouble in the first place (snake included).

www.stallinga.nl
HAMMER IT IN: a nail in the head of the hammer keeps this hook in it's place forever.

www.domodinamica.com
SCIUSCIA: Denis Santachiara's design incorporates an electric shoebrush at the base.

www.leitmotiv.nl
RECYCLING: hangers can be useful in lots of ways, apparently.

www.interiorinternet.com

LIBERIA: a trompe-l'oeil screen, decorated with a detailed painting by Piero Fornasetti.

www.o-to-o.com

RAIN CURTAIN: a delicate fibreglass mosquito screen with an integral blown-glass vase creates a buzz.

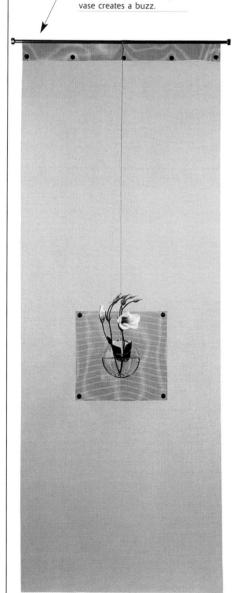

www.interiorinternet.com

ARENGA: Annemette Beck's design in linen and wood fibres allows the light to filter through.

www.talisman-trading.co.uk

MOROCCAN STYLE: a wrought-iron screen that can transform the room into a palace from the Arabian Nights.

www.porada.it

ALHAMBRA: a door carved with Moorish designs, complete with mirror.

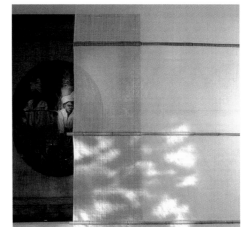

www.zaafdesign.com

BUBBLES: seven lamps trapped between two surfaces create an unusual stream of light.

www.acova.fr

CLARIAN: one of Acova's large range of radiators that act as semi-partitions.

www.raumgestalt-en.de

DREAM SCREEN: soothingly pale screens help create a space in which to meditate.

www.nobilis.fr

AUTUMN, an atmospheric silk veil from the Silk Cocoon Collection by Nobilis, specialists in fabrics for interiors.

www.soca.fr

BAMBOU: Éric Raffy designed this attractive screen in metal cloth.

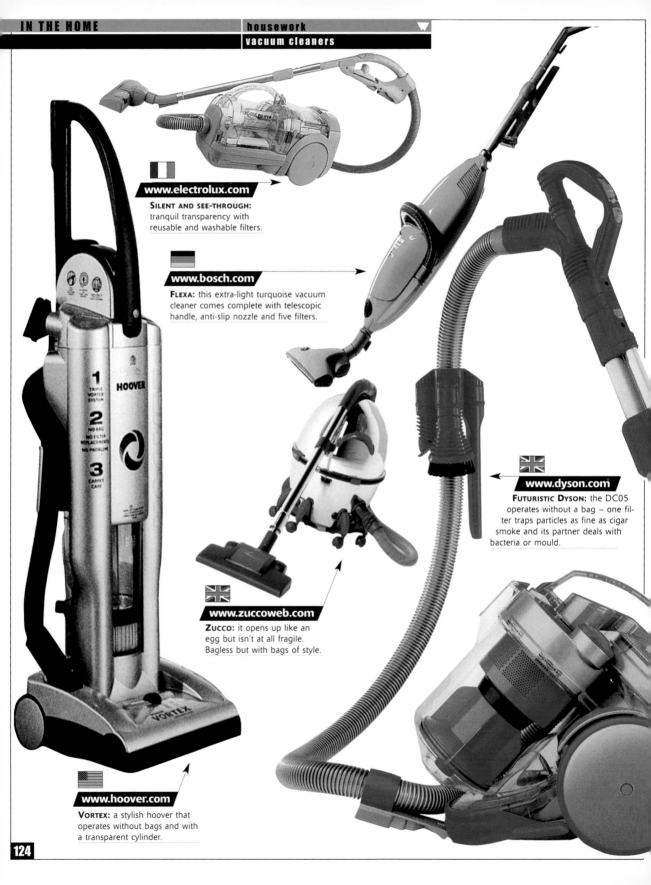

www.electrolux.com

SILENT AND SEE-THROUGH: tranquil transparency with reusable and washable filters.

www.bosch.com

FLEXA: this extra-light turquoise vacuum cleaner comes complete with telescopic handle, anti-slip nozzle and five filters.

www.dyson.com

FUTURISTIC DYSON: the DC05 operates without a bag – one filter traps particles as fine as cigar smoke and its partner deals with bacteria or mould.

www.zuccoweb.com

ZUCCO: it opens up like an egg but isn't at all fragile. Bagless but with bags of style.

www.hoover.com

VORTEX: a stylish hoover that operates without bags and with a transparent cylinder.

www.princess.nl

PRINCESS: a miniature vacuum cleaner (23cm high) that does a royal job of quick clean-ups.

www.samsung.com

SUBCOMPACT: a sky-blue vacuum cleaner in the Micro Veloce range, with four levels of filtration and hand-held remote controls.

www.polti.it

LECOLOGICO: it operates with a water filter rather than bag and can even handle moist particles.

www.viceversashop.com

LITTLE GEM: a chrome-plated, circular and compact machine.

www.lge.com

SANI PUNCH from LG Goldstar: a household appliance that looks like a toy. It's small, circular and colourfully translucent.

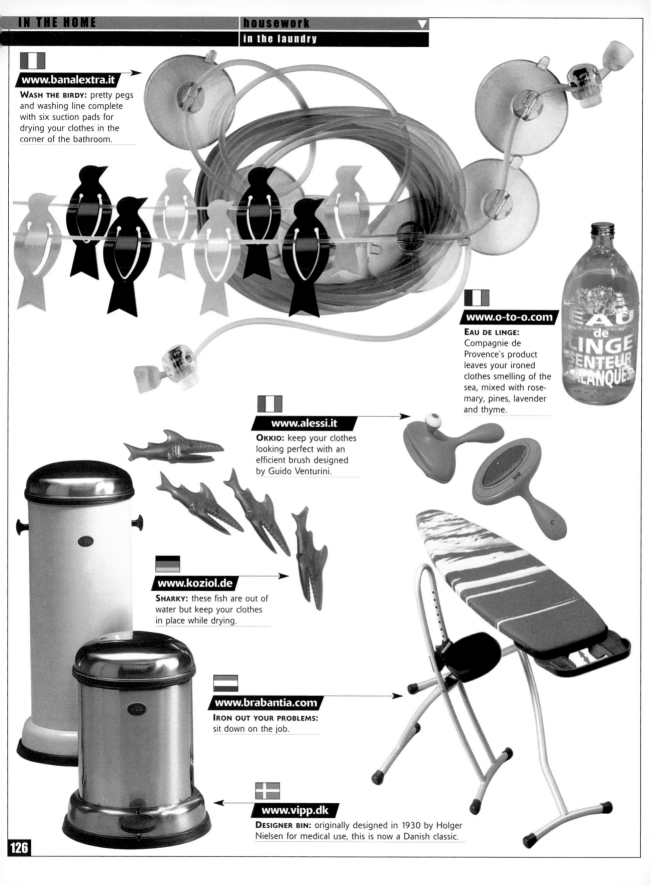

www.banalextra.it

WASH THE BIRDY: pretty pegs and washing line complete with six suction pads for drying your clothes in the corner of the bathroom.

www.o-to-o.com

EAU DE LINGE: Compagnie de Provence's product leaves your ironed clothes smelling of the sea, mixed with rosemary, pines, lavender and thyme.

www.alessi.it

OKKIO: keep your clothes looking perfect with an efficient brush designed by Guido Venturini.

www.koziol.de

SHARKY: these fish are out of water but keep your clothes in place while drying.

www.brabantia.com

IRON OUT YOUR PROBLEMS: sit down on the job.

www.vipp.dk

DESIGNER BIN: originally designed in 1930 by Holger Nielsen for medical use, this is now a Danish classic.

www.planetdesign.nl
EXOTIC: a washing basket in woven plastic, inspired by Thai designs.

www.perigot-fr.com
PHARAOH: a wooden brush with horse hair that reaches high-up places where others fear to go.

www.petiteplanet.com
MISTER QUIET AND MISTER TONIC: Anne Chédeville's soft dolls, made of felt or flannel, are filled with aromatic plants. Pop one in the wardrobe.

www.benzadesign.com
ZAGO: collapsible bins in recycled cardboard are decorated with appropriate designs.

www.efx.co.uk
ECOBIN: recycle your shopping bags in style and save a tree.

www.margherita2000.com
MARGHERITA 2000: the Merloni group's Ariston Digital washing machines can be remotely programmed from a dedicated Internet site.

www.dyson.co.uk
CONTRACTOR: Dyson takes on the world of washing machines following its enormous success with vacuum cleaners.

127

 ❶

www.arclinea.it

ARTUSI: arranged around a central unit complete with sink, hotplates, rubbish bin and shelving.

 ❷

www.whirlpool.com

SLOT-IN KITCHEN: a union of Whirlpool's high-quality equipment and stylish, adjustable design.

 ❸

www.binova.it

SINTESI: the kitchen bar is a new space-saving design.

 ❹

www.lineaquattro.com

CLIO: available in a range of colours, glossy or matt.

 ❺

www.valcucine.it

RICICLA, the eco kitchen, uses ten times less wood than other comparable kitchens and does not use chemical products.

 ❻

www.boffi.it

WORKS: a central multi-purpose unit with professional sink for those with space and style.

 ❼

www.poggenpohl.fr

ALU 2000: the first totally aluminium kitchen from Poggenpohl. Endlessly brilliant.

 ❽

www.snaidero.it

OLA: a curved unit, including hob and sink flush with the worktop.

 ❾

www.bulthaup.com

SYSTEM 25: an innovative yet classic kitchen design.

www.gorenje.com

COLD AS METAL: a curvaceous refrigerator designed in Slovenia.

www.generalelectric.com

AMERICAN STYLE: complete with ice and water dispensers and a quick service hatch.

www.whirlpool.com

CLOCKY WATCH: a refrigerator with something to say for itself.

www.electrolux.com

SCREEN FRIDGE: programmed to monitor its contents and warn when stocks are low on its interactive screen.

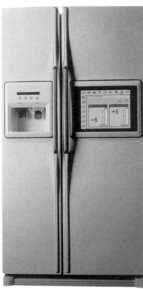

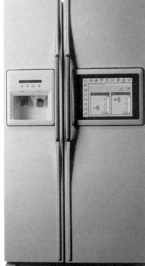

www.zanussi.com

OZ: the shapely door opens courtesy of a large black ball. Inside there's a magical orange light.

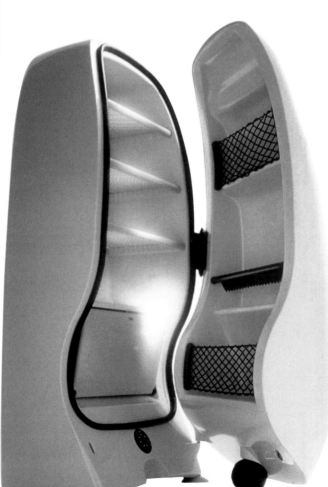

www.samsung.com

FRIDGNET: tomorrow's fridge has a computer linked to the internet to help control it, find recipes, read e-mails or watch televison.

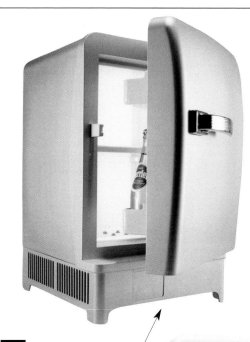

www.minicooler.com

MINICOOLER: only 29cm in height, a pocket fridge that slips easily into a bedroom, office or even a car (connected to the cigarette lighter).

www.daewoo.com

MAGIC MIRROR: push a button and the opaque door becomes transparent.

www.electrolux.com

LEGENDARY: retro in design but forward-looking in eco-technology, the Legend introduces the latest development of absorption technology.

www.smeg.it

BACK TO THE 1950s: design returns to the post-war golden days with this range of fridges in gentle shades of blue, green and cream with soft angles.

www.electrolux.com

COOL NOMAD: the first absorption refrigerator with detachable wheels. The Powerfridge operates by electricity or gas.

www.smeg.it

OPERA: a vitreous ceramic oven top with a multi-function electric oven. Hot stuff.

www.lacanche.com

FONTENAY: Lacanche cookers are equipped with five rings, hotplates, bains-marie and huge ovens. They are described as chefs' pianos and come in a range of ten colours.

www.lacornue.com

CHÂTEAU 80: an old-style stove made by La Cornue, experts in the field since 1908.

www.molteni-france.com

P 145 EVOLUTION: designed by Molteni, this range is for those keen on authenticity and the real art of cooking. Adapted for domestic use, this model has all the features of a professional industrial oven.

www.godin.fr

LA SOUVERAINE 1100: equipped with five rings, one of them covered, a large oven and an integrated hood.

www.aga-rayburn.co.uk

AGA COOKER: invented in 1922 by Gustav Dalen, winner of the Nobel prize for Physics, the Aga maintains a constant temperature day and night. Powered by gas or electricity, it accumulates and stores heat and allows you to steam, grill, stew, roast, braise or fry without pressing any buttons.

•**INSULATED COVERS** keep the hotplates warm and protected.

•**BOILING HOTPLATE:** cooks so quickly that vegetables are ready in an instant without losing their colour and flavour.

•**SIMMERING HOTPLATE:** large enough for several pans at once, it remains at a constant and low temperature for slower cooking.

•**THE BURNER**

•**ROASTING OVEN:** for roasting and baking. Some models have four hot ovens.

•**SIMMERING OVEN:** for long slow cooking and keeping plates warm.

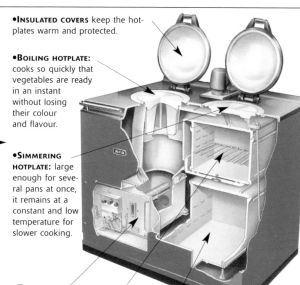

www.effeti.it

VOLA: perfect for worktops positioned in the middle of the room.

www.lacanche.net

SALAMANDRE: an electric grill, complete with spit for cooking crispy and succulent chicken. It attaches to the wall and is available in white, blue, red or green.

www.valcucine.it

ARTEMATICA CERASUS: easy to maintain, this extractor hood is stylishly curved.

www.smeg.it

FOR THE PROFESSIONALS: five gas rings that combine performance with style.

www.novy.com

ESCADE: like all Novy hoods, this one is wonderfully quiet.

www.dedietrich.com

CLASSIC DESIGN: enjoy the effectiveness of horizontal and vertical extraction.

www.faber-flaminia.com

BRIO: a hood with a choice of three speeds, high noise absorption and a cassette aluminium grease filter.

www.zanussi.com

TEO: a prototype oven from Zanussi. The flames on the door window are for artistic effect.

www.fosterspa.it

ALIEN: four gas rings arranged in the arc of a circle for easier simultaneous use.

www.kueppersbusch.de

TWO INNOVATIONS FROM KUEPPERSBUSCH: built-in hotplates in a protective recess (as shown here) or in a drawer that can be hidden away under the worktop.

www.dedietrich.com

LOTUS FLOWER: each of the four rings has eight gas outlets for a more effective and efficient distribution of heat.

www.whirlpool.com

THE SHAPE OF THINGS TO COME: eight different international designs that have revolutionised the traditional microwave.

MICRO MOBILE: a cordless machine, by the Brazilian designer Mario Fioretti.

VERTIGO by the American designer Mark Baldwin operates by hydraulic power.

PIC NIC by Ricardo Giovanetti from Italy. A clever disguise.

SOUND WAVE comes complete with radio. Designed by James Irvine from England.

PICARD created by the Dutch designer Jacco Bregonje.

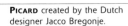

CHEF, the work of Konstantin Grcic from Germany.

POTS PANS, by Frenchman Christophe Pillet.

www.samsung.com

FOUR ON-LINE: a prototype machine that can store five recipes in its memory, downloaded from the Web, and cook the food for the appropriate length of time.

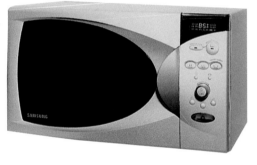

TROLLO, created by the Swedish designer Bjorn Goransson.

www.samsung.com

SAM JUNIOR: following the translucent trend of the last century, this small microwave comes in green, orange or blue.

www.sharp-usa.com

HALF PINT R120DK: red, green, blue, orange or purple, this microwave is currently availably only in the USA. It excels at making popcorn, naturally.

www.samsung.com

MICRO-MOBILE: a powerful microwave that weighs less than 10kg. It can be plugged into the mains or a cigarette lighter. It even works on batteries.

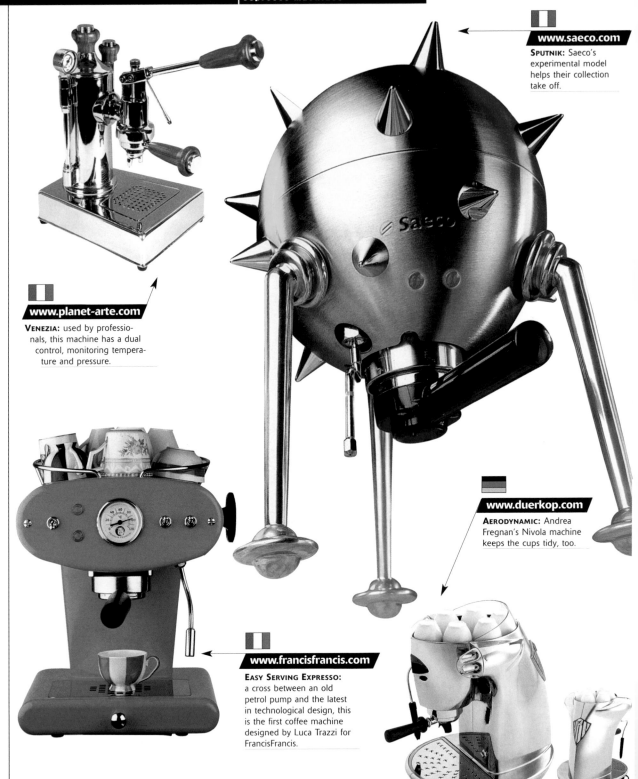

www.saeco.com

SPUTNIK: Saeco's experimental model helps their collection take off.

www.planet-arte.com

VENEZIA: used by professionals, this machine has a dual control, monitoring temperature and pressure.

www.duerkop.com

AERODYNAMIC: Andrea Fregnan's Nivola machine keeps the cups tidy, too.

www.francisfrancis.com

EASY SERVING EXPRESSO: a cross between an old petrol pump and the latest in technological design, this is the first coffee machine designed by Luca Trazzi for FrancisFrancis.

www.magimix.com

ROBOT: this machine grinds the coffee, measures the amount of water and removes the dregs. Automatically easy.

www.lapavoni.com

TURBO CAPPUCCINO: the milk is sucked up from its bottle through a pipe and then emulsified by a special turbine.

www.krups.com

ORCHESTRO: measures the amount of water, monitors the strength of the coffee and can be programmed a day in advance.

www.duerkop.com

MURAL: a new concept in coffee machines that can be attached to the wall. An invention from the Italian architect Grazia Gambino and the Dutch designer Fram van Eeden.

www.lapavoni.com

THE MIDAS TOUCH: an 18-carat gold coffee machine from the legendary Italian company – La Pavoni.

www.coffee4you.com

CAFETINO: this machine makes a true ceremony of coffee breaks.

www.younggeneration.de

SOLAR COFFEE: a solar-powered cappuccino machine adds sunshine to your cup.

www.delonghi.com

MULTI-SKILLED: make filter coffees, cappuccinos or milky coffee – the choice is yours. You can even programme your order electronically up to a day in advance.

www.riviera-et-bar.fr

PALLADIO makes filter coffee and espressos and is the design of Riviera & Bar, inventors in 1969 of the electro-magnetic pump-actioned espresso machine.

www.krups.com

AROMA CONTROL THERM TIMER: keeps coffee warmer for longer due to its isothermal pourer.

www.mono.de

CAFINO is designed along the same lines as a teapot. The coffee infuses in the double filter, which is then removed from the top.

www.bodum.com

SANTOS 3000: the modern electric version of the famous Bodum cafetière from the sixties. Its slanted design is intended to prevent the coffee from burning.

www.bodum.com

SANTOS: the boiling water is sucked into the top compartment, where it mixes with the coffee before being filtered. Designed in 1958 by the architect Kaas Klaeson, this cafetière has been popular ever since.

www.stelton.com

STELTON CAFE-TIÈRE: designed by Arne Jacobsen.

www.guzzini.it

LOLA: a characteristically stylish Italian coffee maker.

141

www.aristonchannel.com

LEON@RDO: WRAP (Web Ready Appliances Protocol) has been developed by the Merloni group to connect electrical appliances to the Internet. Leon@rdo allows you to programme your entire house from a distance.

Don't forget to call Maria!

Bruno, Your friend

www.kitchenaid.com

ROBOT ULTRA POWER: this machine whips, beats, slices, grates and minces in nine stylish colours.

www.siemens-electromenager.com

DESIGNER MIXER: Siemens has commissioned a series of electrical appliances from the designers of Porsche products.

www.belpasta-trattorina.com

WAFFLE MAKER: perfect for making those wonderfully fine and crunchy Italian ice-cream cones.

www.seb.fr

ELECTRONIC SAUCE MAKER: this useful machine heats and mixes all by itself. Free yourself from the stove.

www.viceversashop.com

CHROME MINI-OVEN: for bachelors with style.

www.kenwood.com

ELECTRONIC STEAMER: it works on the same principle as the Chinese bamboo steamer, with three levels for rice, vegetables and fish.

www.lequip.com

CITRUS: this electric juice extractor decants its wares into two glasses.

www.magimix.fr

SYSTEM 5100: invented nearly thirty years ago, the latest Magimix is the machine used by professionals and amateurs alike to prepare food quietly and quickly. This model is chromium-plated.

www.philips.com

METAL FRYER: efficient and stylish, this deep fryer holds four litres.

www.cristel.fr

CAPITELLO: stainless steel and wood in harmony in a versatile kettle design.

www.ikea.com

HOTT: an original and practical union of stainless steel and plastic.

www.stelton.com

NICKEL: a practical, elegant and stylish kettle from Stelton.

www.oxo.com

UPLIFT: just tilt the whistling kettle with the handle and the water pours out easily.

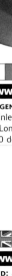

www.delonghi.com

ARGENTO: a cordless stainless steel kettle from DeLonghi that swivels 360 degrees.

www.kenwood.com

CLOUD: a Kenwood kettle inspired by clouds of steam.

www.metrokane.com

CUPID: an angel trumpets the arrival of tea for two. Confirmed bachelors can be alerted by a dragon.

www.rowenta.fr

MAGNUM: practical, powerful and perfectly pretty.

www.bodum.com

CURL: a classic black kettle, cool, cordless and curvaceous.

www.riviera-et-bar.fr

GLOSSY: cordless, ergonomic and equipped with three anti-burn mechanisms.

www.allclad.com

TEA KETTLE: an elegant design from the famous US pan designer.

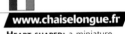

www.allclad.com

COPPER CHEF: a collection of professional copper pans.

www.tefal.fr

THERMOSPOT: the red circle indicates when the frying pan is at the same temperature as the hotplate.

www.chaiselongue.fr

HEART-SHAPED: a miniature pan for romantic breakfasts.

www.lagostina.it

METEORITE FRYING PAN: Lagostina's non-stick masterpiece.

www.evasolo.com

GLASS SAUCEPAN: delight another of your senses when cooking.

www.mauviel.com

PRESERVING PAN IN BEATEN COPPER: Mauviel has been preserving the tradition of high-quality cooking utensils since 1830.

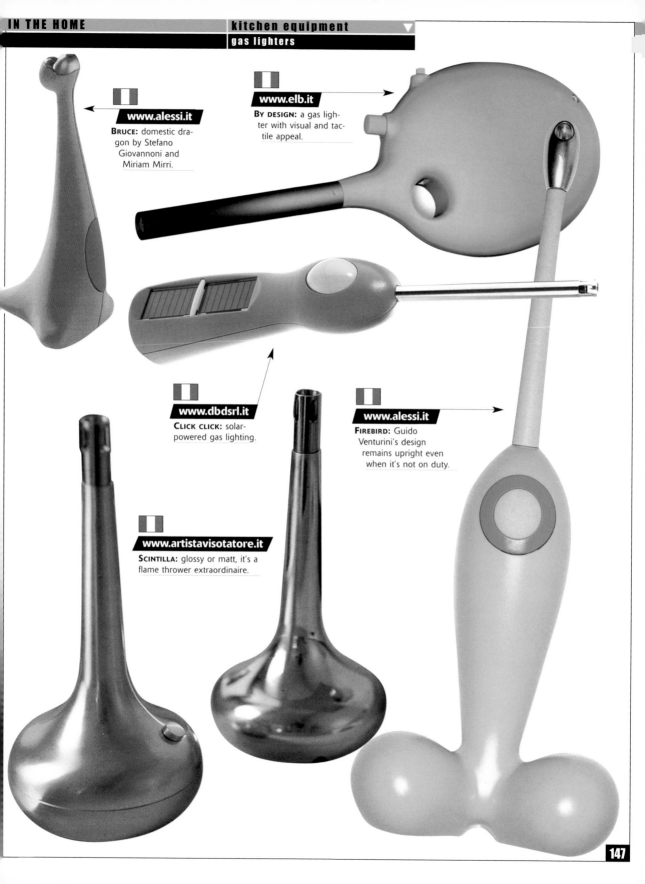

www.alessi.it

BRUCE: domestic dragon by Stefano Giovannoni and Miriam Mirri.

www.elb.it

BY DESIGN: a gas lighter with visual and tactile appeal.

www.dbdsrl.it

CLICK CLICK: solar-powered gas lighting.

www.alessi.it

FIREBIRD: Guido Venturini's design remains upright even when it's not on duty.

www.artistavisotatore.it

SCINTILLA: glossy or matt, it's a flame thrower extraordinaire.

147

www.ronnebybruk.com

ANCESTRAL DESIGN: the Swedish company Ronneby Bruk has been making old-style iron pots since the 19th-century. Eternal, simple and practical.

www.fratelliguzzini.com

ITALIAN STYLE: a pasta cooker designed by Bruno Geccelin for Guzzini, with a lid that doubles as a sieve.

www.seb.fr

UNDER PRESSURE: Seb's Cocotte Minute pressure cooker, produced since 1953, is a universal classic. One of its descendants, Clips, is oval-shaped and perfect for cooking poultry and roasts.

baumalu@dial.oleane.com

IDEAL: Baumalu's voluptuous cooker has a valve that regulates the pressure.

www.evasolo.com

SILVER DOME: for simmering with style.

www.norpro.com

PAN WITH POURER: Krona's pan comes complete with practical pourer that allows the food to drain and remain hot.

www.alessi.it

VAPOUR-SET: Massimo Morozzi's pot incorporates a steamer.

www.magimix.com

ARCADE-WOK: this wok can reach temperatures of up to 400°C due to its built-in cooker.

SOUP OF THE DAY written on the pot: Dualit HotPot SOUP OF THE DAY

www.dualit.com

SOUP OF THE DAY: make soup the old-fashioned way, thanks to today's technology.

www.petiteplanet.com

WALL SPONGE HOLDER with
a pair of safe stainless
steel hands.

www.oncook.fr

STEEL SOAP:
Mastrad's celebrated
soap eliminates all
odours – eternally.

www.ibb-aghifug.com

ORNAMENTAL: a soap dispenser
in glass and metal.

www.koziol.de

SALTO: a clean balancing act.

www.marc-newson.com

DISH DOCTOR: a plastic
drainer by Marc Newson.

www.zanussi.com

MINIATURE DISHWASHER:
perfect after dinner for four.

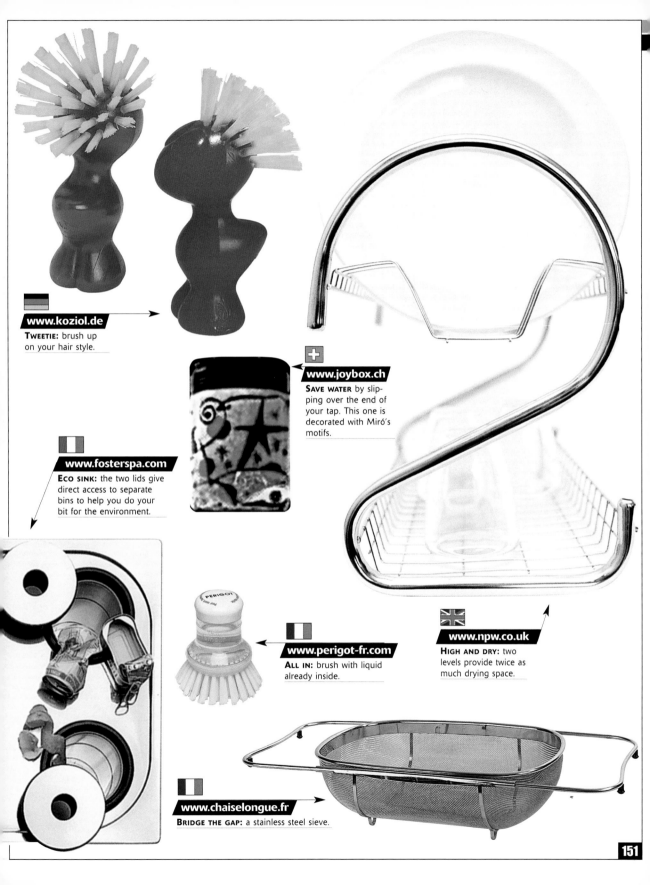

www.koziol.de

TWEETIE: brush up
on your hair style.

www.joybox.ch

SAVE WATER by slip-
ping over the end of
your tap. This one is
decorated with Miró's
motifs.

www.fosterspa.com

ECO SINK: the two lids give
direct access to separate
bins to help you do your
bit for the environment.

www.perigot-fr.com

ALL IN: brush with liquid
already inside.

www.npw.co.uk

HIGH AND DRY: two
levels provide twice as
much drying space.

www.chaiselongue.fr

BRIDGE THE GAP: a stainless steel sieve.

www.biessecasa.it

ROUND AND PASTEL: visually appealing, what would this design score on a scale of one to ten?

www.viceversashop.com

PURE AND SIMPLE, and as shiny as a mirror. Scales designed by Luca Trazzi.

www.soehnle.com

TULIP opens up its four petals to weigh items of different sizes.

www.soehnle.com

FOOD PILOT: these scales can store the nutritional value of 400 food items in their memory and calculate the calorific content. Ideal for healthy eaters, they can even be connected to a PC.

www.wellman.com

FLAT OUT STYLE: perfectly flat, these scales weigh things up in style with numbers that appear on the screen.

www.alessi.it

MOLLY, symmetrical and colourful, a design by Stefano Giovannoni.

www.artistavisitatore.it

GRAMMA: totally aluminium.

www.soehnle.com

MEASURE UP TO THIS: the first set of electronic wall scales in the world. Soehnle have specialised in precision tools since 1868.

www.chaiselongue.fr

MARKET STRATEGY: a range of traditional designs in a wide choice of colours.

www.soehnle.com

SATELLITE SENSITIVITY: Trio is a minimalist design capable of such accuracy it can even weigh letters.

www.duerkop.com

EQUILIBRIUM: designed by Sebastian Conran, son of Sir Terence Conran, these scales operate with nine weights in the form of chrome-plated pebbles.

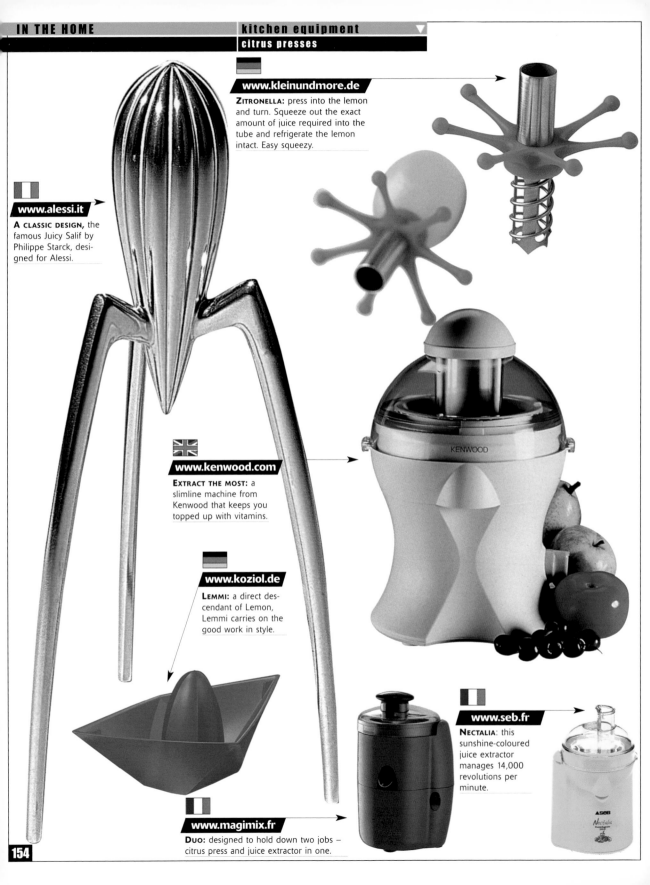

www.kleinundmore.de

ZITRONELLA: press into the lemon and turn. Squeeze out the exact amount of juice required into the tube and refrigerate the lemon intact. Easy squeezy.

www.alessi.it

A CLASSIC DESIGN, the famous Juicy Salif by Philippe Starck, designed for Alessi.

www.kenwood.com

EXTRACT THE MOST: a slimline machine from Kenwood that keeps you topped up with vitamins.

www.koziol.de

LEMMI: a direct descendant of Lemon, Lemmi carries on the good work in style.

www.seb.fr

NECTALIA: this sunshine-coloured juice extractor manages 14,000 revolutions per minute.

www.magimix.fr

DUO: designed to hold down two jobs – citrus press and juice extractor in one.

www.viceversashop.com

CORNUCOPIA: a horn of plenty available in blue, green or red. Designed by Massimo Casola.

www.evasolo.com

TWO IN ONE: a citrus press that acts like a bottle top with a stylish carafe to catch every drop. A fresh idea from Evasolo.

www.metrokane.com

JUICE MACHINE: a curvaceous chromium-plated design.

www.metrokane.com

SPORTING SECRETS: a domestic professional.

www.le-webstore.com

FRIDGE FUN: twelve plastic sheets of wipe-clean magnetic reminders.

www.oxo.com

GOOD GRIP SCOOPS: part of a range of utensils with larger than average grips for increased practicalilty.

www.dbdsrl.it

IGLOO: when placed in the refrigerator, it absorbs odours and puts an end to garlic-flavoured milk.

www.atypyk.com

COWSTICK: bring a rural feel to your city kitchen with six large self-adhesive patterns.

www.chaiselongue.fr

ICE CRUSHER EXTRAORDINAIRE: a small tool with big results.

www.leonardo.de

VENETIAN GLASS: a rainbow of possibilities in this range of glass ice-cream spoons.

www.evasolo.com

PUMPKIN: the supple plastic lid forms an ice-tray while the serving bowl keeps the cubes cold. The tongs fit neatly in the centre.

www.ikea.com

THINK OUTSIDE THE SQUARE with these flexible moulds that make shapely and fun cubes for parties.

www.banalextra.it

VERY COOL SPOONS:
1) fill the plastic mould with water;
2) store in refrigerator;
3) place in glass like a spoon and chill your drink with style.

www.yoshikin.co.jp

GLOBAL: a Japanese brand recommended by the professionals for its anti-slip handle (even when gripped by wet hands).

www.fratelliguzzini.com

EXCALIBUR: Ross Lovegrove was inspired by the legendary sword for his design.

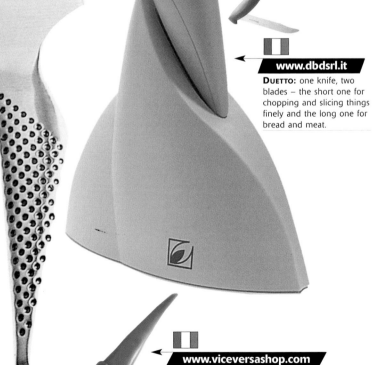

www.zwilling.com

ERGONOMIC: just the feel of the handle is enough to make you want to own one.

www.dbdsrl.it

DUETTO: one knife, two blades – the short one for chopping and slicing things finely and the long one for bread and meat.

www.evasolo.com

MISSION CONTROL: three fruit knives – one to remove the core, the second to peel and the third to cut. All you need to do is lend a hand.

www.viceversashop.com

IN AT THE SHARP END: a knife sharpener with teeth, designed by Giovanni Guacci.

www.sievert-line.de

CLEAR CUT: a transparent plastic knife holder that makes your choice of utensil easier.

www.adhoc-design.de

CERAMIC KNIVES that are 30 per cent stronger than steel and never need sharpening. Designed by Eberhard Hagman.

www.muninidesign.com

FISH KNIFE: so convincing you may be tempted to put it in the aquarium.

www.dozorme-claude.fr

HAUTE CUISINE: a top-quality steel knife good enough for the top professionals.

www.oncook.com

AXOS by Mastrad: a knife that combines precision, quality, comfort and safety.

www.artistavisitatore.it

TAIO SET: a bread knife, a meat knife and a serving fork held in place between rolls of wood.

www.legnoart.it

KATANA: these ziconium oxide knives are said to be indestructible. Only a diamond tip could damage their blade.

www.typhooneurope.com

ROOKIE STIX: a complete and colourful range of plastic chopsticks, joined at the hip.

www.forkchops.com

UFO: East meets West, somewhere in the middle.

www.koziol.de

YUMMI AND HANNI: the squirrel's tail gets in a jam and the bee works the honey pot.

www.oncook.fr

OROS: a peeler-zester designed by Mastrad.

www.simplicitas.se

PLUS: a butter knife designed by Olof Söderholm that works as smoothly and naturally as an extension of your hand.

www.mono.com

ONE POTATO, TWO POTATO: the knife peels and the unusual fork keeps the vegetable in its place.

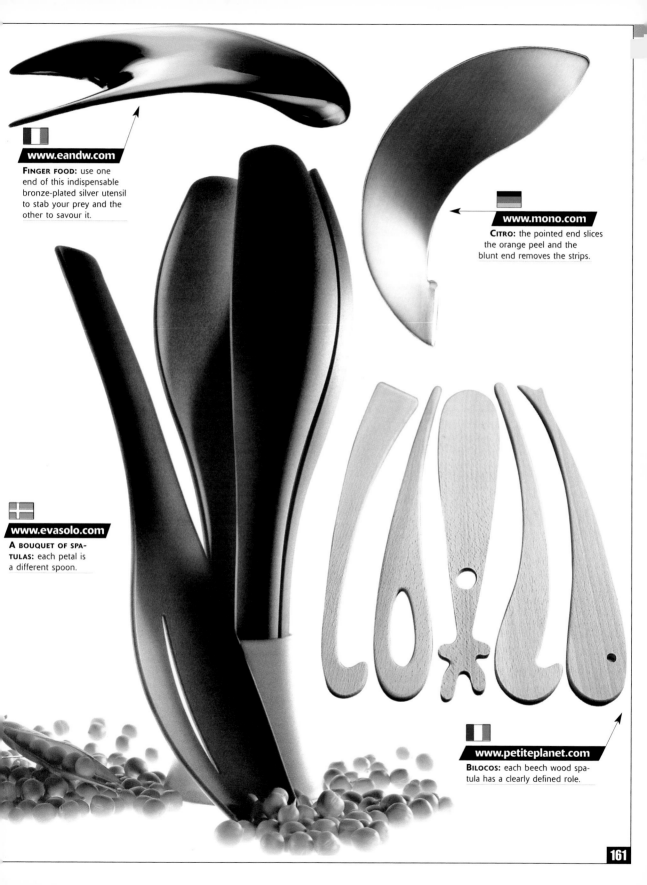

www.eandw.com

FINGER FOOD: use one end of this indispensable bronze-plated silver utensil to stab your prey and the other to savour it.

www.mono.com

CITRO: the pointed end slices the orange peel and the blunt end removes the strips.

www.evasolo.com

A BOUQUET OF SPATULAS: each petal is a different spoon.

www.petiteplanet.com

BILOCOS: each beech wood spatula has a clearly defined role.

www.duerkop.com

OYSTER SET: a metal glove and knife ensure safe enjoyment of this seafood delicacy.

www.pylones.fr

WING IT: a butterfly tin opener that makes the task an art form.

www.oncook.com

CRAB: a crustacean bottle-opener from Mastrad.

www.banalextra.it

HAND IT OVER: silicone oven gloves resist temperatures of up to 250°C.

www.journee-france.com

SNAIL POT: starve the snails by adding flour and thyme.

www.oncook.com

A STYLISH HAND WHISK, complete with a caged canary.

www.moulinex.fr

HANDY GRATER: designed to grate almost everything.

www.alessi.it

FOLPO: a measuring jug with an octopus-shaped whisk, designed by Marta Sansoni.

www.exemplaire.fr

RICE BOWL: a much larger version of a tea infuser.

www.typhooneurope.com

SHARK: gets his teeth into corks and shows no mercy.

www.muninidesign.com

CHESTNUT CUTTER: small retractable teeth slice through chestnut skins.

www.chaiselongue.fr

DOMESTIC ANIMAL and table sculpture, this stylish piece combines function with form. And it cracks nuts.

www.koziol.de

MC CRACKER: this little fellow has strong teeth. Just one turn of the handle and the problem is cracked.

www.details-produkte.de

CRACKING IDEA: two simple nutcrackers that work on the simple principle of leverage.

www.bodum.com

NUT MILL: the genius lies in the base where all the broken shells are collected.

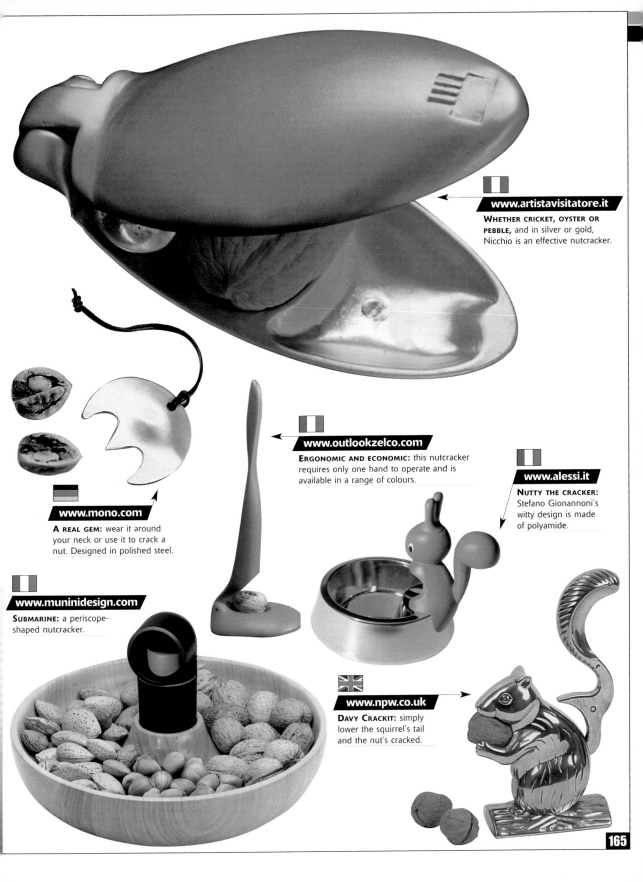

www.artistavisitatore.it

WHETHER CRICKET, OYSTER OR PEBBLE, and in silver or gold, Nicchio is an effective nutcracker.

www.outlookzelco.com

ERGONOMIC AND ECONOMIC: this nutcracker requires only one hand to operate and is available in a range of colours.

www.alessi.it

NUTTY THE CRACKER: Stefano Gionannoni's witty design is made of polyamide.

www.mono.com

A REAL GEM: wear it around your neck or use it to crack a nut. Designed in polished steel.

www.muninidesign.com

SUBMARINE: a periscope-shaped nutcracker.

www.npw.co.uk

DAVY CRACKIT: simply lower the squirrel's tail and the nut's cracked.

www.leitmotiv.nl

CUCCI LUCCI: part kitchen chandelier, part utensil hanger.

www.alessi.it

MULTI-PURPOSE: a chopping board with a smaller surface for slicing vegetables.

www.alessi.it

ALPHONSE: Sowden's attractive design for Alessi emits a melodic reminder that the cooking time is up.

www.bodum.com

TRANSPARENT TIMER: a green drop of water to attach to your window with a suction pad. Wait 99 minutes and the bleep will sound.

www.studiofusion.co.uk

KITCHEN COMPANION: an elevated bin topped by a chopping board. An excellent idea by Antonio Arevalo.

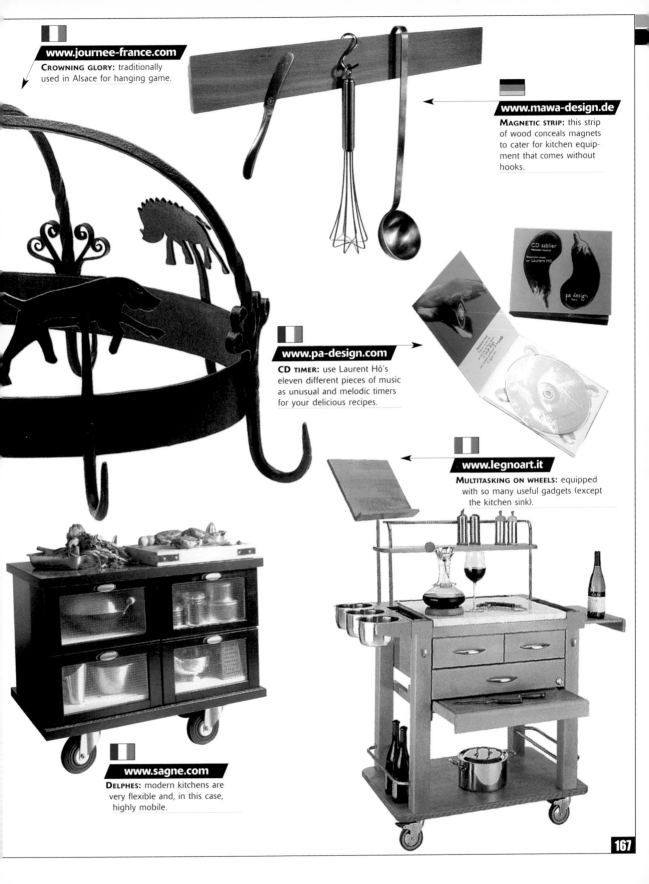

www.journee-france.com

CROWNING GLORY: traditionally used in Alsace for hanging game.

www.mawa-design.de

MAGNETIC STRIP: this strip of wood conceals magnets to cater for kitchen equipment that comes without hooks.

www.pa-design.com

CD TIMER: use Laurent Hô's eleven different pieces of music as unusual and melodic timers for your delicious recipes.

www.legnoart.it

MULTITASKING ON WHEELS: equipped with so many useful gadgets (except the kitchen sink).

www.sagne.com

DELPHES: modern kitchens are very flexible and, in this case, highly mobile.

www.kenwood.com

GRATI: Kenwood's latest design – a cordless electric grater with push-button control for use at the table.

www.biessecasa.it

PASS THE CHEESE PLEASE: easy to handle and pass to fellow diners. Just grab the handle and the lid does the rest.

www.hogri.com

SAY CHEESE! This little chap has to stick his tongue out for a living.

www.koziol.de

TOPOLINO keeps a lid on things.

www.stelton.com

STYLISH: a simple and elegant design.

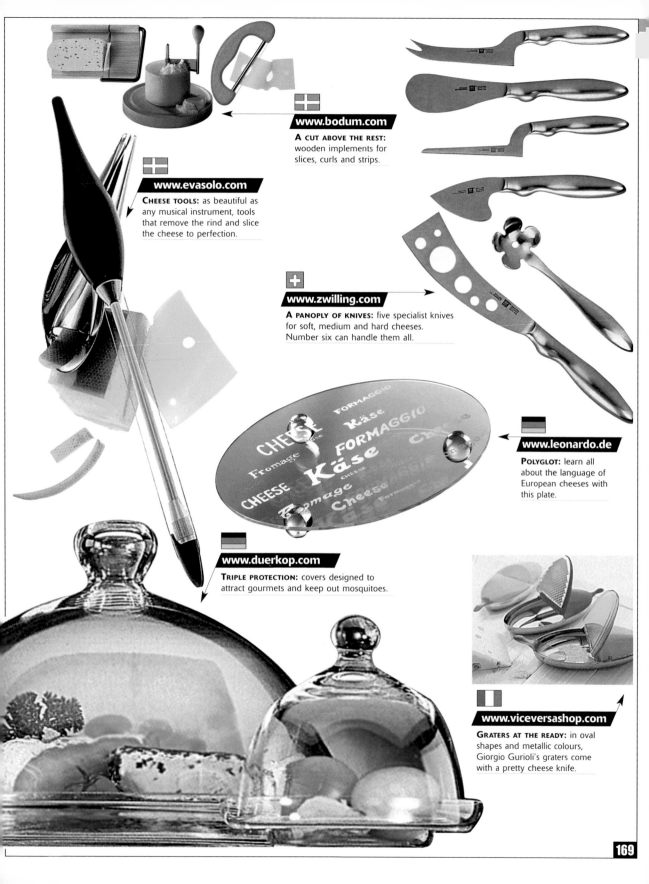

www.bodum.com

A CUT ABOVE THE REST: wooden implements for slices, curls and strips.

www.evasolo.com

CHEESE TOOLS: as beautiful as any musical instrument, tools that remove the rind and slice the cheese to perfection.

www.zwilling.com

A PANOPLY OF KNIVES: five specialist knives for soft, medium and hard cheeses. Number six can handle them all.

www.leonardo.de

POLYGLOT: learn all about the language of European cheeses with this plate.

www.duerkop.com

TRIPLE PROTECTION: covers designed to attract gourmets and keep out mosquitoes.

www.viceversashop.com

GRATERS AT THE READY: in oval shapes and metallic colours, Giorgio Gurioli's graters come with a pretty cheese knife.

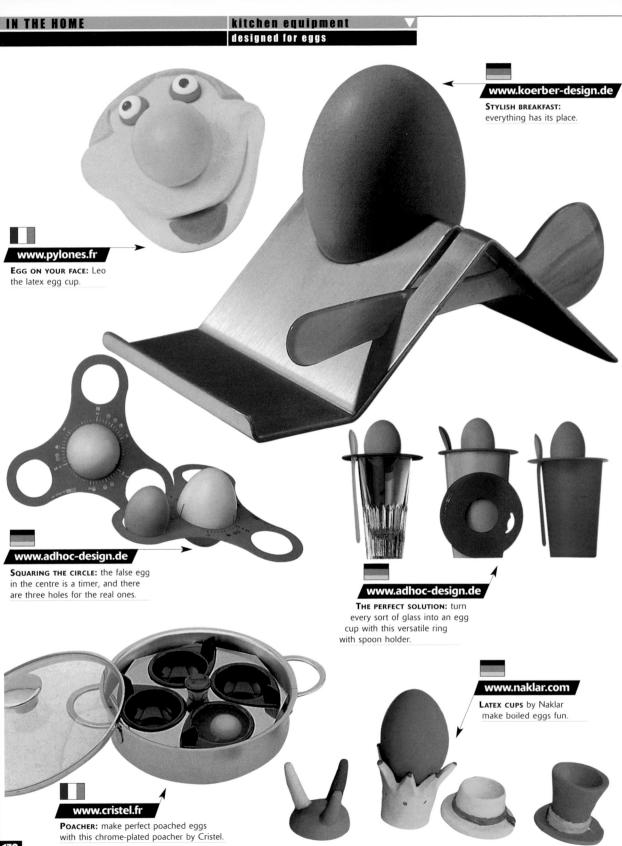

www.koerber-design.de

STYLISH BREAKFAST: everything has its place.

www.pylones.fr

EGG ON YOUR FACE: Leo the latex egg cup.

www.adhoc-design.de

SQUARING THE CIRCLE: the false egg in the centre is a timer, and there are three holes for the real ones.

www.adhoc-design.de

THE PERFECT SOLUTION: turn every sort of glass into an egg cup with this versatile ring with spoon holder.

www.naklar.com

LATEX CUPS by Naklar make boiled eggs fun.

www.cristel.fr

POACHER: make perfect poached eggs with this chrome-plated poacher by Cristel.

www.freudlemos.com

IN THE BALANCE: display your eggs stylishly.

www.banalextra.it

TAKE THE PLUNGE: a safe and stylish plunger for the perfect egg..

www.leonardo.de

EARLY BIRD: an egg cup cleverly disguised as a flower-pot.

www.funandfantasy.de

EGG LEGS: put your best foot forward at the start of the day with these fun cups.

www.pa-design.com

DIY EGG CUP: use this invention to make your own egg holder and then eat it.

www.inflate.co.uk

KEEP YOUR EGGS AFLOAT in this lifebelt after rescuing them from the boiling water.

www.bodum.com

Uovo: this egg cup, complete with spoon, comes in a range of colours.

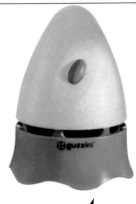

www.guzzini.it

ELECTRIC CRUMB COLLECTOR: a green genie that whisks crumbs away before your eyes.

www.funandfantasy.com

TOAST RACK: bring a bit of romance back to Monday mornings.

www.chaiselongue.fr

ROUND, RED AND READY FOR ACTION, this toaster comes in black, blue and yellow.

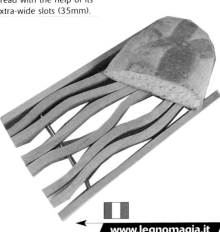

www.anteprimamilano.com

EARLY MORNING BARBECUE: slip your slice of bread in the individual grills and and no more burnt fingers.

www.seb.fr

TOAST THE MOST: this toaster defrosts, reheats and grills all types of bread with the help of its extra-wide slots (35mm).

www.artistavisitatore.it

BAGHETTO: a bread bin that looks more like a soap container. It keeps the bread fresh for longer and keeps it smelling good.

www.legnomagia.it

WAVE DESIGN: a wooden chopping board on steel rods.

www.muninidesign.com

TOAST HOLDER: stylishly protects your fingers from burning.

www.outlookzelco.com

PANINO, by Matteo Tresoldi and Michela Pagani: perfectly designed for picking up crumbs at the table.

www.delonghi.com

SIXTIES STYLE: monitor and regulate the intensity of heat using the panel. Grill toast to perfection.

www.quelle.de

BREAD MACHINE: just pour in the ingredients and the machine does the rest. Programme it the night before for freshly made bread at breakfast.

www.elie-arnaud-denoix.com

ELIE ARNAUD DENOIX: luxury liquids and spirits in beautiful bottles.

www.wedgwood.com

WEEKDAY WEEKEND: an inseparable pair of finely-worked porcelain bottles.

www.modusdesign.com

IDENTICAL WHITE LADIES: two tall porcelain bottles with only their initials to tell them apart.

www.kleinundmore.de

PORCELAIN IGLOO: oil, vinegar, salt and pepper – each has its own container.

www.oncook.fr

OIL SPRAY: practical, efficient and healthy.

www.droogdesign.nl

NO CHEMISTRY: the two liquids don't mix, hence the separate pourers.

🇬🇧
www.typhooneurope.com
Duo: as impressive as an abstract oil painting in a glass frame.

🇫🇷
www.chaiselongue.fr
Nostalgic design: a French reproduction of an old-style olive oil can.

www.leonardo.de
Arteessi: an oil pourer with a very precise aim.

🇫🇷
www.ardi.fr
Java: oil and vinegar do the tango.

www.raumgestalt-en.de
Symmetry and simplicity: simply beautiful containers for oil and vinegar.

www.tonfisk-design.fi

PILOTIS: a stylish and functional union of porcelain and cork.

www.exemplaire.fr

SALT POT: a Provençal terracotta pot that absorbs all the humidity and preserves the contents.

www.propagandaonline.com

A PINCH OF SALT: a splendidly literal design in porcelain.

www.duerkop.com

SMOOTH AND TAPERED: salt and pepper grinders, designed in tactile wood by Katrin Amend (23cm long).

www.j-me.co.uk

MAGIC WANDS: Just tap the ends and abracadabra – the flavour pours out.

www.kleinundmore.de

FLYING SAUCERS: two metallic dishes resting on a wooden base – one for pepper, the other for salt. Tell them apart by the design of the holes.

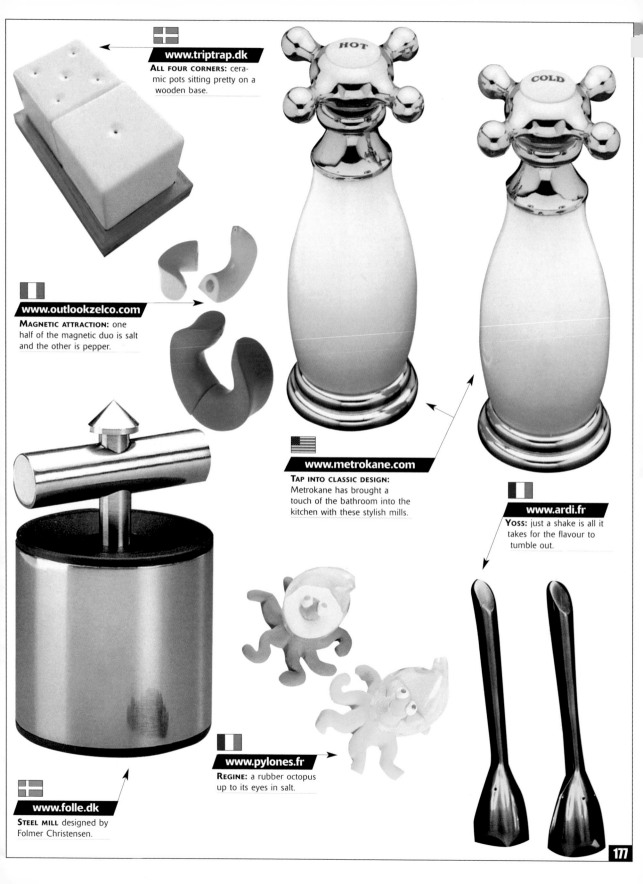

www.triptrap.dk

ALL FOUR CORNERS: ceramic pots sitting pretty on a wooden base.

www.outlookzelco.com

MAGNETIC ATTRACTION: one half of the magnetic duo is salt and the other is pepper.

HOT

COLD

www.metrokane.com

TAP INTO CLASSIC DESIGN: Metrokane has brought a touch of the bathroom into the kitchen with these stylish mills.

www.ardi.fr

YOSS: just a shake is all it takes for the flavour to tumble out.

www.folle.dk

STEEL MILL designed by Folmer Christensen.

www.pylones.fr

REGINE: a rubber octopus up to its eyes in salt.

www.tohubohu.fr

RATTAN CASE: twelve spices in recycled glass jars, each with its own spoon.

www.brabantia.com

WINDOW BOX: stainless steel, stylish and practical.

www.ronnebybruk.com

PESTLE AND MORTAR: an old-style spice grinder.

www.adhoc-design.de

SPICE MILL: grind dried spices with this colourful machine.

www.modusdesign.com

KULFON: small sensual pots.

www.museesdefrance.com

PEWTER BOX with three compartments: a replica of an 18th-century piece.

www.bodanova.com

WINDOW ON WORLD OF SPICES: frosted and clear glass containers.

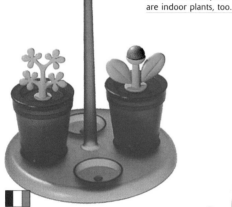

www.alessi.it

HAPPY SPICES: spices are indoor plants, too.

www.o-to-o.com

SEA SALT COCKTAIL: salt, coriander, citrus peel and star anise are all ready to spice up your cooking.

www.alessi.it

OVOLINI: a stylish nutmeg grater.

Domaine du Soleil Couchant
Sel de mer épicé poids net:
350g
Méditerranée

Ingrédients : Sel de mer, Badiane Etoilée, Coriandre torréfié Zestes d'agrumes
Produit de France - Les Fruits du Vin Sarl 11200 St André de Roquelongue

www.legnomagia.it

IGLOO: a felt bag for those delicate purchases.

www.tohubohu.fr

TO THE SHOPS TO THE SHOPS: a woven-effect blue PVC shopping basket with rattan handles.

www.momastore.org

WIRE BOWL: the future of shopping as predicted by Ole Palsby.

www.eandw.com

TROMPE-L'ŒIL: soft suede disguised as simple brown paper. Bags of style.

www.comebike.com

CITY BUG: the ideal scooter for a housewife (or househusband, of course), complete with shopping basket.

www.viceversashop.com

TRANSPARENT: a trolley that tells you when the deal is in the bag.

www.themut.com

MESH: a lightweight and durable storage basket sold by the Museum of Useful Things in America. Use it for shopping, too.

www.koziol.de

TASCHE: made of translucent and soft plastic.

www.anteprimamilano.com

BAGS OF COLOUR: cheerful and bright plastic baskets.

www.intercycles.com

TROKOLO: a tricycle equipped with a large basket for major shopping expeditions.

181

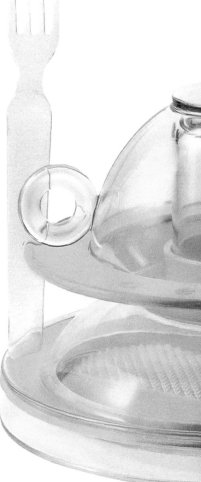

www.ritzenhoff.de

MILK: Emmeke Van der Put's milk glass has amusing taste.

www.bienjoue.com

AVIATOR SET: makes learning to eat properly more fun.

www.eveiletjeux.com

BIRTHDAY CAKE: a dress-shaped mould with a doll's bust to put on top.

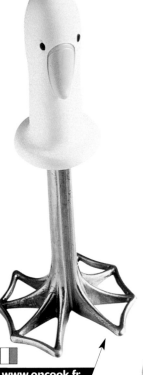

www.oncook.fr

POTATO MASHER: Mastrad's duck has designs on your potato dishes.

www.pylones.fr

HOOK A FISH: cutlery complete with hooks and eyes.

www.momastore.org

No place like home: a ceramic dish designed by Patrick Martinez for children but loved by all.

www.rosendahl.com

Baby cutlery: modern ergonomic design for tiny hands.

www.guzzini.it

Kiddy: Furio Minuti's set includes plates, cutlery, cup, glass and apple grater.

www.mono.de

Get a handle on children: the flattened ends make the cutlery easier for little hands.

www.bebeconfort.com

Multi-purpose cup: designed for choice and safety.

www.outlookzelco.com

Tommy: one for baby and one for teddy.

183

www.ritzenhoff.de

IT'S TEA TIME: a collection of cups and tins by Michael Shalev.

www.modusdesign.com

WHITE AS SNOW: a minimalist and elegantly designed tea set, including sugar bowl and milk jug.

www.artistavisitatore.it

SPLENDOR: a professional grill complete with section for crumbs.

www.wedgwood.com

SUGAR SHAKERS: Wedgwood allow us another opportunity to enjoy Clarice Cliff's lovely designs in high-quality porcelain.

www.graines-baumaux.fr

BLUE CORN: if you plant Cutie's blue seeds, this is what grows. Use to decorate or eat.

www.chaiselongue.fr

ORIGINAL SIN: the Temptation Collection includes a sugar bowl and six spoons. Sssinful!

http://le-village.ifrance.com/anyduroy

CERAMIC SHAKERS: sugar delicately flavoured with cinnamon, lavender and vanilla from Anysetier's du Roy.

www.bodum.com

CEYLON: this iced tea jug with vertical filter infuses as it serves.

www.propagandaonline.com

CHO: an attractive equation – a sugar bowl and cream jug.

www.journee-france.com

APPLE TOASTER: for cooking fruit and vegetables the Breton way.

185

www.pylones.fr

OPTICAL ILLUSION: this mirrored cup reflects and illuminates the distorted image in the saucer. Bruno Contensou's vision.

www.francisfrancis.com

NOCTURNAL: a limited edition of six cups designed by Ettore Sottsass. They come complete with a little book of erotic poetry.

www.chaiselongue.fr

SQUARE CUP: an original design with a square saucer and special slot for the spoon.

www.tonfisk-design.fi

A HANDLE ON STYLE: curved cups without handles that achieve perfect balance when placed in their saucer.

www.bodum.com

TRANSPARENT: a cup that looks more like a cafetière.

www.fragile.fr

CLOSE UP: a trompe-l'œil leather-look cup with gold padlock, designed by Patricia Deroubaix.

www.ibride.fr

TRAY CHIC: an aluminium tray that has a special slot embedded in it to hold each component, even the spoon.

www.ph-deshoulieres.com

GLORIOUS TUSCANY: dream of Italy with cypress trees against a warm golden background.

www.mono.com

NIGHT AND DAY: the porcelain handles are so translucent that the delicate sun and moon designs shine through.

www.eandw.com

WHEN IN ROME: Laurent Corio designed this enamelled ceramic cup with insulation to protect fingers from the heat.

www.bodum.com

SHIN CHA SET: a modern teapot that combines simplicity with function.

www.tonfisk-design.fi

KEEP WARM: a walnut casing protects the ceramic teapot.

www.evasolo.com

TRANSPARENT: no illusion in this infusion.

www.blomus.com

OPTICAL ILLUSION: half teapot, half warmer – wholly original.

www.mono.com

TEA LIGHT: elegance and warmth integral to a healthy alternative.

www.tefal.com

MAGIC TEA: teapot and cordless kettle in one.

www.raumgestalt-en.de

TEA AND FLAME: makes a ceremony of teatime.

TEFAL

MAGIC TEA

www.modusdesign.com

KUM-KUM SET: an organic design to a T.

www.o-to-o.com

5 O'CLOCK: the metal frame has a heat-protection role while emphasising the form.

www.le-webstore.com

IL LITRO, designed by Nicolaï Carels, complete with protective silicone handle.

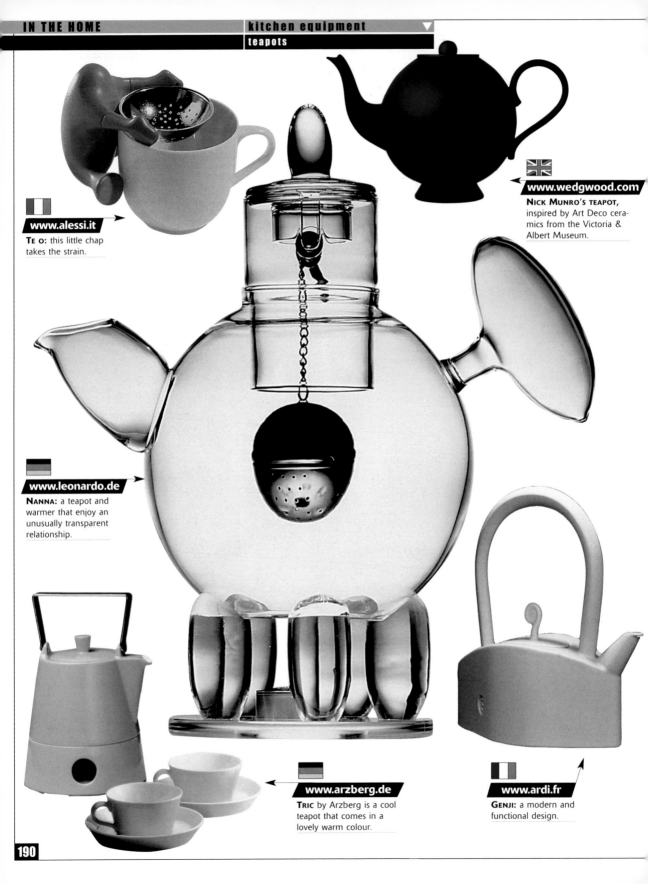

www.wedgwood.com

NICK MUNRO'S TEAPOT, inspired by Art Deco ceramics from the Victoria & Albert Museum.

www.alessi.it

TE O: this little chap takes the strain.

www.leonardo.de

NANNA: a teapot and warmer that enjoy an unusually transparent relationship.

www.arzberg.de

TRIC by Arzberg is a cool teapot that comes in a lovely warm colour.

www.ardi.fr

GENJI: a modern and functional design.

www.pordamsa.com

TEA SERVICE: perfectly round porcelain.

www.hering-berlin.de

DELICATE CERAMICS: size and design mean this teapot isn't too hot to handle.

www.rosenthal.de

SARASTO: a tapered teapot with beautiful bas-relief.

www.vignelli.com

SILVER TEA SET: Cleto Munari's tea service has a very Egyptian feel.

www.formgeber-berlin.de

BIG DIPPER: four different porcelain compartments join forces to make a saucy selection.

www.bodum.com

COLLEGE BOWL SET: bowl and cups at the ready for happy hour.

www.koziol.de

DOLCE VITA: keep tabs on your glass of champagne.

www.fly.fr

BAR MALIBU: it looks like a refrigerator but actually it's a drinks cabinet with a mirror at the back.

www.bodanova.com

WARM RECEPTION: ideal for mulled wine, this set was designed by Ulf Hanses and Lavisa Wattman.

www.abblownglass.fr

TEQUILA CARAFE: salt, lemon and tequila are all in one place, ready to mix a delicious and traditional Mexican cocktail.

www.metrokane.com

BULLET: the 1930s cocktail shaker is back.

www.propagandaonline.com

HEART: pierced by arrows (in the form of cocktail sticks).

www.weinbrecht.de

SHOW TRAY: a tray on wheels that transports delicacies and delights at parties. Move the olives along please.

www.bellieforti.com

PALLINO keeps paper serviettes firmly but stylishly in place.

www.adhoc-design.de

ORION: no danger of losing this bottle-opener – it fixes to the wall.

www.david.se

PULL THE WOOL: rollneck jumpers that are reminiscent of Thermos flasks. Ideal for blind tastings.

www.artistavisitatore.it

AMBROGIO: a foolproof aluminium bottle-opener by Alessandro Artizzu and Federica Saisi.

www.kleinundmore.de

COLUMBUS: a cork that pays tribute to the theory that a spoon in the neck of the bottle keeps the bubbles in.

www.trust-design.de

SLIMLINE DESIGN: a streamline bottle-opener available in silver and other colours.

www.jgdurand.com

BILOBA: clear as a bell, this crystal cone fits any bottle with its different-sized rings.

www.benzadesign.com

PEACOCK HANGING: table mats and coasters to hang on the wall when not in use. Designed by Giovanni Pellone.

www.elladoran.co.uk

TABLE DESIGN: Ella Doran's wide range of table mats and coasters with colourful graphics.

www.details-produkte.de

DRESS FOR DINNER: it's extra large, complete with buttons and a collar and machine washable, but it's not a shirt.

www.reisenthel.de

PHOTOGRAPHIC STENCIL: plastic mats available in a range of colours.

www.raumgestalt-en.de

BREAD & SALT: wooden slats and a small salt bag roll up in a convenient felt pouch.

www.conmoto.com

ULBER: decorate the table with a plate warmer in the style of a Chinese lantern.

www.artistavisitatore.it

BIBO, OLLI AND LINA: three aluminium hotplates with a farmyard feel.

www.evansandwong.com

GAZ DE PARIS: an aluminium hotplate in the design of a Parisian manhole cover.

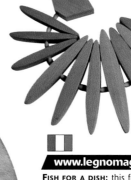

www.legnomagia.it

FISH FOR A DISH: this fish is able to move and adapt to the shape of the plate.

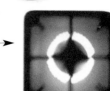

www.elladoran.co.uk

TROMPE-L'ŒIL: a melamine hotplate that reflects what's cooking.

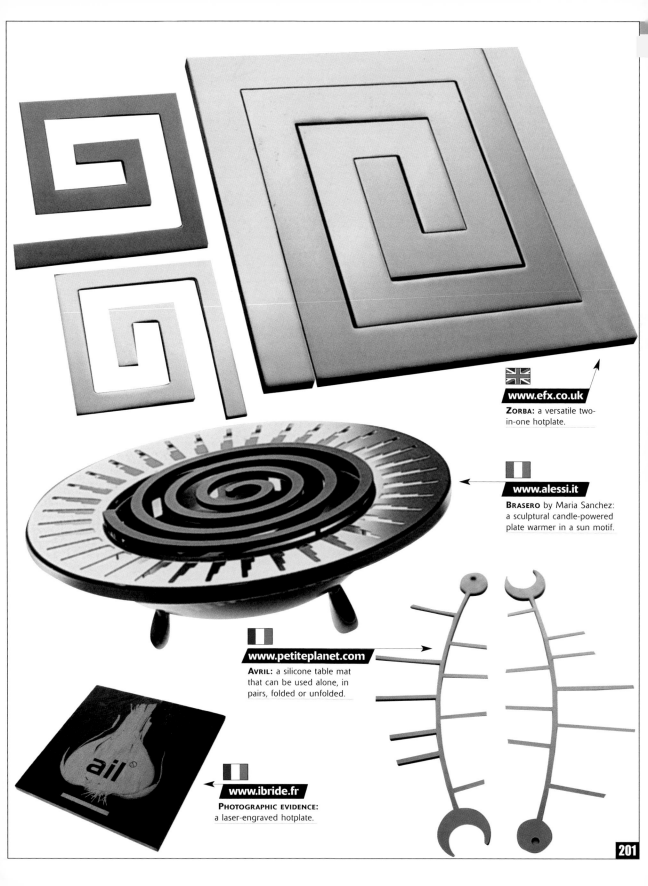

🇬🇧 **www.efx.co.uk**

ZORBA: a versatile two-in-one hotplate.

🇮🇹 **www.alessi.it**

BRASERO by Maria Sanchez: a sculptural candle-powered plate warmer in a sun motif.

🇮🇹 **www.petiteplanet.com**

AVRIL: a silicone table mat that can be used alone, in pairs, folded or unfolded.

🇮🇹 **www.ibride.fr**

PHOTOGRAPHIC EVIDENCE: a laser-engraved hotplate.

ail

 www.genevievelethu.fr

GALILÉO: sunshine on your plate

 **www.tohubohu.fr**

METAL AND RATTAN: a porcelain plate on a metal base decorated with rattan.

 **www.bernardaud.fr**

MATISSE: Bernardaud's tribute to the master.

www.gien.com

JARDIN BLEU: a trompe-l'oeil vegetable design on a blue background.

www.fragile.fr

PORTHOLE: exotic fish swim by.

www.rosenthal.de

TREASURES OF THE SEA: beautiful designs by Gianni Versace.

www.journee-france.com

ALSACE DESIGN: a different approach to plate design.

www.evasolo.com

PERFECT FIT: a round-bottomed bowl and three different sizes of flat plates make up this perfectly balanced set.

www.y-blayo.com

DJOLO: this collection was inspired by African flora and fauna.

www.emauxdelongwy.com

GRIGRI: enamelled plates by Patricia Ascenzio, who draws on the motifs and colours of her native Africa.

www.costa.tm.fr

ROAD SIGNS: an entire collection based on road warnings.

www.o-to-o.com

TWO BECOME ONE: together the plates complete the French poem in Limoges porcelain.

www.villamarais.com

OPTICAL ILLUSION: a collection designed by D. Jos that will make you look twice.

www.alessi.it

FAITOO: plates designed by Philippe Starck to hang on a rail.

www.propagandaonline.com

CONE: the six pieces in this collection can be stored in the shape of a pyramid.

www.kostaboda.se

LIMONCINO: transparently fruity plates and bowls.

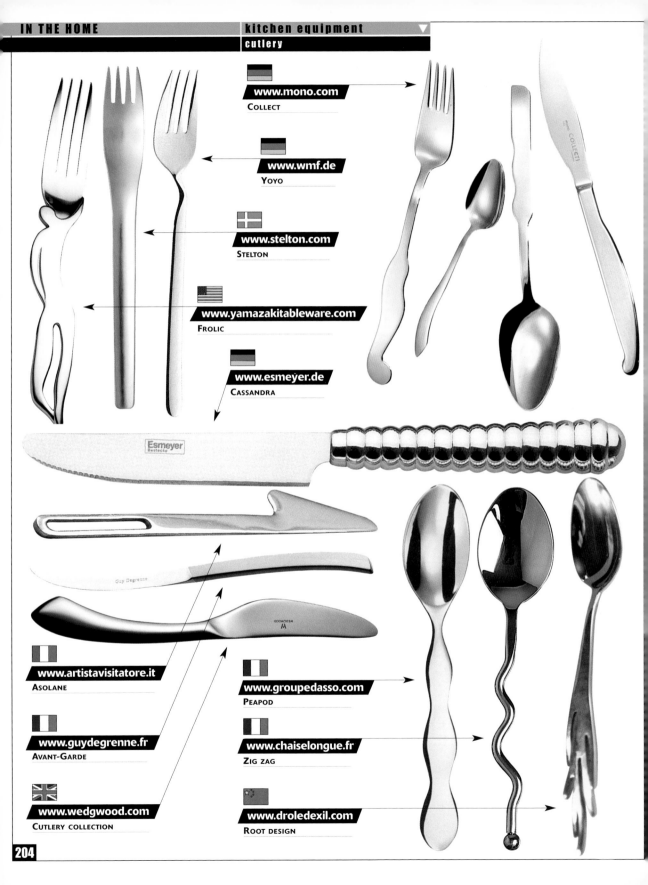

www.mono.com

COLLECT

www.wmf.de

YOYO

www.stelton.com

STELTON

www.yamazakitableware.com

FROLIC

www.esmeyer.de

CASSANDRA

www.artistavisitatore.it

ASOLANE

www.guydegrenne.fr

AVANT-GARDE

www.wedgwood.com

CUTLERY COLLECTION

www.groupedasso.com

PEAPOD

www.chaiselongue.fr

ZIG ZAG

www.droledexil.com

ROOT DESIGN

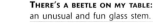

www.pylones.fr

THERE'S A BEETLE ON MY TABLE: an unusual and fun glass stem.

www.leonardo.de

BABYLON: glasses with an Oriental flavour in party colours.

www.evansandwong.com

DON'T DRINK A DROP: the beauty of the design lies in the details – on the rim of the glass.

www.ritzenhoff.de

AQUA GLASS: a collection that pays tribute to the transparent elixir of life.

www.marc-newson.com

TRIO: a collection of three glasses designed by Marc Newson.

www.leonardo.de

Swing: rainbow-coloured glasses with attitude.

www.propagandaonline.com

Help, Hungry and Hope: the humour flows even when the glasses are empty.

hope!

help!

hungry!

www.evansandwong.com

Travel mementoes: six coasters with different manhole covers from various cities around the world.

www.o-to-o.com

Pearl: the pearl is trapped between the two layers of glass in this design from Tungstène.

Manhole Cover Coasters

www.egizia.it

Aia Circo: hand-painted animal motifs created on a silk screen have been applied to these pretty blue-tinted glasses.

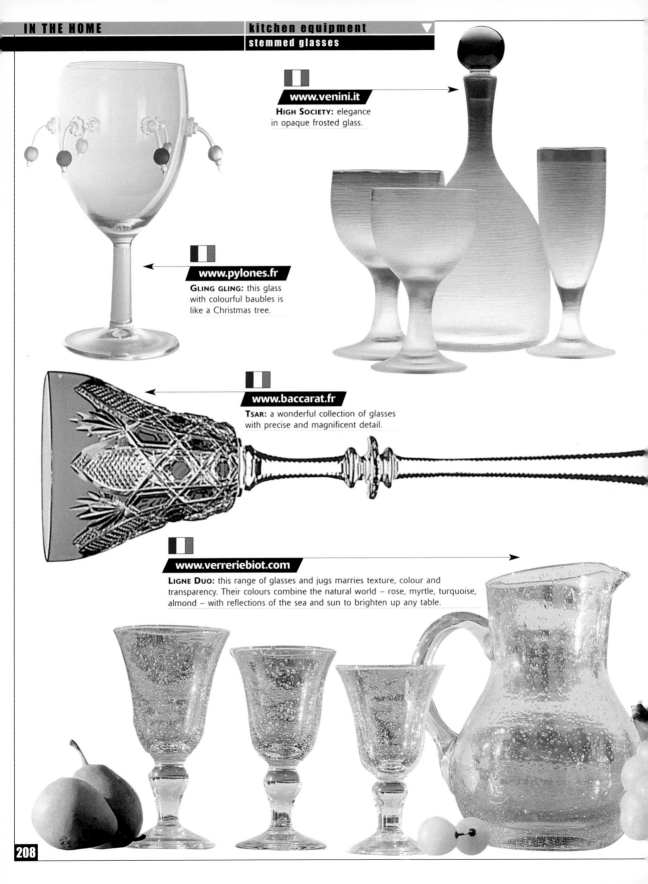

www.venini.it

HIGH SOCIETY: elegance in opaque frosted glass.

www.pylones.fr

GLING GLING: this glass with colourful baubles is like a Christmas tree.

www.baccarat.fr

TSAR: a wonderful collection of glasses with precise and magnificent detail.

www.verreriebiot.com

LIGNE DUO: this range of glasses and jugs marries texture, colour and transparency. Their colours combine the natural world – rose, myrtle, turquoise, almond – with reflections of the sea and sun to brighten up any table.

www.leonardo.de

POLLUX: one champagne flute inside another, an accomplished design from Ron Arad.

cristalsaintlouis@aol.fr

COSMOS: blue crystal glasses with long stems for elegant dinner parties.

www.baccarat.fr

TRANQUILITY: a stemmed glass that plays subtly with colour.

www.verreriebiot.com

FROST: mysterious and enigmatic in frosted pastel shades and with bubbles that never burst, these glasses are produced by La Verrerie de Biot.

www.rmn.fr

MUCHA: two Bohemian crystal glasses, hand enamelled, gilded and decorated with one of the famous painter's motifs.

www.leonardo.de

BIG BANG: each rocket/
champagne flute has a lid
with a message inside.

www.ercuis.com

CHAMPAGNE BUCKET: the
party glasses are attached
to the edge.

www.christian-de-nardi.com

MANTIS: inspired by the
insect world, this cutlery set
was designed by Ludovic
Shoepen and Renato Saleri.

www.letrefle-limoges.com

SPOON REST: designed by Claude
Bromet in Limoges porcelain,
bringing together form and function.

www.ritzenhoff.de

CHAMPUS: Belicta
Castelblanco's party designs.

www.mathon-fr.com

DAINTY DELIGHTS: pretty
presentations from 6 to
11cm in length.

www.etainsducampanile.com

SAUCEBOAT: made in pewter with
all the allure and sparkle of silver.

www.carlharrison.com

PLATE CUPS: attach them
to the edge of your plate
for condiments and sauces.

www.modusdesign.com

LIQUID FORMS: pure and perfect porcelain pourers.

www.raison-de-plus.com

PUMPKIN SOUP TUREEN: designed by a ceramic artist passionate about his craft.

www.cinna.fr

DERVICHE: a pedestal table with an integrated compartment in the tray in which to keep flowers fresh or bottles chilled.

www.folle.dk

MINIATURES: salt and pepper pots with individual style.

www.jgdurand.com

CELEBRATION: an ice bucket and champagne flute set with extra bubbles and in-built fun.

211

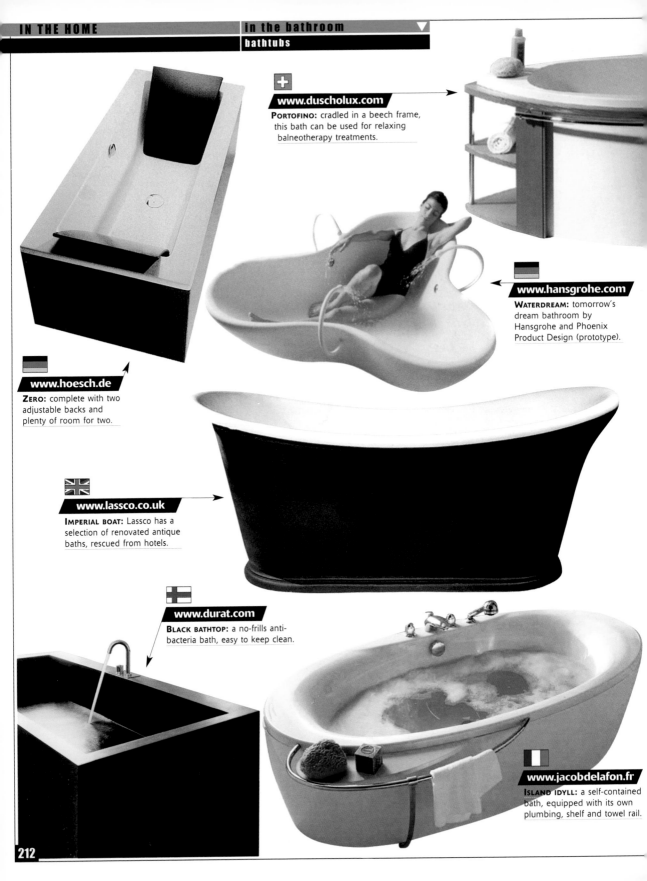

www.duscholux.com

PORTOFINO: cradled in a beech frame, this bath can be used for relaxing balneotherapy treatments.

www.hansgrohe.com

WATERDREAM: tomorrow's dream bathroom by Hansgrohe and Phoenix Product Design (prototype).

www.hoesch.de

ZERO: complete with two adjustable backs and plenty of room for two.

www.lassco.co.uk

IMPERIAL BOAT: Lassco has a selection of renovated antique baths, rescued from hotels.

www.durat.com

BLACK BATHTOP: a no-frills anti-bacteria bath, easy to keep clean.

www.jacobdelafon.fr

ISLAND IDYLL: a self-contained bath, equipped with its own plumbing, shelf and towel rail.

www.aquamass.com

FLEUR DU TEMPS: traditional design meets avant-garde.

http://perso.wanadoo.fr/sbr

RETRO: from a studio that restores antique baths and reproduces traditional designs.

www.lichting98.nl

CLIMB ABOARD: this bath tub comes in a kit and is easy to assemble and move around.

www.kohlerco.com

IRON WORKS TELLIEUR: the wooden frame embraces a metal bath with stylish simplicity.

www.astonmatthews.co.uk

CAST-IRON BATH: a cast-iron and porcelain bath, following a design tradition that dates back to 1823.

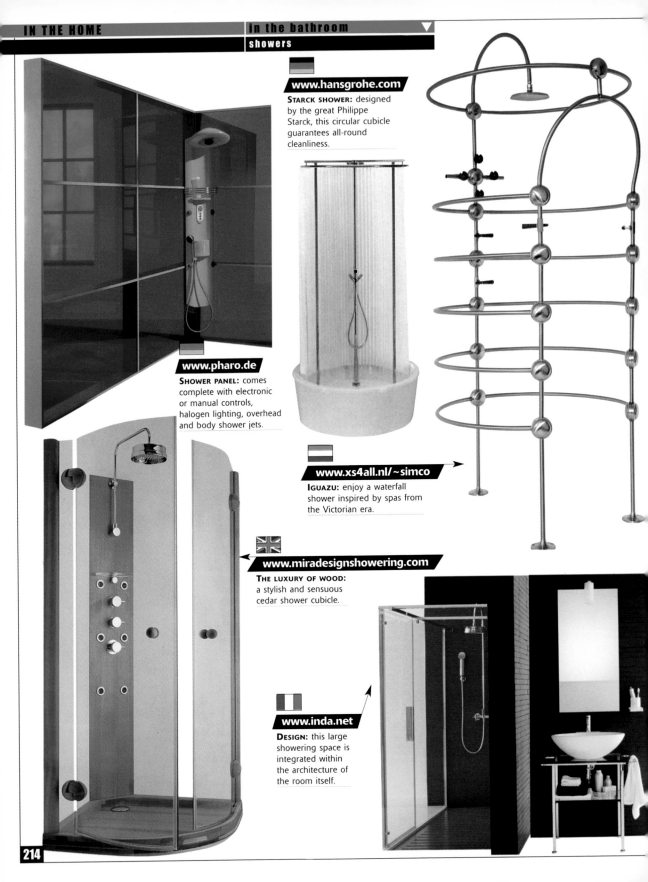

www.hansgrohe.com

STARCK SHOWER: designed by the great Philippe Starck, this circular cubicle guarantees all-round cleanliness.

www.pharo.de

SHOWER PANEL: comes complete with electronic or manual controls, halogen lighting, overhead and body shower jets.

www.xs4all.nl/~simco

IGUAZU: enjoy a waterfall shower inspired by spas from the Victorian era.

www.miradesignshowering.com

THE LUXURY OF WOOD: a stylish and sensuous cedar shower cubicle.

www.inda.net

DESIGN: this large showering space is integrated within the architecture of the room itself.

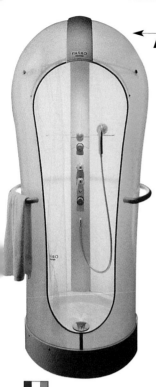

www.pharo.de

COCOON: complete with lighting and massage jets, a cubicle designed to fit the human shape, allowing free movement of the upper body.

www.neomediam.fr

CAMPO: it takes two to tango in this double cubicle with mood lighting, music and massage jets as well as a steam option.

www.dornbracht.de

GIANT: for tropical showers in the comfort of your own home.

www.pharo.de

TEMPLE: equipped with overhead, hand and body showers, this design is futuristic and functional.

215

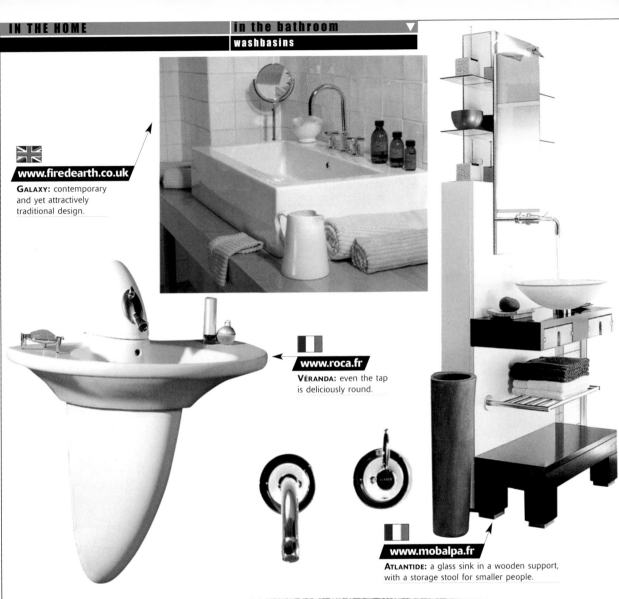

🇬🇧

www.firedearth.co.uk

GALAXY: contemporary and yet attractively traditional design.

www.roca.fr

VÉRANDA: even the tap is deliciously round.

www.mobalpa.fr

ATLANTIDE: a glass sink in a wooden support, with a storage stool for smaller people.

www.kohlerco.com

BANDANA: this sink design is based on a china porcelain plate from the Qing dynasty (16th century).

www.sprint-france.fr

SPRING: a glass basin held aloft by a stainless steel helicoid structure, designed by Belinox.

www.pyram.fr

CHADÉ: a harmonious composition in alder, rattan, stainless steel and slate.

www.hoesch.de

DREAMSCAPE: from a dream bathroom design by Michael Graves.

www.kohlerco.de

CRUCIBLE: inspired by Danish design from an abstract sculpture from the 50s and 60s.

www.durat.com

RECYCLABLE: a collection of rectangular basins from Durat – 50 per cent recycled plastic, 100 per cent recyclable.

www.duravit.de

GIORNO: sensual from top to toe, designed by Massimo Losa Ghini.

www.dmd.products.com

SOFT WASHBOWL: a polyurethane bowl, designed by Hella Jongerius of Droog Design.

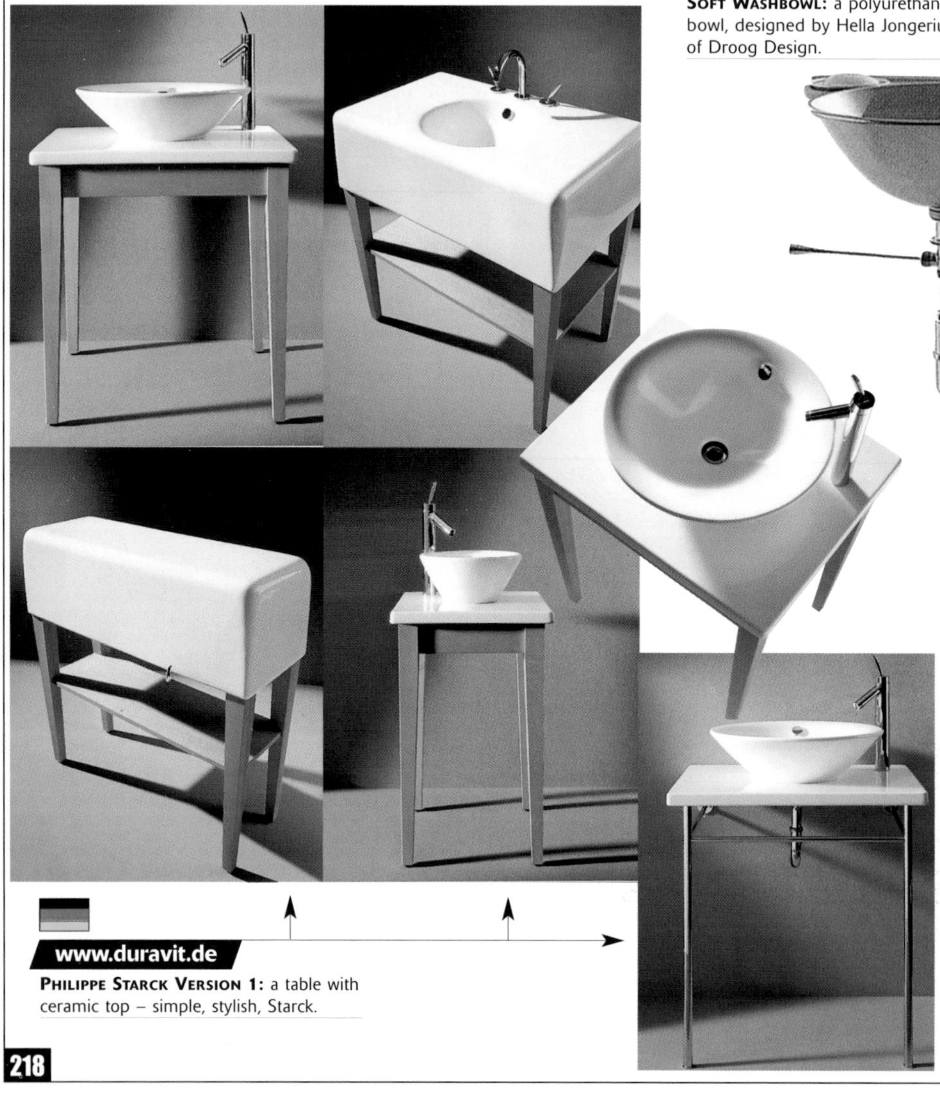

www.sprint-france.fr

AQUA BY BELINOX: both waste pipe and support, the central shaft can be placed in the middle of the room.

www.duravit.de

PHILIPPE STARCK VERSION 1: a table with ceramic top – simple, stylish, Starck.

www.sanijura.fr

DÉCLIC: semi-sunken ceramic sink surrounded by cubic chic.

www.tendadorica.it

LAVABOLO: off-centre, colourful and easy to clean.

www.idealstandard.com

SEMI-CIRCULAR SPACE SAVER: a stylish unit designed in pear tree wood, complete with towel holder and tidy basket, all on wheels.

www.kohlerco.com

SPUN GLASS: a glistening glass bowl brings a touch of traditional hand-crafted design to the bathroom.

www.lineabeta.com

APELLE: two chromium-plated washbasins that are twice as bright.

www.jbermanglass.com

GLASS BASINS by an expert on the subject, Joël Berman.

www.sanijura.fr

IMAGINE: dreamy colours for morning and night routines.

www.pyram.fr

TAO: maple wood and white ceramic – an arranged marriage.

www.ambiancebain.com

A'TOLL: simple, sober and stylish lines.

www.ceramicaflaminia.it

TWIN SET: twin basins designed by Roberto Palomba.

www.corian.com

MADE OF CORIAN: a new material with a bright future in interiors.

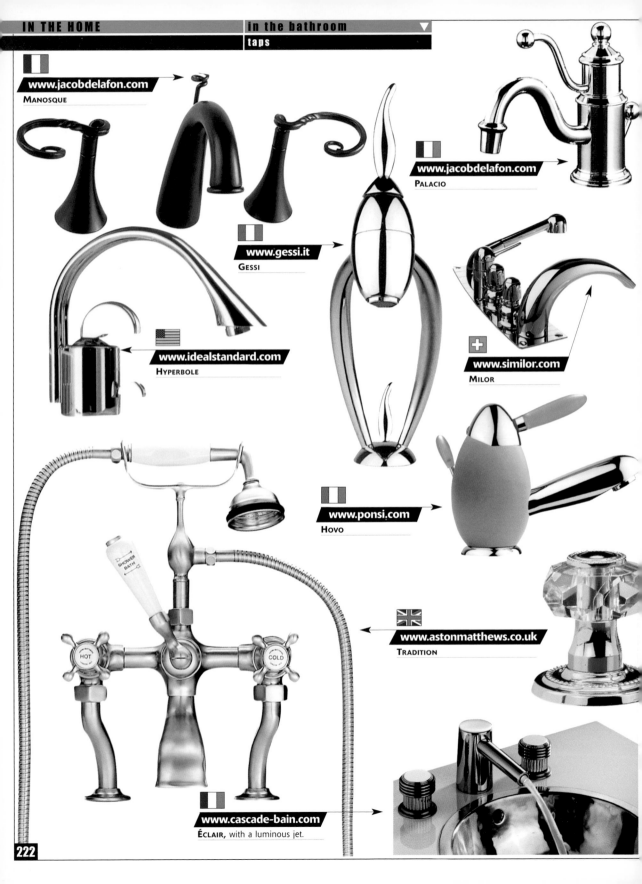

www.jacobdelafon.com

MANOSQUE

www.jacobdelafon.com

PALACIO

www.gessi.it

GESSI

www.idealstandard.com

HYPERBOLE

www.similor.com

MILOR

www.ponsi.com

HOVO

www.astonmatthews.co.uk

TRADITION

www.cascade-bain.com

ÉCLAIR, with a luminous jet.

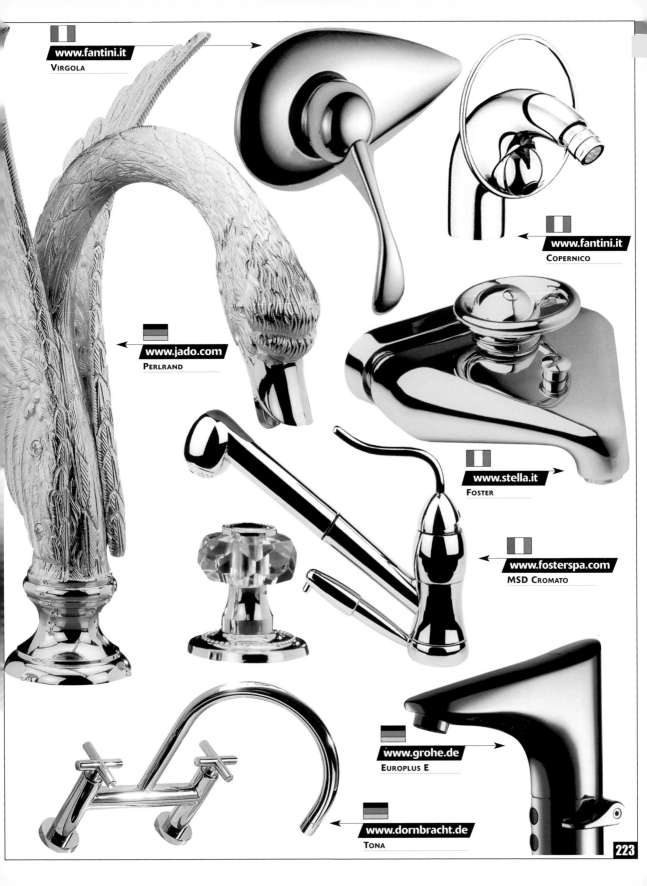

www.fantini.it
VIRGOLA

www.fantini.it
COPERNICO

www.jado.com
PERLRAND

www.stella.it
FOSTER

www.fosterspa.com
MSD CROMATO

www.grohe.de
EUROPLUS E

www.dornbracht.de
TONA

223

NATURAL TERRACOTTA is great for massaging the feet.

www.radius-design.de

PSICOSIS: relive THAT famous scene, if you dare.

www.dornbracht.de

TARA: Sieger Design's streamlined wall installation has a fixed shower head and ring and is available in chrome, platinum or brass.

www.propagandaonline.com

TISSUE OF LIES: a shower curtain with deceptively revealing moments.

www.sharperimage.com

SHOWER COMPANION: at last there's a water-resistant CD player/radio/clock for those who can't live without music in the bathroom.

www.viveversashop.com

DULY: hang this clock in your shower and you need never be late for work again.

www.aiwa.com

RADIO SPLASH PROOF: this radio is happy to join you in the shower.

www.outlookzelco.com

SPLASH: a non-slip mat that lives up to its name.

www.octopus-bath.com

MULTI-COLOURED: a lively bath mat to greet your feet after showering.

www.aquamass.com

OCEAN SPRAY: place the seaweed capsules in the shower and you'll be all at sea.

Affusion d'Algues de Bretagne

Aux Trois Algues Fucus, Laminaria, Ascophyllum

• Relaxe
• Reminéralise
• Ressource

Brittany Seaweed Spa Shower

A UTILISER DANS
L' Aqua · Énergiseur

Daniel Jouvance

LABORATOIRES DE BIOLOGIE MARINE

ALOE VERA
BODY WASH
ALL SKIN TYPES
With soothing aloe vera gel, to help leave the skin feeling refreshed

THE BODY SHOP
tea tree oil
BODY WASH
NORMAL, OILY OR BLEMISHED SKIN
250 ml

www.thebodyshop.com

BODY WASH: aloe vera and tea tree oil help you stay clean and fresh.

www.allia.fr

SAMARCANDE: a retro bath with lion's feet and old-fashioned taps.

www.inflate.co.uk

ANTI-SLIP MAT: one water spillage you won't slip on.

www.solmet.com

ARTÙ: a soap dispenser, a toothbrush holder and a glass, supported by a metal base.

www.natureetdecouvertes.com

LOOFA: a fruit from North Africa that makes a perfect sponge.

www.radiatingstyle.co.uk

RETRO: an old-style chrome-plated towel rail.

www.interiorinternet.com

BUBBLE SQUARE: bubbles captured on ceramic tiles.

www.bodyshop.com

AFRICA SPA: bath salts with plant extracts create an exotic feel in the bathroom.

www.kardelen.se

CHRISTIAN: round linen bath gloves.

www.anteprimamilano.com

MASSAGE MAT: therapeutic pebbles do their stuff indoors.

www.porada.it

SALVIA: stylish towel rack in cherry wood.

www.solmet.com

GRIFO: an elegant combination of wood, metal and glass in a cabinet that is attached to the ceiling and the floor.

www.propagandaonline.com

GIANT MOLAR: where else would you want to keep your toothbrush?

www.eandw.com

HIS, HER AND THEIRS: sponge towels in 100 per cent cotton. You'll know which one to use.

www.koziol.de

ARIEL: this self-adhesive mermaid enjoys a day on the tiles.

www.pylones.fr

FLOWER MIRROR: a jolly latex sunflower that reflects your own mood.

www.alessi.it

OTTO: dispensers with no hair but plenty of dental floss.

www.inflate.co.uk

TONSIL: this pot opens wide for your toothbrush.

www.koziol.de

STRUPPI: really puts his back into providing effective nail care.

www.chaiselongue.fr

FLOATING RADIO: small, round and translucent waterproof radios.

www.neomediam.fr

COROT: this shapely bath has built-in steps and shelves.

www.thebodyshop.com

EXFOLIATING BODY WASH: almost as sensual as bathing in crushed strawberries.

JASMINE
EXFOLIATING
BODY WASH

Gel douche exfoliant au jasmin

ALL SKIN TYPES

Polishes and smooths skin
powdered walnut shells

150 ml

STRAWBERRY
EXFOLIATING
BODY WASH

www.sevi.com

CLOWN SANDGLASS: checks that teeth are brushed for three minutes exactly.

www.alessi.it

MR SUICIDE is ready to jump into the water, tied to the plug.

229

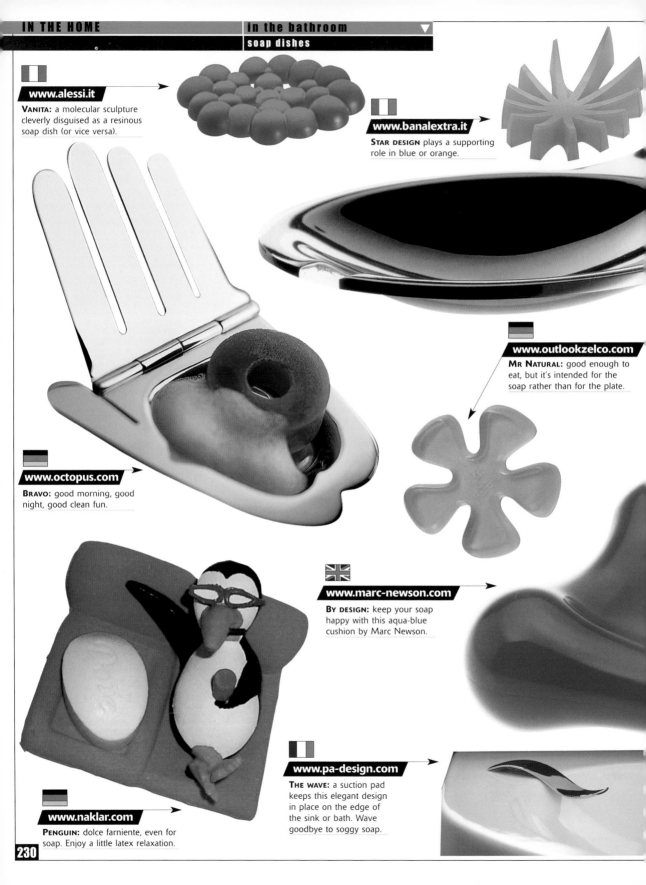

www.alessi.it

VANITA: a molecular sculpture cleverly disguised as a resinous soap dish (or vice versa).

www.banalextra.it

STAR DESIGN plays a supporting role in blue or orange.

www.octopus.com

BRAVO: good morning, good night, good clean fun.

www.outlookzelco.com

MR NATURAL: good enough to eat, but it's intended for the soap rather than for the plate.

www.marc-newson.com

BY DESIGN: keep your soap happy with this aqua-blue cushion by Marc Newson.

www.pa-design.com

THE WAVE: a suction pad keeps this elegant design in place on the edge of the sink or bath. Wave goodbye to soggy soap.

www.naklar.com

PENGUIN: dolce farniente, even for soap. Enjoy a little latex relaxation.

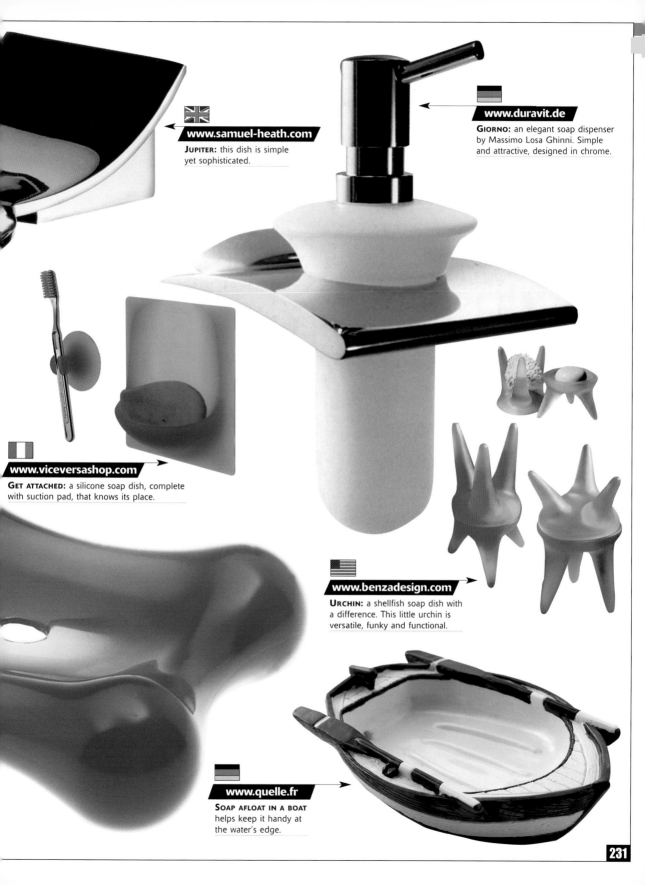

www.samuel-heath.com

JUPITER: this dish is simple yet sophisticated.

www.duravit.de

GIORNO: an elegant soap dispenser by Massimo Losa Ghinni. Simple and attractive, designed in chrome.

www.viceversashop.com

GET ATTACHED: a silicone soap dish, complete with suction pad, that knows its place.

www.benzadesign.com

URCHIN: a shellfish soap dish with a difference. This little urchin is versatile, funky and functional.

www.quelle.fr

SOAP AFLOAT IN A BOAT helps keep it handy at the water's edge.

www.perigot-fr.com

SOAP LIKE IT USED TO BE: for those nostalgic for the old style soap on the wall.

www.kreativsape.no

CREATIVE SOAP: visit this Norwegian site for all the information you need on making your own soap.

www.smithandhawken.com

SWEET ORANGE: keep your hands clean, soft and smelling of summer fields with essential oils of orange and lavender.

www.primalelements.com

SLICES OF SOAP: a selection of fruity, scented and spicy soaps.

🇬🇧 **www.ou-b.com**
STIMULATING SOAK: a range of bath oils that relax, revive or refresh.

🇫🇷 **www.savon-de-marseille.com**
MARSEILLE SOAP: pure vegetable soap, made according to a venerable 18th-century recipe.

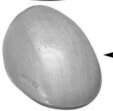

www.leonardo.de
SOAPWORLD: keeps an eye on what's happening in the bathroom.

🇫🇷 **www.loccitane.com**
SCULPTED SOAP: a vegetable-oil soap in the shape of a wooden pebble.

🇫🇷 **www.chaiselongue.fr**
NOËL: it can be Christmas in July with this soap bubble.

🇯🇵 **www.muji.co.jp**
NATURAL BATH SALTS: perfumed with essence of Japanese cypress, salts that restore the three 'V's – vitality, verve and vigour.

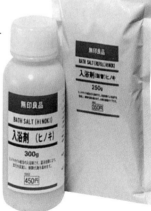

www.octopus.com
SOAP OPERA: bathing beauties, bubbles and massage soaps plus a ring on which to hook them to keep dry.

www.duravit.de

GIORNO: simple and modern designs by Massimo Losa Ghini.

www.roca.fr

MULTICLIN incorporates automated hygiene by washing and drying the seat using jets of water or air at regulated temperatures.

www.kuhfuss-sanitaer.de

FRESHEN UP: a stainless-steel base with transparent (or wooden) lid brings minimalist design to the bathroom.

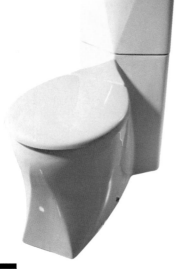

www.lassco.co.uk

FLORAL: old-style romantic designs for the smallest room in the house.

www.studiofusion.co.uk

TOILET: a prototype design for keeping the bathroom tidy.

www.details-produkte.de

MINIATURE: a small footstool with an important role (or roll).

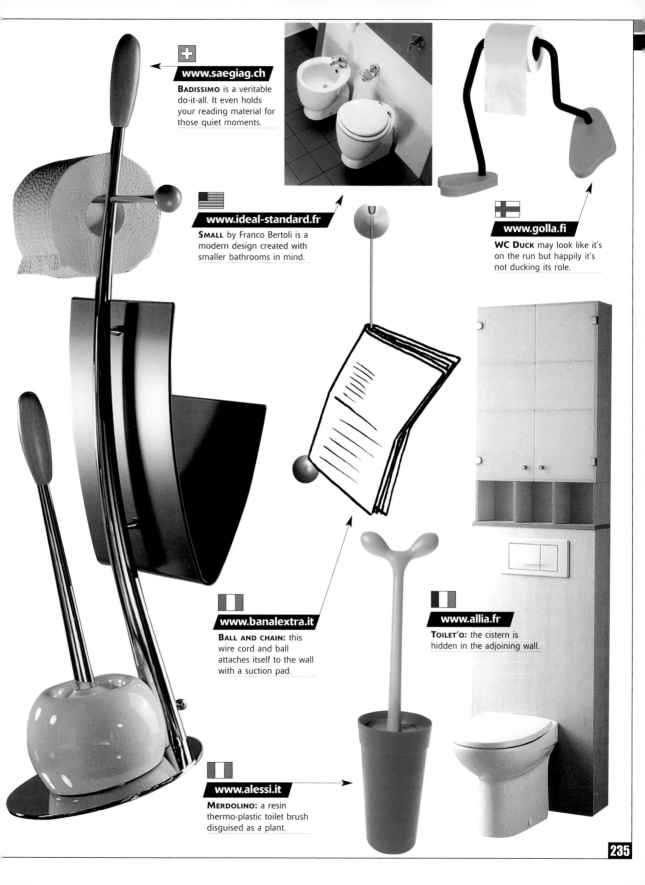

www.saegiag.ch

BADISSIMO is a veritable do-it-all. It even holds your reading material for those quiet moments.

www.ideal-standard.fr

SMALL by Franco Bertoli is a modern design created with smaller bathrooms in mind.

www.golla.fi

WC DUCK may look like it's on the run but happily it's not ducking its role.

www.banalextra.it

BALL AND CHAIN: this wire cord and ball attaches itself to the wall with a suction pad.

www.allia.fr

TOILET'O: the cistern is hidden in the adjoining wall.

www.alessi.it

MERDOLINO: a resin thermo-plastic toilet brush disguised as a plant.

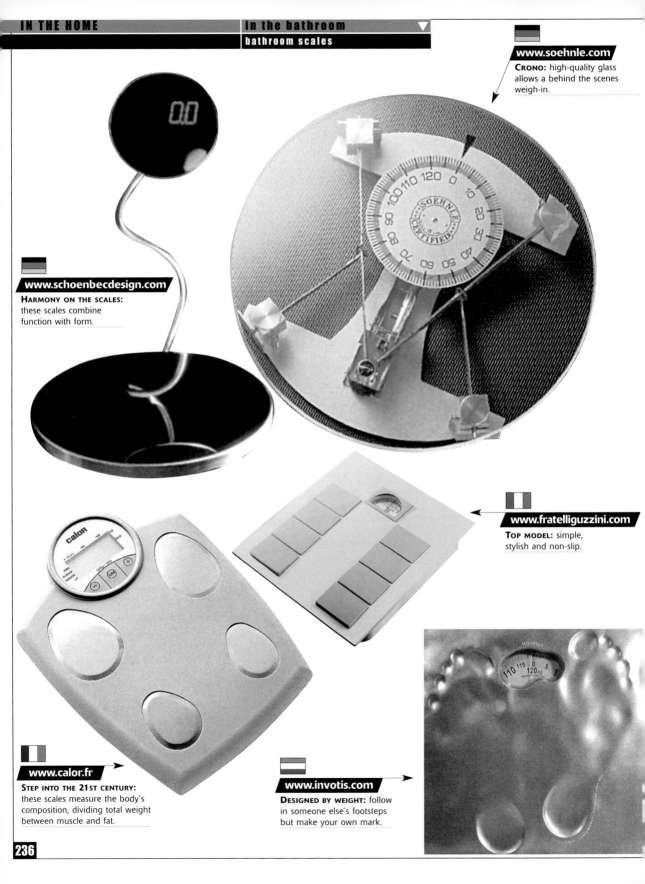

www.soehnle.com

CRONO: high-quality glass allows a behind the scenes weigh-in.

www.schoenbecdesign.com

HARMONY ON THE SCALES: these scales combine function with form.

www.fratelliguzzini.com

TOP MODEL: simple, stylish and non-slip.

www.calor.fr

STEP INTO THE 21ST CENTURY: these scales measure the body's composition, dividing total weight between muscle and fat.

www.invotis.com

DESIGNED BY WEIGHT: follow in someone else's footsteps but make your own mark.

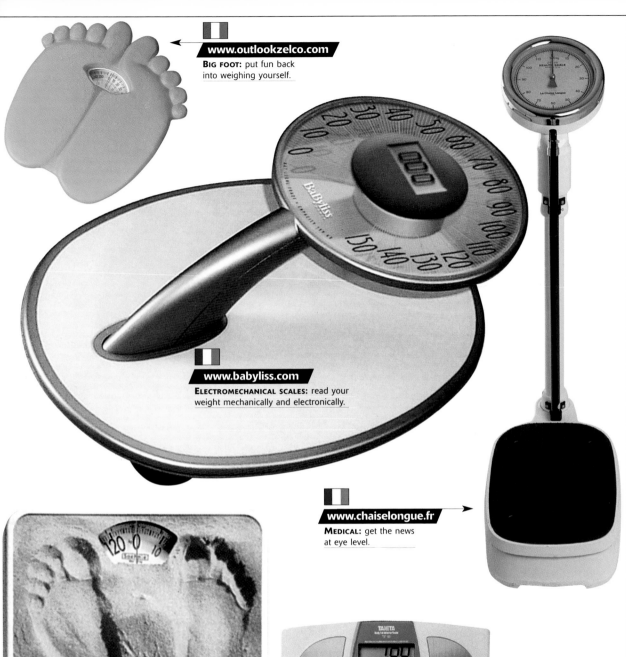

www.outlookzelco.com

BIG FOOT: put fun back into weighing yourself.

www.babyliss.com

ELECTROMECHANICAL SCALES: read your weight mechanically and electronically.

www.chaiselongue.fr

MEDICAL: get the news at eye level.

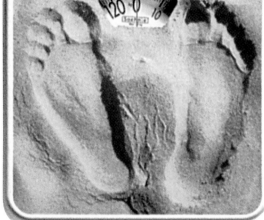

www.tanita.com

DIET DETAILS: these scales weigh body fat to the nearest 0.1 per cent.

www.soehnle.com

JUMP ABOARD: wear your beachwear when you step on these scales.

www.wegdwood.com

HIDDEN TREASURE: an ornate porcelain box that opens to reveal a pocket mirror.

www.limoges-diffusion.com

LIMOGES PILL BOXES: just three of the hundreds of miniature masterpieces.

www.baccarat.fr

RENDEZ-VOUS: the combined delicacy of a powder dish and crystal ring holder.

www.venini.it

MONOFIORI: glass bottles with creative stoppers, dreamed up by Laure de Santillana.

www.victoria-jill.com

REEDS: this bath oil comes in an elegant and minimalist bottle.

www.authenticmodels

MARINE ART: originally painted by artistic sailors, these miniature boxes with painted lids may conceal many secrets.

www.moeve.de

AT YOUR FINGERTIPS: an efficient and stylish ring holder.

www.baccarat.fr

ONE SUMMER IN LIVADIA: a magical name for an elegant perfume bottle.

www.verreriebiot.com

VISUAL SYMPHONY: master glaziers display their creations at the Biot glassworks in southern France. Thousands of people visit every year to watch the craftsmen at work.

www.remington.co.uk

WAX SPA: citrus blend aromatherapy paraffin wax softens the skin on your hands, elbows and feet.

www.fondamental.com

RELAXATION CAPSULE: float in a sound-proofed cocoon on a waterbed covered in a deliciously silky fabric that moulds to your body. Recommended by many relaxation therapists.

www.esteban.fr

ENERGY KIT: contains an exfoliating glove, pumice stone, bath marbles, body oil and a coloured resin massage tool.

www.bodyshop.com

SENSUAL: aromatherapy bath and massage oil for tender, intimate moments.

www.natureetdecouvertes.com

MASSAGE BALM: a solid perfume made of essential oils and wax. Dab it on your wrist and temples.

www.remington.co.uk

VIGORO: an electric massager complete with two aromatherapy oils – one relaxing and the other stimulating.

www.fondamental.com

THE DREAMER: an audiovisual light and sound stimulation device with glasses, equipped with intermittent diodes and small audio headphones. An all-in-one mental relaxation centre.

www.accakappa.it

MASSAGE BATH BRUSH: made of natural silk and biodegradable acetate balls.

www.outlookzelco.com

TRANQUIL MOMENTS: an electric diffuser of natural sounds, including rain, waterfalls and summer evenings.

www.babyliss.com

INFRAFORM: equipped with eight fingers that deliver a heated deep massage.

www.thinktank.com.sg

PATHFINDER: a flotation tank for deep relaxation, with underwater stereo sound system, vaporiser, adjustable lighting and video playback system for in-tank relaxation or accelerated learning programmes. The complete at home relaxation experience.

241

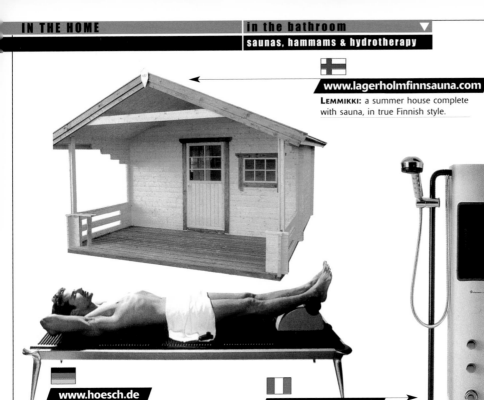

www.lagerholmfinnsauna.com

LEMMIKKI: a summer house complete with sauna, in true Finnish style.

www.hoesch.de

BODYSWING: a day bed equipped with a vibrating cushion to place under your legs during or after your time in the sauna.

www.vismaravetro.it

BABELE JUNIOR: an aluminium column with hand shower, three to five movable jets and a mixer tap.

www.harvia.fi

CHROMOTHERAPY: therapeutic lighting from Harvia saunas: yellow for depression, blue for concentration, red for stimulation and green for inner peace.

www.teuco.it

SAUNA SHOWER: pop into the shower after the sauna (or vice versa).

www.tylo.com

SAUNA TŸLO: this sauna comes in kit form, in cedar or spruce, complete with windows and lighting. A truly Swedish experience.

www.tylo.com

MIXED HEAT: Tÿlo's technological revolution can be used in dry or humid saunas.

www.duscholux.com

DUSCHODRIVE: a multi-functional shower with massage ducts for head and back together with a hammam option.

www.tylo.com

TŸLO DOES IT ALL: scented steam bath, hydromassage, showers of varying intensity – all controlled electronically.

www.jacuzzi.com

FIORE: a luxury bath equipped with a jacuzzi with six ducts, a hand shower and a shelf with mirror for your bathing bits and pieces.

www.allia.fr

BIOPROJECT: enjoy balneotherapy with essential oils while you listen to a CD.

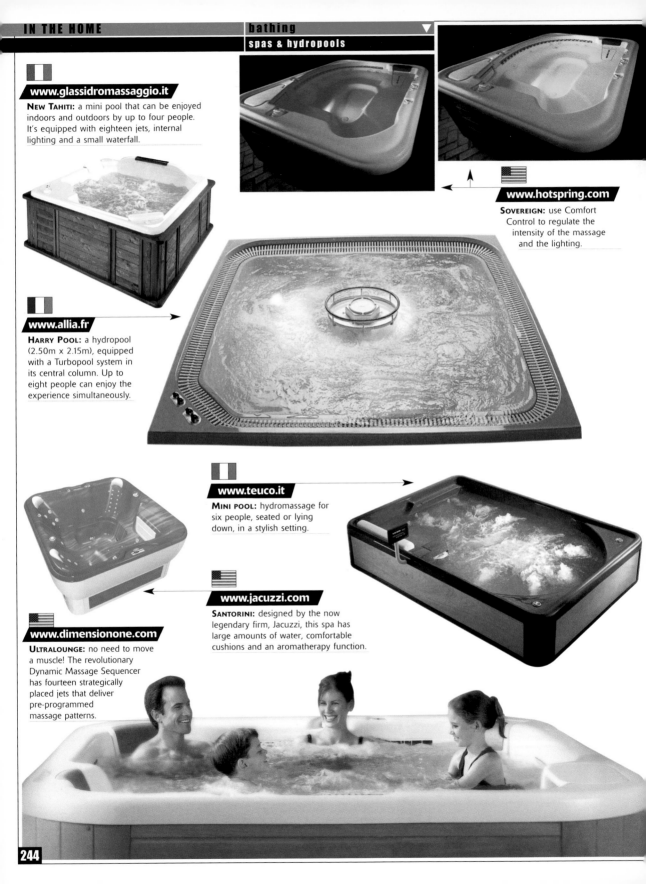

www.glassidromassaggio.it

NEW TAHITI: a mini pool that can be enjoyed indoors and outdoors by up to four people. It's equipped with eighteen jets, internal lighting and a small waterfall.

www.hotspring.com

SOVEREIGN: use Comfort Control to regulate the intensity of the massage and the lighting.

www.allia.fr

HARRY POOL: a hydropool (2.50m x 2.15m), equipped with a Turbopool system in its central column. Up to eight people can enjoy the experience simultaneously.

www.teuco.it

MINI POOL: hydromassage for six people, seated or lying down, in a stylish setting.

www.jacuzzi.com

SANTORINI: designed by the now legendary firm, Jacuzzi, this spa has large amounts of water, comfortable cushions and an aromatherapy function.

www.dimensionone.com

ULTRALOUNGE: no need to move a muscle! The revolutionary Dynamic Massage Sequencer has fourteen strategically placed jets that deliver pre-programmed massage patterns.

www.storvatt.com

STORVATT: an authentic Norwegian pool made of Western Red Cedar wood, heated by an aluminium stove so that you can enjoy it even in the mid-winter… Aesthetic and energising.

www.carrebleu.net

CARRÉ BLEU: design your own pool and integrate it perfectly into the environment, using the expertise of a European network that operates in France, Belgium, Switzerland and Portugal. The reinforced concrete overflow pool shown here, Carré Bleu (Blue Square), won the silver medal in the international NSPI competition in the United States in 1999.

www.waterair.com

WATERAIR: choose from fifty-six designs (with over a thousand variations) of leisure or sports pools. The Escatop Balneo System incorporates several functions, including massage and balneotherapy and transforms your pool into a health spa.

• **ESCATOP BALNEO SYSTEM**

www.pool-design.co.uk

POOL DESIGN: this company specialises in converting old buildings into indoor pools.

www.californiapools.com

CALIFORNIA POOLS AND SPAS design landscaped pools so you can have your own lagoon, complete with natural and synthetic rocks, waterfalls and gently sloping bottoms. They also do pools with fountains, if you prefer.

www.naturalsettings.com

NATURAL SETTINGS: this company specialises in truer-than-life natural settings with rocks, waterfalls and lush greenery.

fashion & beauty

watches
pens
sunglasses
rings
handbags
fashion accessories
cosmetics
aromatherapy
hand & nail care
sports shoes

delaneau@delaneau-watch.com

STARMASTER: equipped with a patented, automatic movement.

www.mulberry.com

CLASSIC: both timepiece and objet d'art, this fob watch is used by men and women.

www.breguet.com

HORA MUNDI: an 18-carat yellow-gold nautical watch.

www.pulsarwatches.com

TWO TIMER: monitors time conventionally and digitally.

www.oakley.com

TIME BOMB: a high-tech watch that uses your own wrist movements to operate.

www.bellross.com

VINTAGE: a four-counter chronograph with secure fastener, in stainless steel.

www.zenithwatches.ch

COLLECTION CLASS ELITE: 18-carat pink-gold case with a transparent sapphire face.

www.bulgari.com

BOLD ALLIANCE: aluminium, rubber and steel come together in this stylish design from Bulgari.

www.eterna.ch

GALAXIS: minimalist design with a battery that lasts three years.

www.audemarspiguet.com

KNOW IT ALL: an automatic perpetual calendar showing day, date, month, moon phases and leap years.

www.rado.com

CERIX: a futuristic design that plays with colours not time.

PAT: aluminium and titanium in high-tech harmony.

TOURBILLON: a manual wrist watch with visible movement, complete with 18-carat gold crown.

CHRONOSWISS: combines Swiss precision with quality.

SWISS MOVEMENT: elegant and sporty with a practical rubber bracelet.

CAPELAND: water-resistant to 100 metres, this watch has an alligator-skin bracelet.

TIME ZONE: globe-trotters can enjoy different time zones, with this model.

UNIQUE: an unusual stick with an 18-carat gold watch and a sword in a rosewood sheath.

NAVITIMER: Breitling have been solving navigation calculations since 1952.

V-TRONIC: a high-precision chronometer that is powered by the movement of its lucky owner's arm.

KIRIUM Ti5: this avant-garde chronograph has high-tech components, including titanium, carbon fibre and vulcanised rubber.

CHRONOBIKE: the French football team's official chronometer.

TITANIUM CHRONOGRAPH: Porsche's flagship design for Eterna combines the durability of titanium with precision technology. Water-resistant to 120 metres.

DIGITAL DISPLAY: a favourite with top athletes and containing fibres used in bulletproof vests, this watch is hard wearing but light.

HYDRO-CHALLENGER: the first watch to use liquid silicone in its case, allowing it to be water resistant to 11,100 metres. Clear dial with fluorescent hands.

HEMIPODE: a steel chronometer-watch with brutal precision, fluorescent orange and luminous hands, rubber strap and unique fastening system.

www.storm-watches.com

FUTURISTIC: watch, barometer, compass and torch – all in steel.

www.nike.com

HRM TRIAX 100: the watch for keen runners – it's both chronometer and heart-rate monitor.

www.technomarine.com

MILLENIUM SNAKE: equipped with a real snakeskin strap, mother-of-pearl face and nearly a carat of diamonds.

www.casio.com

FILM WATCH: this ultra-thin watch (6mm slim) operates as a chronometer, holds up to thirty messages in its memory, tells the time in as many as twenty-seven capitals and illuminates with a simple movement of the wrist.

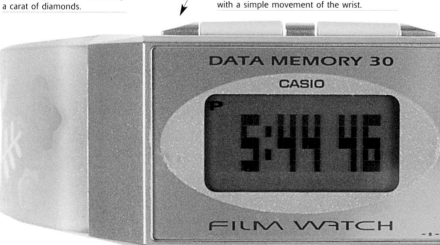

DATA MEMORY 30

CASIO

P

5:44 46

FILM WATCH

www.piaget.com

MISS PROTOCOLE: 18-carat white gold with a mother-of-pearl face and interchangeable straps.

www.bulgari.com

BULGARI BEAUTY: a steel serpent watch with Tubogas strap.

delaneau@delaneauwatch.com

THREE IN ONE: this watch tells you the time, day and month and is set with diamonds and four sapphires around an 18-carat gold face.

www.eluxury.com

FABULOUS FRED: platinum and diamonds from the famous Fred label.

www.parmigiani.com

BASICA: a mother-of-pearl face surrounded by 260 sapphires.

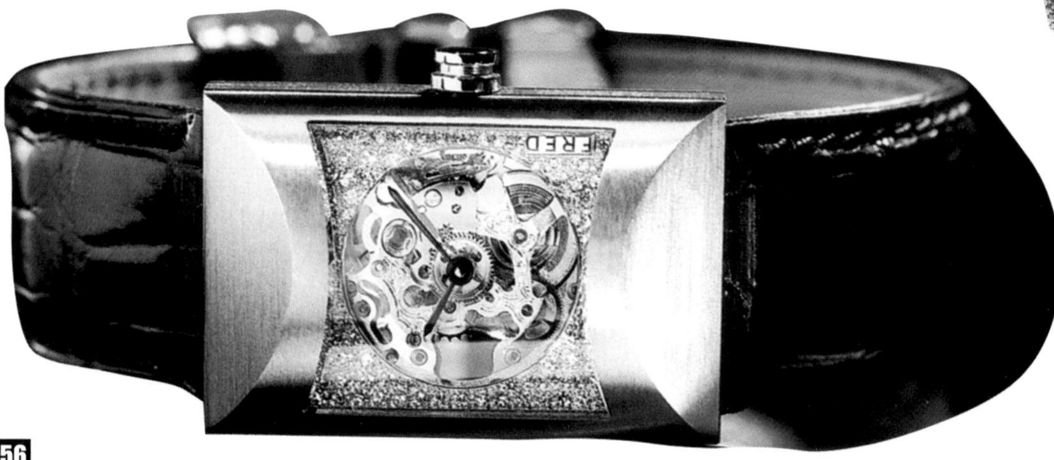

www.tagheuer.com

ALTER EGO: polished steel bracelet with blue dial. Water resistant to 100 metres.

www.raymond-weil.com

MINI: a stainless-steel watch set with more than fifty-four diamonds, weighing 0.27 carats.

www.montres-jaguar.com

JAGUAR: combines precision, elegance and stylish design.

www.dior.com

MALICE: exchange the camouflage-effect strap for a Christian Dior link bracelet with ease.

www.gucci.com

CLASSIQUE: Gucci's star timepiece has an 18-carat gold-plated case and black or brown leather strap.

www.longines.com

DOLCE VITA: an 18-carat face set with forty-eight diamonds.

www.mauboussin.com

LADY M: a rainbow collection, with or without diamonds.

www.cartier.com

PANTHÈRE AND MINI-BAIGNOIRE: these white-gold models are water resistant to thirty metres.

www.rado.com

BLUE FASCINATION: the latest in the Coupole range brings together gold, sapphire and diamonds.

www.bulgari.com

TRIKA: white gold and diamonds, rectangle and curve. Timeless and shapely beauty.

www.vancleef.com

CADENAS: a padlock watch in gold sporting a tartan strap keeps time Scottish-style.

www.harry-winston.com

DIAMONDS ARE FOREVER: a cascade of gems from 'The King of Diamonds', Harry Winston.

www.tissot.ch

BELLFLOWER: a steel watch with sapphire face.

www.cartier.fr

PANTHÈRE: available in several sizes, it's as sleek as its namesake.

www.chopard.ch

RIVER OF DIAMONDS: six diamonds on the dial and 740 on the bracelet. Who could ask for more?

www.pulsarwatches.com

SPOON: reflect on time with a digital display.

www.animal.co.uk

FUTURE LINE: Animal's extreme sports watch with a titanium face on a sturdy rubber strap.

www.swatch.com

NEANDA: a colourful range of watches with detachable faces on flexible metal bracelets.

www.swatch.com

PINK JELLY SKIN: ultra flat and thin, this watch has a transparent face and can be worn by women between seven and seventy.

www.citizenwatch.com

COUNT THE MINUTES AND THE HOURS: a luminous abacus-style watch for alternative time-keeping.

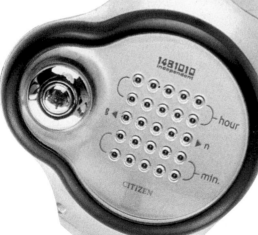

www.weals.com

MAKE YOUR WATCH: design your own watch and Weals produce it to order. Have your own time on your hands.

www.eandw.com

MONTRES EVANS & WONG: minimalist and imaginative design.

www.seiko.com

AIR PRO: pump air into the strap for extra comfort.

www.timex.com

MYSTERY: this fun watch has a mystery answer feature. Ask a question, press a button and receive one of fourteen random answers.

www.fossil.com

BRAIN: a design with seven different alarms and chrono stopwatch. It can also store up to thirty memos, each with thirty-two characters.

www.seiko.com

FREQUENCY: this watch contains six variable batteries that allow it to act as a metronome.

www.lexon-design.com

DESIGNER BRACELET: wrist action by F. Lintz.

261

www.waterman-pens.com

SERENITY: a curved collection available in matt silver or 18-carat gold.

www.visconti.it

TAJ MAHAL: this luxurious pen is made of gold and ivory, encrusted with 210 diamonds.

www.montblanc.com

YEHUDI MENUHIN: a limited edition pen designed for charity in honour of the great musician and conductor. The clip is shaped like a violin neck and the pen bears the great master's signature.

www.montegrappa1912.com

MAROSTICA: write letters as you practise your chess moves.

www.cartier.fr

DANDY: this pen is also a calendar and a watch.

www.namiki.com

COBRA: Namiki celebrates 2000, the Year of the Snake, with this limited edition fountain pen.

www.faber-castell.com

PORSCHE DESIGN FOR FABER-CASTELL: superior style in steel, designed by Porsche.

www.deltapen.it

SAXOPHONE: a collection that pays tribute to Adolphe Sax, inventor of the famous instrument.

www.ferraridavarese.com

KONYA: a stylish collection that includes a fountain pen, paper knife and photo holder.

www.hysek.com

DIAMONDS: a fountain pen and ink bottle in alligator skin, encrusted with diamonds. Designed by Jorg Hysek.

www.conwaystewart.co.uk

FLORAL: only fifty copies of this hand-painted 18-carat gold enamel pen were made.

www.yardoled.com

ART DÉCO 33: solid silver nostalgic style.

www.st-dupont.com

OLYMPIO: a fountain pen in black lacquer with a palladium-plated lid.

www.acmestudio.com

RINGS: designed by Robert and Trix Hausmann in a series of rings.

www.carandache.com

METWOOD: this pen is made of rose wood, brass and rhodium, a precious stainless metal.

www.cross.com

ION: the latest pen from Cross is compact, velvety and equipped with a transparent window through which to monitor the ink level.

263

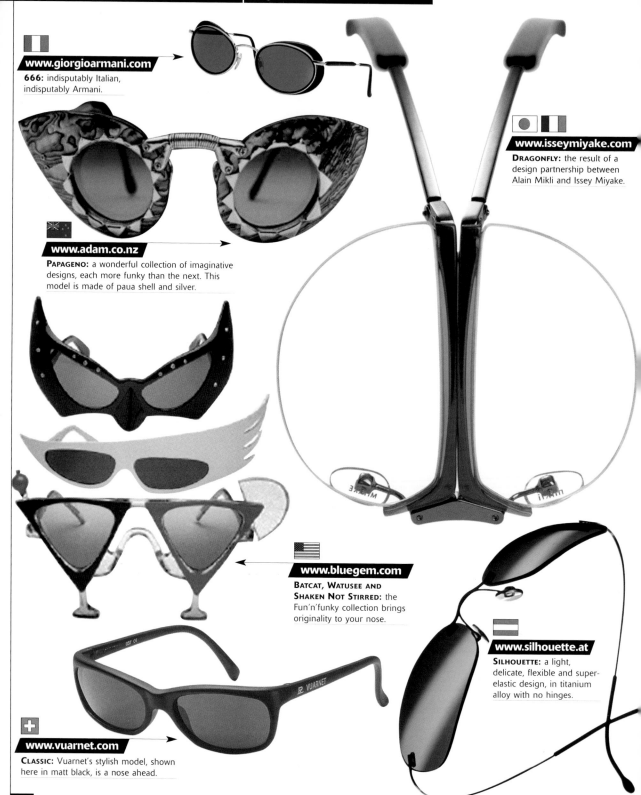

www.giorgioarmani.com

666: indisputably Italian, indisputably Armani.

www.adam.co.nz

PAPAGENO: a wonderful collection of imaginative designs, each more funky than the next. This model is made of paua shell and silver.

www.isseymiyake.com

DRAGONFLY: the result of a design partnership between Alain Mikli and Issey Miyake.

www.bluegem.com

BATCAT, WATUSEE AND SHAKEN NOT STIRRED: the Fun'n'funky collection brings originality to your nose.

www.silhouette.at

SILHOUETTE: a light, delicate, flexible and super-elastic design, in titanium alloy with no hinges.

www.vuarnet.com

CLASSIC: Vuarnet's stylish model, shown here in matt black, is a nose ahead.

www.cutlerandgross.com
CUTLER AND GROSS: unique style meets eye-catching colour.

www.scott-europe.com
SNAKE MASK: home to a horror hologram.

www.briko.com
JUMPER: designed for those who enjoy outdoor activities.

www.bodyspecs.com
EYERODZ: psychedelic and protective.

www.shades4u.com
SUNSPOT: anti-UV screens that you cut to fit your glasses. They stay in place due to static electricity.

www.oakley.com
OVER THE TOP: enjoy a wide range of vision and extraordinary clarity with Oakley's futuristic sunglasses.

www.bolle.com
VIGILANT: supple and hard-wearing sunglasses in metal and nylon, from the Action Sport range.

www.stilic-force.com
STILIC EYES: flexible, soft and adjustable, these glasses know their place.

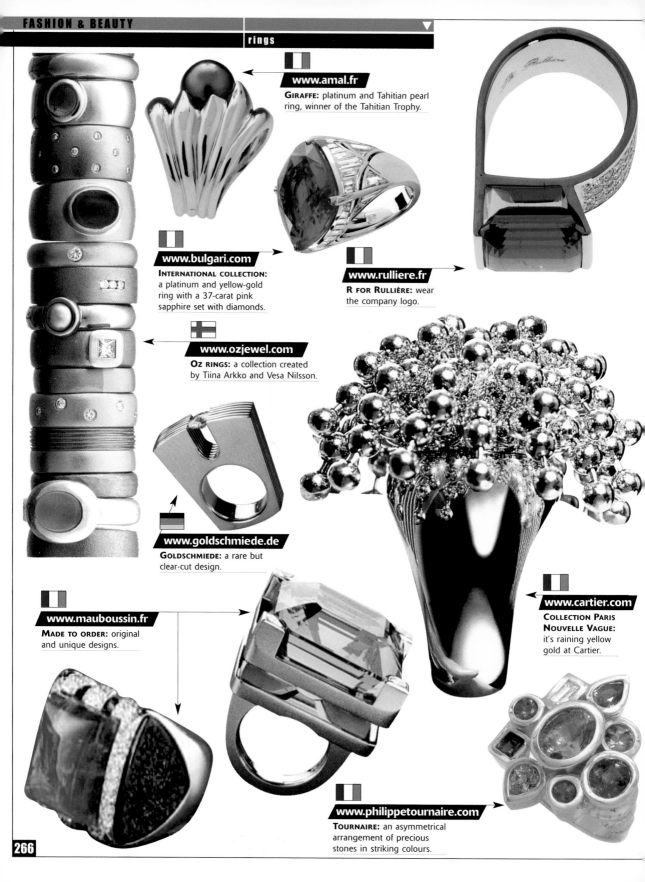

www.amal.fr

GIRAFFE: platinum and Tahitian pearl ring, winner of the Tahitian Trophy.

www.bulgari.com

INTERNATIONAL COLLECTION: a platinum and yellow-gold ring with a 37-carat pink sapphire set with diamonds.

www.rulliere.fr

R FOR RULLIÈRE: wear the company logo.

www.ozjewel.com

OZ RINGS: a collection created by Tiina Arkko and Vesa Nilsson.

www.goldschmiede.de

GOLDSCHMIEDE: a rare but clear-cut design.

www.cartier.com

COLLECTION PARIS NOUVELLE VAGUE: it's raining yellow gold at Cartier.

www.mauboussin.fr

MADE TO ORDER: original and unique designs.

www.philippetournaire.com

TOURNAIRE: an asymmetrical arrangement of precious stones in striking colours.

www.boblbee.com

LOCK SOLID: this rucksack shuts firmly and safely.

www.viahero.com

THREE IN ONE: a range that includes wellington boots, umbrella and bag. Sponge clean and keep forever (so they claim).

www.lollipops.fr

FLASHY KICK: fun fake-fur adds a finishing touch to kitsch fashion.

www.buguk.com

MILLENNIUM BUG: make your point with a spiky rucksack by Craig Morrison.

www.o-to-o.com

TWO BY TWO: Zora La Fée's bag has a transparent outer case, a Zen garden at the base and a black nylon upper section.

www.karinedupont.com

KADEAU: a square bag that opens up to reveal its hidden contents.

271

www.jalucine.com

PORTABLE SCULPTURES: a practical and attractive range of bags with strong wooden frames.

www.bijouxrigaux.com

CRAFTED IN METAL AND STONE: original and lovely jewellery designs.

www.sandsofparadise.com

A TOUCH OF PARADISE: these earrings contain grains of sand from the paradise island of your choice.

www.le-webstore.com

PAGODA: a limited series of handbags made of moleskin on a hand-carved palm wood base and lined with silk.

www.anteprimamilano.com

BUCOLIC: three umbrellas that bring a ray of sunshine even to grey skies.

www.dadoudesign.com/lolita.pompadour
DIVA: wear this synthetic rose in your hair or wrapped around your arm.

www.baccarat.fr
HORTENSIA: topaz flowers on gold wire make a delicate necklace.

www.pylones.fr
RURAL SUPPORT: latex braces for all sizes.

www.knowear.net
BASEBALL: a plywood baseball cap designed by Peter Allan and Carla Murray.

www.natureetdecouvertes.com
CAP HORN: a watch powered by the movement of your own arm.

Cousteau
AUTOMATIC
100M
WATER RESISTANT

www.burtsbees.com
SALAD DAYS: a different natural soap for each type of complexion.

BURT'S BEES
Garden Tomato
COMPLEXION
SOAP
for oily and troubled skin
4 oz. (113 g)

BURT'S BEES
Garden Carrot
COMPLEXION
SOAP
for mature and sun-damaged skin
4 oz. (113 g)

BURT'S BEES
Wild Lettuce
COMPLEXION
SOAP
for dry and sensitive skin
4 oz. (113 g)

www.paticoandco.com

HARD LIFE: this metal brooch is the answer to virtual headaches.

www.raumgestalt-en.de

ALADDIN: do your own divining with this felt-encased game.

www.fashionguillarme.com

SAY IT WITH SILK: a pretty choker bearing motifs and messages.

www.quartdepoil.com

DOUBLE VIE: when closed, it's a document file but when unfolded, voilà an extra seat.

www.eandw.com

WHO IS THE FAIREST OF THEM ALL? A modern version of the mythical magical mirror.

http://marion.ch.free.fr

BODY CHIC, BODY FRIEND: Marion Chopineau's exotic creations are designed to caress and complement you.

www.apc.fr

OLDER IS BETTER: this sandpaper glove will age your denim jeans in a flash.

www.camper.es

TWINS: giant steps for design.

www.tateossian.co.uk

BRAVE YOUNG BLADES: wear this masculine jewellery at your own peril.

www.eandw.com

LUMINOUS: the pendant contains fluorescent liquid to light up your evenings.

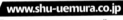

www.shu-uemura.co.jp

REVOLUTIONARY LOTION: oil and water combine to deep cleanse and freshen the skin.

www.giorgioarmani.com

IMMACULATE COVER: a new range of cosmetics that brightens your skin without adding colour.

www.le-webstore.com

PORTE-BONHEUR: this ring is made with a whole dollar note folded by hand and varnished twice for luck and longevity.

designed for lovers

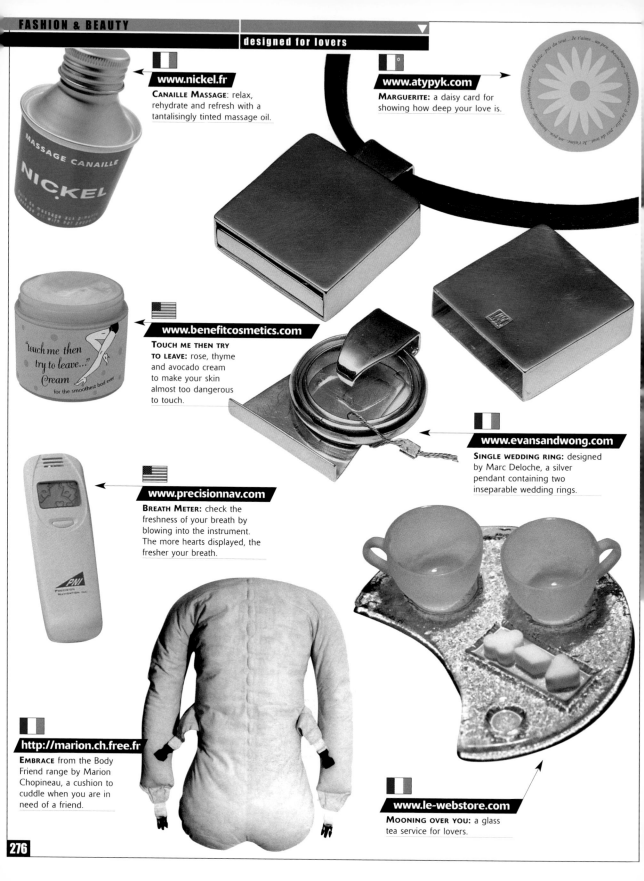

www.nickel.fr

CANAILLE MASSAGE: relax, rehydrate and refresh with a tantalisingly tinted massage oil.

www.atypyk.com

MARGUERITE: a daisy card for showing how deep your love is.

www.benefitcosmetics.com

TOUCH ME THEN TRY TO LEAVE: rose, thyme and avocado cream to make your skin almost too dangerous to touch.

www.evansandwong.com

SINGLE WEDDING RING: designed by Marc Deloche, a silver pendant containing two inseparable wedding rings.

www.precisionnav.com

BREATH METER: check the freshness of your breath by blowing into the instrument. The more hearts displayed, the fresher your breath.

http://marion.ch.free.fr

EMBRACE from the Body Friend range by Marion Chopineau, a cushion to cuddle when you are in need of a friend.

www.le-webstore.com

MOONING OVER YOU: a glass tea service for lovers.

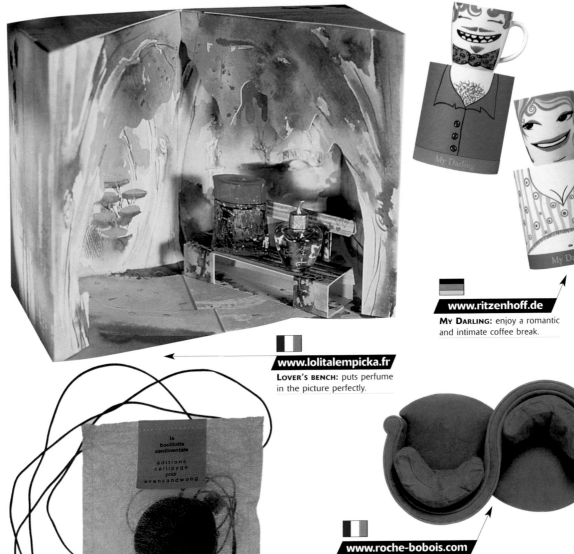

www.ritzenhoff.de

MY DARLING: enjoy a romantic and intimate coffee break.

www.lolitalempicka.fr

LOVER'S BENCH: puts perfume in the picture perfectly.

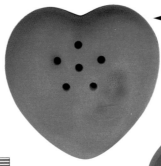

www.roche-bobois.com

LUDIVINE: a conversation chair in stylish leather – close but not too close for comfort.

www.chaiselongue.fr

PLAY IT CLOSE TO YOUR HEART: keep track of whispered sweet-nothings on a tape recorder.

www.eandw.com

HEART-WARMING STUFF: a Pyrex hot-water bottle encased in felt.

www.revlon.com

RED FOR ROMANCE: inflammatory aroma in a flask.

www.tateossian.co.uk
RAINBOW: colourful glass cufflinks – handle with care.

www.eandw.com
TIEPINS À LA FRANCAISE: in gold, silver and platinum, as marked.

www.dalvey.com
PLAYING CARD: round cards in a lovely chrome-plated steel case

www.cosmalia.com
IMPERIAL: authentic eau de cologne as worn by Napoleon I in St Helena.

www.burtsbees.com
BAY RUM: traditional eau de cologne in a whisky bottle. Smells good, tastes bad.

www.ricochet.fr
INTERNET JEWELLERY: necklace, bracelet and cufflinks, designed by Simon Santoni to keep up with the latest technology.

www.authenticmodels.com

BOSCO: this type of copper and brass whistle was originally used by crew captains on boats. Whistle while you work.

www.rmn.fr

BRITANNICUS: a small box with a lid that's a clock, inscribed by a quote from the 17th-century French dramatist Racine.

www.tateossian.co.uk

CUFFLINKS: keep heading in the right direction with these compasses.

www.eshave.com

E-SHAVE: put a stylish end to designer stubble.

www.acmestudio.com

CAMPBELL TIE: Andy Warhol's paintings inspired this tie design.

www.o-to-o.com

KEEP IT CLEAN: made in Syria, this alum stone has healing and disinfecting properties.

www.shu-uemura.co.jp

DEEPSEAWATER: a Japanese eau de toilette collection made with sea water found 300 metres beneath the surface.

www.danieljouvance.com

OXYGEN: day and night cream, an oxygen spray and cleansing tablets.

www.burtsbees.com

AFTERSHAVE: a soothing balm that leaves the skin supple and smooth.

www.parfums-azzaro.com

HYDRATE: trace elements and Vitamin E keep the skin moist and healthy.

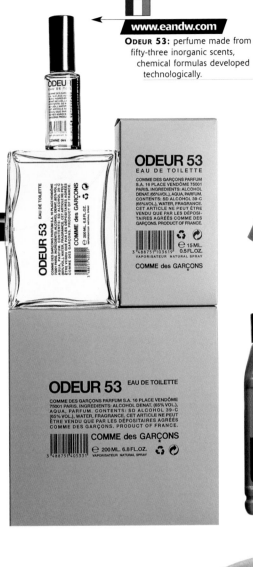

www.eandw.com

ODEUR 53: perfume made from fifty-three inorganic scents, chemical formulas developed technologically.

ODEUR 53
EAU DE TOILETTE

COMME DES GARÇONS PARFUM S.A. 16 PLACE VENDÔME 75001 PARIS. INGREDIENTS: ALCOHOL DENAT. (65% VOL.), AQUA, PARFUM. CONTENTS: SD ALCOHOL 39-C (65%VOL.), WATER, FRAGRANCE. CET ARTICLE NE PEUT ÊTRE VENDU QUE PAR LES DÉPOSITAIRES AGRÉÉS COMME DES GARÇONS. PRODUCT OF FRANCE.

℮ 15 ML.
0.5 FL.OZ.
VAPORISATEUR NATURAL SPRAY

COMME des GARÇONS

ODEUR 53 EAU DE TOILETTE

COMME DES GARÇONS PARFUM S.A. 16 PLACE VENDÔME 75001 PARIS. INGREDIENTS: ALCOHOL DENAT. (65% VOL.), AQUA, PARFUM. CONTENTS: SD ALCOHOL 39-C (65% VOL.), WATER, FRAGRANCE. CET ARTICLE NE PEUT ÊTRE VENDU QUE PAR LES DÉPOSITAIRES AGRÉÉS COMME DES GARÇONS. PRODUCT OF FRANCE.

COMME des GARÇONS

℮ 200 ML. 6.8 FL.OZ.
VAPORISATEUR NATURAL SPRAY

www.nickel.fr

MADE FOR MEN: brush, massage oil, anti-wrinkle cream and 'morning after the party' gel.

www.heavydutyco.com

HEAVY DUTY: body lotion for the very male physique.

BODY LOTION
with ANTIOXIDANTS

HEAVY Duty
BodyLube™

For bodies on the rrrrrun!

Net wt. 8 oz.

THE BODY SHOP

BODY MECHANICS FOR MEN
Everyday
Body Wash
Kick start your day.

www.bodyshop.com

BODY WASH: keeps even car mechanics clean.

www.accakappa.it

SHAVING CREAM: a hand-polished shaving pot with almond soap.

ACCA KAPPA
SAPONE DA BARBA
Salvia
SAGE SHAVING SOAP
SAVON DE RASAGE À LA SAUGE
net WT 1.75 oz
50 g ℮

www.dior.com

LIPS BY DIOR: Dior's divine lipstick combines long-lasting colour, elegant design and luxurious texture.

www.guerlain.fr

METEORITES: these ingenious little balls release a veil of satiny powder.

www.euro-esthetic.com

SPARKLING BODY FOAM: Mary Cohr's innovative product leaves the skin feeling fresh and clean.

www.lancome.com

VINÉFIT: a grape-based moisturiser that revives your skin.

www.givenchy.com

LIPSTICK MIRROR: combines Givenchy's high quality lipstick a mirror lid designed with the sculptor Pablo Reinoso.

www.caudalie.com

VINOLIFT: revitalise and refresh your skin with a product that comes straight from the vines.

www.revlon.com

RED AND ROUGE: enjoy a high-gloss result with gel-based lipstick, enriched with vitamins A and E.

www.thierrymugler.com

SECRET: lovers of Thierry Mugler's Angel perfume can enjoy a face cream in the same range.

www.bodyshop.com

LIPSCUFF: a practical stick that exfoliates and revitalises your lips, ready for a perfect application of colour. Pukka.

www.benefitcosmetics.com

CLASSIC KITTEN: perfumed powder in a puff for cute kittens.

www.cowgirlenterprises.com

COWGIRL: a range of products for outdoor girls.

www.kanebo-cosmetics.com

NEW EYE-LINER: Kanebo's latest product is great for beginners – a precision tool for the eyes.

www.babyliss.com

DIFFUSER LAMP: fills the room with a delicate scent of citronella, vanilla, pine or eucalyptus.

www.primalelements.com

SCENTS AND SENSUALITY: match your perfume with your mood by choosing from fifteen alternatives on this aluminium palette.

www.le-webstore.com

WEAR YOUR HEART ON YOUR SOLE and choose from five aromas for this silk and leather sandal: Seduction, Fidelity, Happiness, Tenderness and Inspiration.

www.loccitane.com

AROMACHOLOGY: apply revitalising balm to pulse points to relax, relieve stress and feel the world's a better place.

www.thebodyshop.com

COLOURTHERAPY: a range of cosmetics that attributes different properties to each of the colours.

www.thebodyshop.com

ESSENTIALLY ELEMENTAL: earth, fire and water body lotions with essential oils to keep the elements in place.

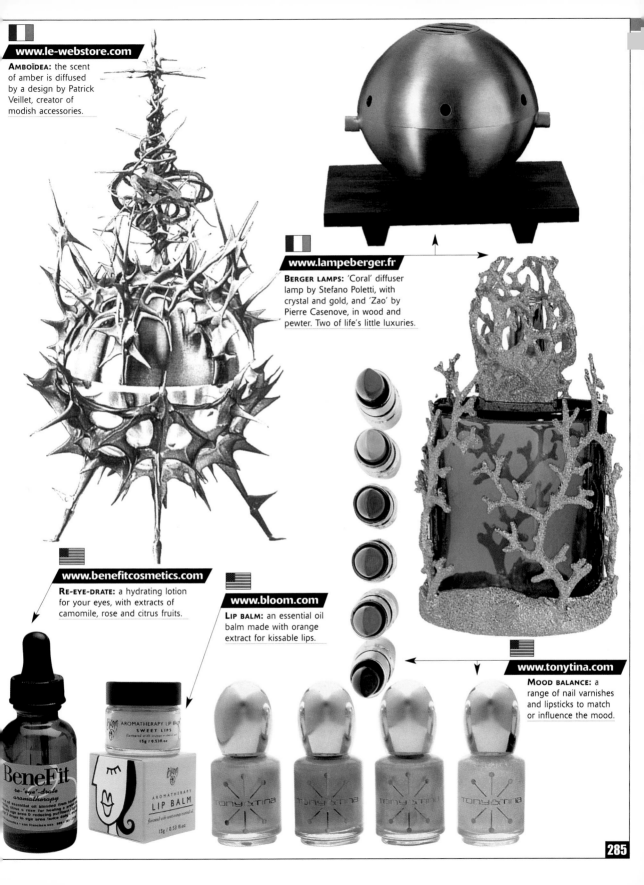

www.le-webstore.com

AMBOÏDEA: the scent of amber is diffused by a design by Patrick Veillet, creator of modish accessories.

www.lampeberger.fr

BERGER LAMPS: 'Coral' diffuser lamp by Stefano Poletti, with crystal and gold, and 'Zao' by Pierre Casenove, in wood and pewter. Two of life's little luxuries.

www.benefitcosmetics.com

RE-EYE-DRATE: a hydrating lotion for your eyes, with extracts of camomile, rose and citrus fruits.

www.bloom.com

LIP BALM: an essential oil balm made with orange extract for kissable lips.

www.tonytina.com

MOOD BALANCE: a range of nail varnishes and lipsticks to match or influence the mood.

BeneFit
re-'eye'-drate
aromatherapy

AROMATHERAPY LIP BALM
SWEET LIPS

AROMATHERAPY
LIP BALM

15g / 0.53 fl.oz

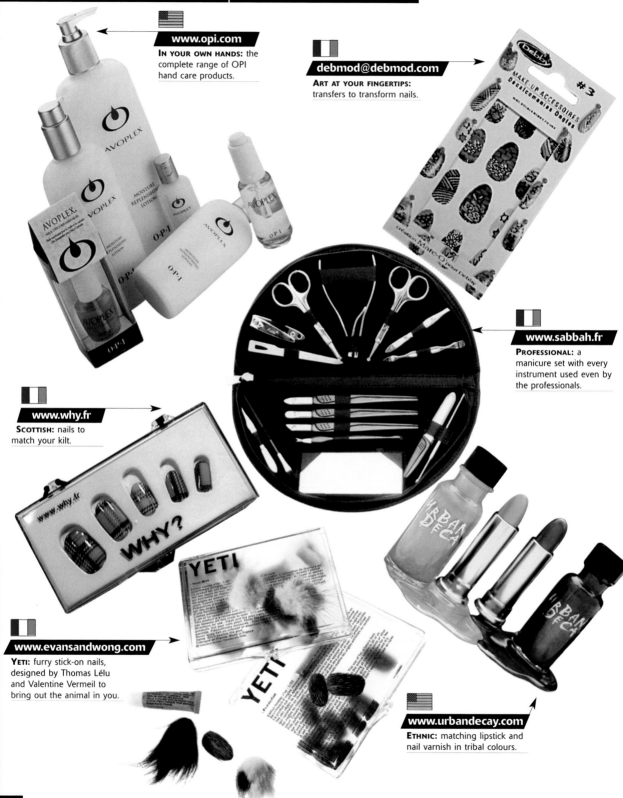

www.opi.com

IN YOUR OWN HANDS: the complete range of OPI hand care products.

debmod@debmod.com

ART AT YOUR FINGERTIPS: transfers to transform nails.

www.sabbah.fr

PROFESSIONAL: a manicure set with every instrument used even by the professionals.

www.why.fr

SCOTTISH: nails to match your kilt.

www.evansandwong.com

YETI: furry stick-on nails, designed by Thomas Lélu and Valentine Vermeil to bring out the animal in you.

www.urbandecay.com

ETHNIC: matching lipstick and nail varnish in tribal colours.

www.escada.com

ESTÉE LAUDER: beautiful in the bottle, beautiful on your nails, a drop of the eternal stuff.

www.urbandecay.com

ROCK AND NAIL: precious stones glued to your fingertips make a statement.

www.yves-rocher.fr

MANUCURE KIT: brush, nail file, varnish and almond oil hand cream keep a hold on perfect-looking hands.

www.peggysage.com

BODY ART: even nails can be pierced and bejewelled. Why should they miss out? Everthing you need in a kit.

www.thebodyshop.com

COLOURINGS: a very precise drop of gold for those with the Midas touch.

www.peggysage.com

NAIL DESIGN: nails by numbers, a different one each day.

www.thebodyshop.com

BIG NAIL FILER: file and buff to a high gloss – a new nail care concept.

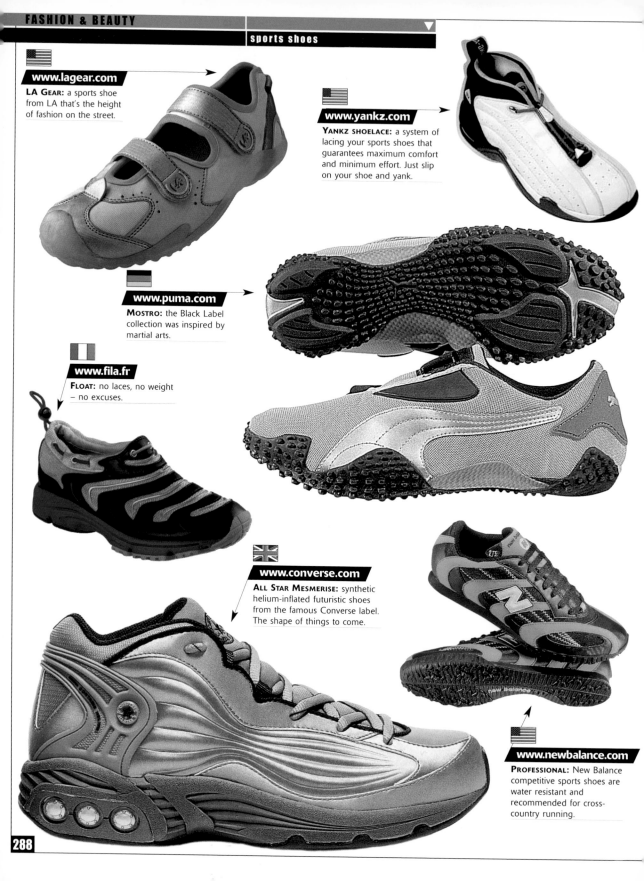

www.lagear.com

LA GEAR: a sports shoe from LA that's the height of fashion on the street.

www.yankz.com

YANKZ SHOELACE: a system of lacing your sports shoes that guarantees maximum comfort and minimum effort. Just slip on your shoe and yank.

www.puma.com

MOSTRO: the Black Label collection was inspired by martial arts.

www.fila.fr

FLOAT: no laces, no weight – no excuses.

www.converse.com

ALL STAR MESMERISE: synthetic helium-inflated futuristic shoes from the famous Converse label. The shape of things to come.

www.newbalance.com

PROFESSIONAL: New Balance competitive sports shoes are water resistant and recommended for cross-country running.

www.reebok.com

FURY: this lace-free shoe is equipped with the Insta Pump system that provides individual support through an inflatable membrane around the foot.

www.adidas.com

THE KOBE : named after NBA champion Kobe Bryant, who helped perfect the design. The inspiration came originally from the Audi TT.

www.nike.com

NIKE SHOX R4: based on Formula One design, the cushion system is made up of four polyurethane columns.

www.zshoes.com

ZCOIL: a sports shoe with extra cushioning and a patented spring suspension system to avoid back and foot injury.

www.lacoste.fr

MISSION: two-tone leather shoes from the casual urban chic collection. Available in a range of colour schemes.

www.lotto.it

EXTREME MICRO: Italian football label, Lotto, has produced a new 'streetwear' shoe with a rubber sole and microfibre upper.

high-tech

www.aiwa.com
PASCAL: five 140-watt satellite speakers and a 120-watt active bass system.

www.a-theater.com
POPCORN MACHINE: for those nostalgic for the good old American movies of the sixties.

www.bose.com
LIFESTYLE: Bose quality is available in an integrated audio system that automatically adjusts the audio signal for the best possible results. Impeccable sound.

www.panja.com
PANJA 1000: a control system for video, audio and computer equipment using just one touch screen remote control – ViewPoint.

www.runco.com
DTV-1101 PROJECTOR: this is the flagship model from Runco – the highest resolution projector on the market, with up to 2,500 x 2,000 pixels.

www.3dmagic.com

SPACE THEATER: contains a 3D internal video projector, surround sound and a screen for use with polarised glasses.

www.goterapin.com

CD VIDEO RECORDER: the first consumer digital video recorder. Transfer your home videos on to CDs and record straight from your camcorder.

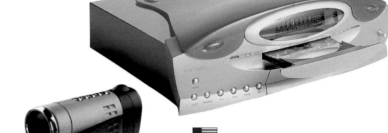

www.tktheaters.com

NO TICKETS REQUIRED: technology alone cannot recreate the atmosphere of a real cinema. The architect Theo Kalomirakis transforms your room into a private cinema.

www.compaq.com

MP2800 PROJECTOR: a portable projector that's easy to use and is equipped with a multi-media PC adaptor. Wonderful picture quality guaranteed.

www.samsung.com

DVD AND VHS COMBO: play CDs, VCDs and CD-DA discs. You can record while you watch a DVD.

www.sharp-world.com

GIANT LC-R60HDE SCREEN: specially adapted for the era of digital television, this LCD screen projects high-definition images on to a 160cm screen.

www.irwinseating.com

SPRINGFIELD CHAIRS: now you can sit in those legendary red velvet chairs in the comfort of your own home.

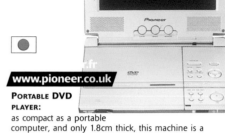

www.pioneer.co.uk

PORTABLE DVD PLAYER: as compact as a portable computer, and only 1.8cm thick, this machine is a DVD player once linked to a television.

www.lge.com

LG PLASMA DISPLAY SCREEN: made in Korea, this is one of the largest plasma screens at 152cm, with impressive brightness and powerful speakers.

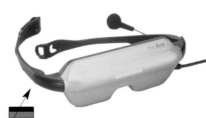

www.olympus-eye-trek.com

EYE-TREK: with these glasses, weighing only 85g, you'll think you're just two metres away from a 52cm screen. Connect to any VCR, DVD player, camcorder or other video source.

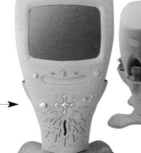

www.tak.fr

THOMSON'S INTERACTIVE TAK: connect to the Internet via your television set. Send emails using the keyboard on the remote control and access information services.

www.islandnet.com/~mercury7

ORBIT: designed by Peter Andringa and available in six colours. Only 500 sets were produced.

www.daewoo.com

OASIS AND BETTY DAVIS EYES: Daewoo's prototypes are set to change the face of television.

www.tamashi.com

MINI TELLY: radio and television set in one, equipped with a 12cm black and white screen.

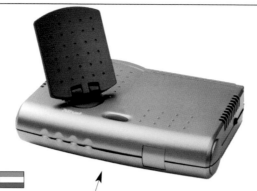

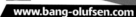

RELAY CONSOLE: sold in pairs, this invention allows you to establish cordless contact between your camcorder, DVD player, computer, hi-fi system and TV. Access the Internet on television or MP3 on your hi-fi. A new flexible friend.

www.bang-olufsen.com

BEOCENTER 1: a complete system with DVD and CD player, radio and television – all operated by a single small remote control.

www.sony.com

GLASSTRON: liquid crystal glasses with 1.55 million pixels, equipped with speakers. Connect to a computer, DVD player or games console.

www.sharp-world.com

LC-28H2E: a high-resolution liquid crystal screen in 16/9 format and 6cm thin – you can use it as a computer or a television.

www.casio.com

MiniTV: this portable TV set looks more like a picture frame. It can operate for three hours at a time and has an integrated aerial.

camcorders

www.canon.com

MV3 MC: weighing in at 395g, this camcorder makes high-resolution digital videos in MultiMediaCard format.

www.hitachi.com

DIGITAL DVDCAM: images are copied directly on to an 8cm DVD.

www.mikli.fr

THIRD EYE: these spectacles are connected to a video recorder.

www.spyzone.com

I SPY: this pen conceals a tiny video camera.

www.sony.com

GV-D900: Digital video recording allows you to record, playback and edit wherever you go. For budding directors.

www.sharp-world.co

DIGITAL RECORDER: the MPEG4 gives digital technology another dimension by allowing images to be transmitted over the Internet.

www.sony.com

DIGITAL POSTPRODUCTION: the DHR-100 video recorder can also develop digital images in DV format.

www.canon.com

XL1 DIGITAL VIDEO CAMCORDER: combines the mini DV format with an interchangeable lens system and a 16x zoom lens to produce top-quality full-motion videos or still images.

www.sharp-world.com

VLCD 20: film others or yourself without a viewfinder and connect to your PC with a special kit.

www.jvc.com

MICRO POCKET GR-DVP3: one of the smallest video cameras in the world, equipped with a 200,000 pixel screen and a 10x optical zoom.

www.i-glasses.com

NUVIEW: attach to your camcorder and within minutes you'll be making 3D videos.

www.jvc.com

DV GY-DV500: combines compact style with high quality results.

www.leica.com

TELEFOTO LENS APO-TELYT-R-1: a uniquely flexible collection – practical and easy to use.

www.hasselblad.com

HASSELBLAD 203 FE: the reference point for medium-format cameras, perfect for portraits and landscapes, with guaranteed results.

www.leica.com

LEICA M6: designed for purists, the M6 favours optimum optical performance over the automatic option.

www.rollei.de

ROLLEIFLEX 6001 PROFESSIONAL: symbolises avant-garde technology in medium-format cameras by combining electronic precision with total reliability.

www.hammacher.com

PHOTO STUDIO AND LABORATORY: everything you need in one place, including enlarger and projector.

www.pentax.com
PENTAX 67: the legendary
Pentax model, equipped here
with a stylish wooden handle.

www.minox-web.de
MINOX LX: its creator wanted to produce a camera
'smaller than a cigar, lighter than a cigarette'.

www.nikon.com
NIKON FX90 PRO: equipped with 3D
matrix metering, a shutter speed of 1/8000
to 30 seconds and a flash control system.

www.canon.com
EOS-1V: the next
generation of
professional SLR
cameras, with
revolutionary
shutter, lightweight
body and both
water and dust
resistance.

www.minox-web.de
MINOX CLASSIC IIIF The dimensions say
it all: 75 x 41 x 38mm. This miniature
camera weighs no more than 93g.

www.polaroid.com

FUN 640: send your favourite images across the world in seconds via the Internet.

www.olympus.com

E-10 DIGITAL: combine ultra-high definition, great optical capabilities and innovative digital features.

www.nikon.com

ERGONOMIC: Coolpix includes several easy-to-use facilities, including a 3x optical zoom and image manipulation software.

www.canon.com

DIGITAL IXUS: combines sophistication with technical prowess.

www.sony.com

UNIQUE: Sony's MVC-CD1 is unique in that it contains a CD-Rom on which images are stored.

www.leica.de

PROFESSIONAL: a top of the range Leica digital camera with easy grip.

www.samsung.com

ALL ROUNDER: the SDC 80 is available in four seductive colours.

www.fujifilm.fr

FINE PIX: a fast and compact point-and-shoot camera with many of the features of today's digital cameras.

www.oregonscientific.com

UNUSUAL: the DS 3868 downloads digital photos to your PC and has software that allows you to modify them first.

www.ricoh.com

MORE THAN JUST A CAMERA: ultra-portable and compact, the RDC-7 can record and play back movie clips as well as record interviews.

www.konica.com

E-MINI M: digital camera, MP3 player, computer cam and audio recorder in one compact package.

www.kodak.com

PALM PIX: a black box that transforms your Handheld Palm into a digital colour camera.

www.oregonscientific.com

DIGITAL DISPLAY: the DV 238 Wallet picture frame allows you to display your digital camera photos elegantly, stored on a mini-disc.

www.canon.com

UNDERWATER VIEWS: a robust camera for sporty types with large buttons and water resistance down to five metres – the Ixus-x-1.

www.canon.com

COMPACT DESIGN: the Ixus Arancia is a limited edition compact camera that is flamboyant and practical – pocket-perfect design.

www.samsung.com

FOUR IN ONE: this small digital camera, the Digimax 35, combines MP3 player, webcam and email facility with capturing important moments.

www.casio.com

WRIST ACTION: the first digital wrist camera capable of storing up to 100 black and white photographs that you can transfer to your PC. Never forget a face again.

www.siliconfilms.com

REVOLUTIONARY: a digital film (not yet on the market) that can be used in all standard cameras.

www.olympus.com

HAND PRINT: easy to carry around, this printer can produce digital images wherever you go.

www.sony.com

NOMAD: a digital picture frame that can be used for stills, slides or video seqences.

www.samsung.com

HYBRID: capable of taking photos as well as recording video sequences with sound.

www.polaroid.com

POLAROID JOYCAM: a compact modern design instant camera with pocketsize photos. Perfect for parties.

www.bang-olufsen.com

BeoSound 9000: play one of six CDs in this (horizontal or vertical) system, accompanied here by BeoLab 8000 loudspeakers.

www.pioneer.co.uk

Pioneer IS-21 M: a futuristic design with horizontal cassette deck, vertical CD player and 3D speaker system.

www.nakamichi.com

Soundspace 9: you can programme three CDs to play in succession in one room or simultaneously in three different rooms.

www.kenwood.com

Avino: this system can be positioned horizontally or vertically.

www.tagmaclarenaudio.com

Turquoise aphrodite: equipped with avant-garde loudspeakers, this hi-fi system is as beautiful to listen to as it is to look at.

www.samsung.com

Samsung SP-2400: a micro CD system with PC access and MP3 player.

www.jvc.com

JVC FS SD1000 R: the aluminium cylinders contain flat loudspeakers that emit a powerful and pure sound.

www.fisherav.com

SLIM 2000: a three-disc CD audio system that can hang on a wall. Its speakers are detachable.

www.grundig.com

GRUNDIG SPACE FIDELITY WITH APOLLO 2000 SPEAKERS: this system on castors is equipped with a three-disc CD changer and spatial overlapping sound.

www.marklev.com

CD PLAYER: Mark Levinson's design is one for the purists.

www.riohome.com

RIO RECEIVER: access music on your PC in any room in the house with a phone connection. One computer can provide music to eight Rio receivers at a time! It also supports MP3.

www.o-d.co.uk

O'HEOCHA: a design that emits a very pure sound.

www.waterfallaudio.com

VICTORIA: transparent glass speakers.

www.pearlaudio.com

ELIPTICA GRANDE: these speakers are as tall as their owners.

www.cabasse.com

ADRIATIS 600 EVOLUTION: produced by the famous company to bring together high-quality sound and innovative design.

www.jmlab.fr

PRESTIGIOUS: made by JM Lab, the Utopia speaker is 1.75m high and weighs in at 186kg.

www.pioneer.com

LINEAR POWER: subwoofers from the Pump series with a futuristic look.

www.infinitysystems.com

MODULUS: a wall speaker that is a versatile part of a top-quality range of equipment for home cinema sound.

www.blueroomdesign.co.uk

MINIPODS: a spherical design on detachable legs.

www.acapella.de

EXCALIBUR: these speakers are interior design features in a room that measures forty square metres or more.

www.tagmclarenaudio.com

CALLIOPE: TAG McLaren's Audio team worked closely with Formula One materials specialists to design a powerful aluminium loudspeaker.

www.roundsound.com

NUCLEUS MICRO: the smallest speaker in the world.

www.sennheiser.de

AUDIO BEAM: due to an ingenious system of overlapping waves, the sound is directed to a very precise spot. One person will hear a clear and strong sound and his neighbour will hear nothing but silence.

www.bang-olufsen.com

BEOLAB 6000: narrow columns (200cm in height) in polished aluminium take up minimal space and emit maximum sound.

www.revelspeakers.com

ULTIMA SALON: a four-way floorstanding system in aluminium emits top-quality sound.

307

portable hi-fi systems

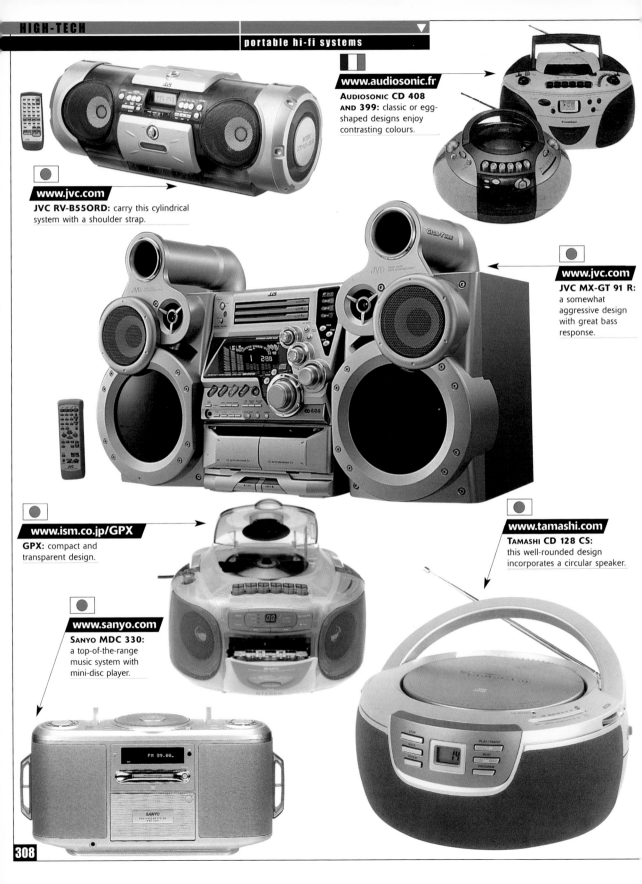

www.audiosonic.fr

AUDIOSONIC CD 408 AND 399: classic or egg-shaped designs enjoy contrasting colours.

www.jvc.com

JVC RV-B55ORD: carry this cylindrical system with a shoulder strap.

www.jvc.com

JVC MX-GT 91 R: a somewhat aggressive design with great bass response.

www.ism.co.jp/GPX

GPX: compact and transparent design.

www.tamashi.com

TAMASHI CD 128 CS: this well-rounded design incorporates a circular speaker.

www.sanyo.com

SANYO MDC 330: a top-of-the-range music system with mini-disc player.

www.sharp-world.com

SHARP QTCD 210: colourful, fun and simple.

www.bang-olufsen.com

BANG & OLUFSEN BEOSOUND 1: now you can carry B&O sound around with you. It has powerful speakers and a vertical CD player.

www.wilsonsports.com

WILSON AND JEEP: unusual packaging for a water-resistant radio, designed by Wilson and Jeep Electronics.

www.daewoo.fr

DAEWOO SUBMARINE: water resistant and very sporty.

www.jvc.com

JVC RS-WP1: wear this design like a rucksack. There's an in-built protective system for the CD player and a remote control.

www.grundig.com

GRUNDIG RR 430 CD: it's compact but extremely powerful.

www.apc.fr

RECORD PLAYER: bring back Happy Days or American Graffiti.

www.jensen.com

JB 15 SPORTSTYLE: wear these headphones at the back of your head – light, comfortable and perfect for jogging.

www.touchtunes.com

DIGITAL JUKEBOX: 750 tunes and Bose speakers for wonderful sounds and perfect choice.

www.philips.com

SBC HC8900: designed for home cinema, this headset has CD quality sound at a distance of 100m.

www.palmgarden.com.tw

CD-203: the headset can be folded and the earphones detached.

www.stantonmagnetics.com

ST 100: a DJ-style deck with aluminium surface and automatic/manual arm.

www.elpj.com

LASER VINYL DECK: the very latest laser technology deciphers vinyl records and allows you to apply all the functions of a CD.

www.sennheiser.com

SURROUNDER SENNHEISER: this invention sits on your shoulders and recreates a 3D virtual world through its four separately controlled speakers. Perfect for video games and home cinema.

www.wurlitzer.de

ONE MORE TIME: this update of the 1946 model takes 100 CDs and offers more than two million possible selections.

www.koss.com

ı40: the plastic support is adjustable and available in several colours.

www.transrotor.de

SUPER7 HIGH END AND GRAVITA: two vinyl record players from the German specialist Transrotor bring together design and performance.

311

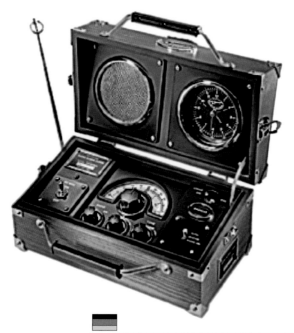

SPIRIT OF SAINT LOUIS: an old style radio, concealed in a case. This is one for aspiring spies.

www.grundig.com

YACHT BOY: a shortwave radio in a leather case, designed by F. A. Porsche.

www.thomson-europe.com.

COLLECTION LINE: a range of radios from the Tim Tom team. The blue version is a radio alarm clock whereas the red model is a radio cassette player.

www.philips.com

AE1000: operated by a wind-up rechargeable generator.

www.windupradio.com

FREEPLAY: this eco-friendly radio was invented for people living in the African bush. Just thirty seconds spent winding up the radio produces an hour of listening, extended by integrated solar panels.

STONE RADIO: hang this design on the wall and control the volume by swinging the cable.

SOUND SPIRAL: a new and hypnotic concept in radio design.

JAZZY: chic, practical and compact.

INTERNET RADIO: equipped with a modem, this radio allows you to listen to programmes on the Internet (without a PC).

RADIO CHALLENGER: the aerial and volume control are on top and the tuning buttons underneath.

SKELETON: a transparent radio that hangs on your belt.

CHOPSTICKS RADIO: this radio has an Asian flavour with its chopsticks aerial.

313

www.riohome.com

RIO VOLT: portable MP3 and CD player plus recorder, with backlit LCD for easy navigation.

www.philips.com

RUSH SA 125: compact MP3 player bundled with 'Real Jukebox' software. Play, manage and transport digital music from the Internet.

www.aiwa.com

CROSSTRAINER: slip this sports watch-radio on to your wrist and switch channels without interrupting your jog.

www.sensoryscience.com

RAVE-MP: an MP3 digital media player that uses removable 'Clik!' discs to store music. Never be without your favourite sounds.

www.fps-inc.co.jp

FDP-2000 GT: it looks like a cassette but in fact it's a digital MP3 player.

www.knowear.com

iVIBE: equipped with Bluetooth technology, these cordless spectacles connect directly to the ivibe.com site and allow you to download and listen to music in MP3 format.

www.thomson.fr

LYRA: a digital personal stereo weighing no more than 150g and equipped with flash memory technology.

www.samsung.com

YEPP: pan audio player for music lovers on the go. No moving parts so no bumps or jilts in the sound.

www.riohome.com

NIKE PSA 120: the first portable digital audio player designed for athletes. It plays MP3 and WMA (Windows Media Audio) formats.

www.sony.com

MINIDISC M-R700: a Walkman recorder with MDLP longtime stereo recording and playback plus rechargeable battery.

www.levistrauss.com

ICD CLOTHING: Philips and Levi have come together to produce clothes equipped with MP3 players and phones that communicate with hidden cables.

www.sony.com

Mw-E5: this very compact player can record, name and edit two hours of digital stereo music.

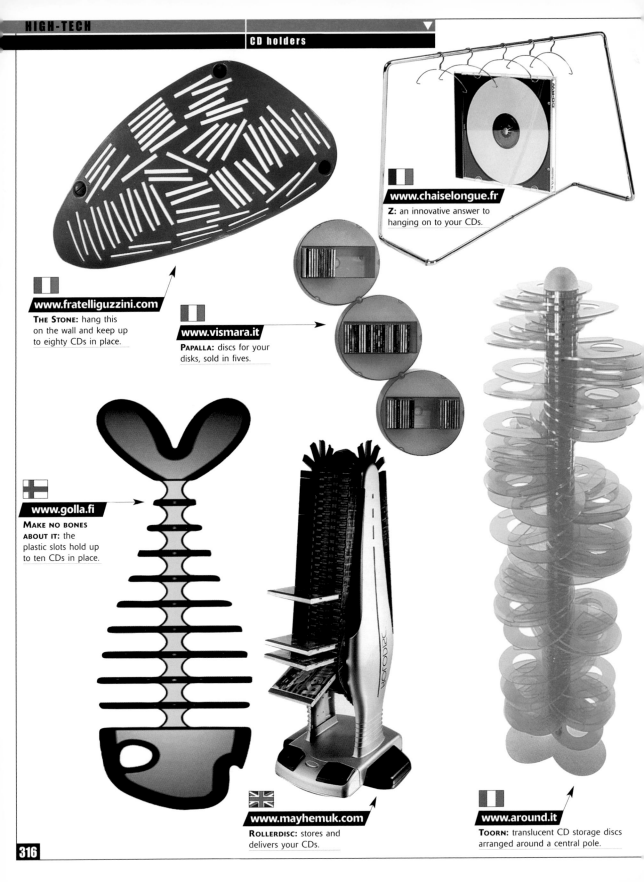

www.chaiselongue.fr
Z: an innovative answer to
hanging on to your CDs.

www.fratelliguzzini.com
THE STONE: hang this
on the wall and keep up
to eighty CDs in place.

www.vismara.it
PAPALLA: discs for your
disks, sold in fives.

www.golla.fi
**MAKE NO BONES
ABOUT IT:** the
plastic slots hold up
to ten CDs in place.

www.mayhemuk.com
ROLLERDISC: stores and
delivers your CDs.

www.around.it
TOORN: translucent CD storage discs
arranged around a central pole.

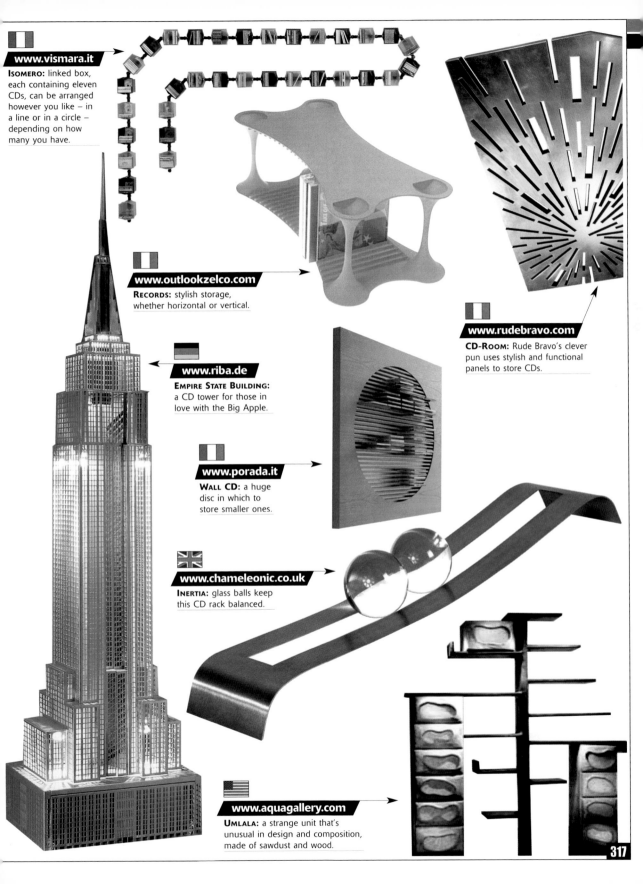

www.vismara.it

ISOMERO: linked box, each containing eleven CDs, can be arranged however you like – in a line or in a circle – depending on how many you have.

www.outlookzelco.com

RECORDS: stylish storage, whether horizontal or vertical.

www.rudebravo.com

CD-ROOM: Rude Bravo's clever pun uses stylish and functional panels to store CDs.

www.riba.de

EMPIRE STATE BUILDING: a CD tower for those in love with the Big Apple.

www.porada.it

WALL CD: a huge disc in which to store smaller ones.

www.chameleonic.co.uk

INERTIA: glass balls keep this CD rack balanced.

www.aquagallery.com

UMLALA: a strange unit that's unusual in design and composition, made of sawdust and wood.

www.cinna.fr

VIVRE by Pascal Mourgue: a tall multi-media cabinet in aluminium and beech, with castors and integrated lamp.

www.leolux.com

PLUGGED FURNITURE: Leolux and Philips have joined forces to introduce their lifestyle technology. The furniture contains all the necessary audio – video equipment, sometimes disguised behind doors equipped with remote control facilities. Cushions, vases and frames are also part of the collection, and a steel ball keeps the cables straight.

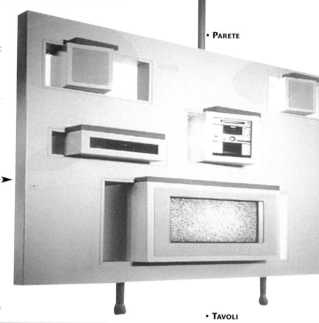

• PARETE

• TAVOLI

• IRONY

www.cattelanitalia.com

LEM: elegant frosted-glass furniture complete with VCR slot.

www.ikea.com

MAMMUT: lots of shelves make this design perfect for children's rooms and audio equipment.

www.le-webstore.com

TABLE PACK: both compact and mobile, this television table was designed by Olivier Gossart.

www.jvc.com

INTERIOR ART: stylish, acrylic, green and integrated. A star of the screen.

www.roche-bobois.com

PARADISIO: the answer to hiding a huge television behind a stylish birch veneer cabinet.

www.around.it

ooLS: removable shelves inside a translucent circular frame. Available in five colour schemes.

www.oma.it/desalto

MOBY: a long, streamlined CD holder attached to the wall, complete with supports for the speakers and music centre. Make a note of it.

www.paceblade.com

PACEBOOK: the first portable notebook computer that can be dismantled. The LCD screen monitor detaches from the keyboard for use in landscape or portrait format, or as a tablet notebook.

www.ibm.com

TRANSNOTE: a portable computer with a touch screen on which you put a sheet of paper. The movements of your pen are then transmitted by radio waves to the PC and translated into text through handwriting recognition software.

www.sozodesign.com

OTTOMAN PC: a new concept in PC furniture, incorporating information technology into your daily lifestyle. Designed by the Sozo agency.

www.apple.com

FLOWER POWER: the iMac goes floral. Meet his psychedelic polka dot cousin Blue Dalmatian (not shown here).

www.xybernaut.com

MOBILE ASSISTANT: a miniature voice-controlled computer connected to a headset with a small screen, headphones and microphone. The US army managed to diagnose a breakdown in a tank within seven minutes instead of the usual seven hours.

www.iiyama.fr

IIYAMA TSA-4634JT: an LCD screen with IPS (In Plane Switching) offering 170 degree horizontal and vertical vision. It rotates 90 degrees, allowing you to view documents in portrait or landscape format.

www.hammacher.com

PANORAMIC SCREEN: three screens controlled by a single USB power point. Perfect for architects and 3D designers.

www.compaq.com

PRESARIO 1400: a compact notebook with impressive screen, CD and DVD player and excellent JBL integrated speakers. It's stylish too.

www.elumens.com

VISION STATION: a hemispherical screen designed like a satellite dish (1.5 x 5m in diameter) with a 180 degree perspective and patented optics technology.

www.onhandpc.com

PC WATCH: according to the Guinness Book of Records, this is the smallest computer that compares favourably with a handheld PC.

www.sony.com

VAIO C1XD: weighing in at 1kg, it boasts a large screen, digital imaging and integrated camera.

www.wacom.de

MOUSE AND PEN SET: a graphic pen, mouse and tablet – all you need for retouching, sketching and writing.

www.typhoonline.com

DS 1040 LOUDSPEAKERS: transform an ordinary computer into a piece of serious hi-fi equipment.

www.digitalpersona.com

URU SENSOR: introducing digital fingerprint recognition and bidding farewell to passwords.

www.casio.com

MINI PRINTER KP-C10: print email addresses or other messages on self-adhesive labels.

http://halfkeyboard.com

HALF KEYBOARD: letters are grouped together on this keyboard, small enough to fit on your wrist.

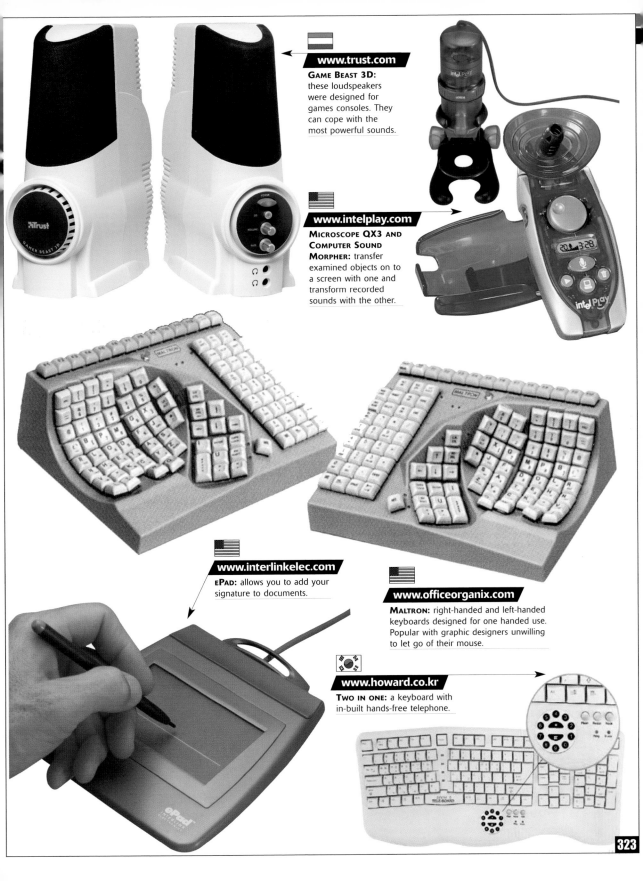

www.trust.com

GAME BEAST 3D: these loudspeakers were designed for games consoles. They can cope with the most powerful sounds.

www.intelplay.com

MICROSCOPE QX3 AND COMPUTER SOUND MORPHER: transfer examined objects on to a screen with one and transform recorded sounds with the other.

www.interlinkelec.com

ePad: allows you to add your signature to documents.

www.officeorganix.com

MALTRON: right-handed and left-handed keyboards designed for one handed use. Popular with graphic designers unwilling to let go of their mouse.

www.howard.co.kr

TWO IN ONE: a keyboard with in-built hands-free telephone.

323

www.logitech.com

TRACKMAN FX: a cordless ergonomic mouse with a large ball for greater precision and digital radio technology for extra freedom.

www.contourdes.com

SHUTTLEPRO: this ultra-flat mouse with thirteen programmable buttons is recommended by designers working on Macs.

www.kensington.com

EXPERT MOUSE PRO: a rectangular chrome-plated mouse with four convenient programmable buttons and an integrated scroll wheel.

www.karnatechnology.com

BOOMSLANG: a new generation of sensitive mice with killer instincts. It's for hardcore gamers, four times faster than an average mouse.

www.lexon-design.com

JERRY: a transparent PC mouse, designed by Marc Berthier.

www.biolinskusa.com

BIOMETRIC MOUSE: equipped with a fingerprint recognition technology as part of its personal identification system.

www.lobotronic.com

GROOVY: a luminous mouse for children (or playful adults).

www.macally.com
iBallPro: transparent and rectangular with two programmable buttons.

www.lindy.com
Cromo: a chrome-plated gem of a mouse.

www.gyration.com
GyroMouse Pro: a cordless mouse with gyroscopes that can sense your natural hand motion.

www.3hird.com
SpaceCat: manipulate virtual 3D objects with this super-sensitive mouse using 'Inductive Spring' technology.

www.apple.com
Apple Pro: this transparent ergonomic mouse with optical sensor suits left- and right-handed users.

www.trust.com
Ami Hand Track: hold this mouse in your hand and operate the ball with your thumb.

www.microsoft.com
Explorer: use your index finger to operate the ball and your thumb to manoeuvre the scroll wheel, located on the side. It combines an optical sensor with advanced ball design.

325

web cameras

www.dexxa.net

DEXXA: a surveillance camera that's small but not small minded.

www.logitech.com

QUICK CAM PRO 3000: this web cam uses its in-built microphone to make live video calls to friends over the Internet and send emails with pictures.

www.trust.com

SPACEC@M 3000: equipped with zoom, microphone and speakers.

www.traxdata.com

TRAXVISION BABYCAM: a digital colour cordless camera with in-built microphone.

www.knowear.net

WEBSTER: a digital camera with microphone and handheld PC aimed at children who can record special moments and share them by email.

www.aiptek.com

PENCAM 2: only slightly larger than a pen, this web camera slips into your pocket. When unconnected, it can be used as a still camera.

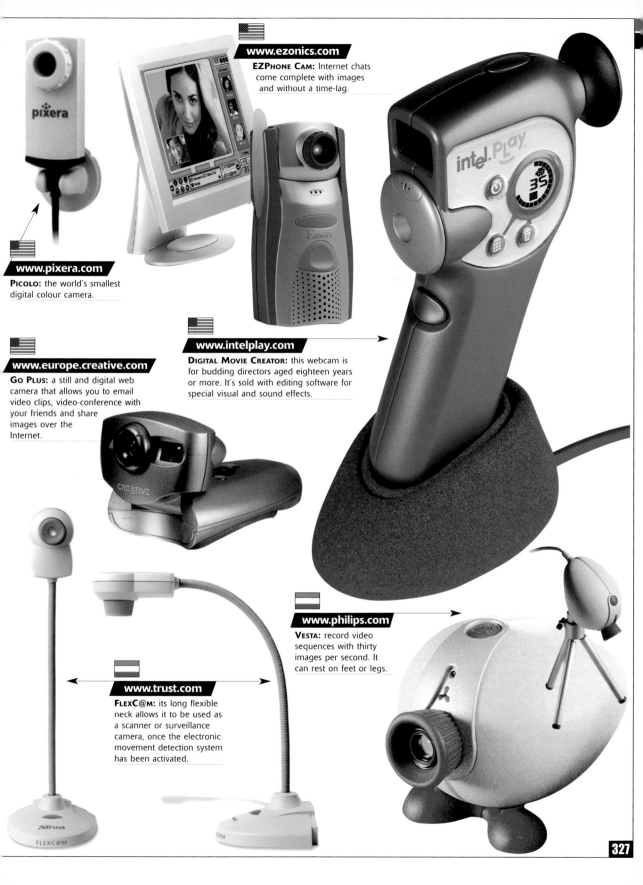

www.ezonics.com
EZPhone Cam: Internet chats come complete with images and without a time-lag.

www.pixera.com
Picolo: the world's smallest digital colour camera.

www.europe.creative.com
Go Plus: a still and digital web camera that allows you to email video clips, video-conference with your friends and share images over the Internet.

www.intelplay.com
Digital Movie Creator: this webcam is for budding directors aged eighteen years or more. It's sold with editing software for special visual and sound effects.

www.philips.com
Vesta: record video sequences with thirty images per second. It can rest on feet or legs.

www.trust.com
FlexC@m: its long flexible neck allows it to be used as a scanner or surveillance camera, once the electronic movement detection system has been activated.

327

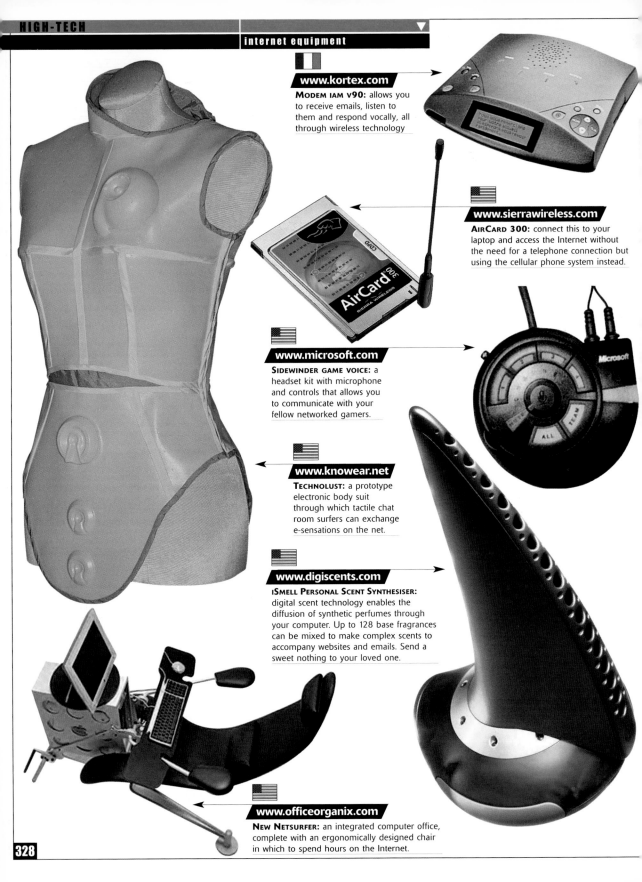

internet equipment

www.kortex.com

MODEM IAM V90: allows you to receive emails, listen to them and respond vocally, all through wireless technology

www.sierrawireless.com

AIRCARD 300: connect this to your laptop and access the Internet without the need for a telephone connection but using the cellular phone system instead.

www.microsoft.com

SIDEWINDER GAME VOICE: a headset kit with microphone and controls that allows you to communicate with your fellow networked gamers.

www.knowear.net

TECHNOLUST: a prototype electronic body suit through which tactile chat room surfers can exchange e-sensations on the net.

www.digiscents.com

iSMELL PERSONAL SCENT SYNTHESISER: digital scent technology enables the diffusion of synthetic perfumes through your computer. Up to 128 base fragrances can be mixed to make complex scents to accompany websites and emails. Send a sweet nothing to your loved one.

www.officeorganix.com

NEW NETSURFER: an integrated computer office, complete with an ergonomically designed chair in which to spend hours on the Internet.

video games

www.thrustmaster.com

FREESTYLER BOARD: an electronic snow- and skateboard, over a metre long. Connect it to your PlayStation, step on, twist and pivot – all in your own home.

www.sony.com

PLAYSTATION2: compact and unpretentious in design, it's also a CD and DVD player and connects to the Internet.

www.zibadesign.com

ROVER: a prototype games console worn like a pair of binoculars for total virtual immersion.

www.xbox.com

X-BOX: the long-awaited new generation of games consoles from Microsoft incorporates cinematic-quality graphics and exceptional sound effects.

www.nintendo.com

GAME CUBE: small and powerful, Nintendo's latest model has a place reserved for a modem.

www.hammacher.com

VIRTUAL FORMULA 1: connect this simulator to the Internet to share the experience of the 100 top racetracks and thirty greatest drivers. Buy your own champagne.

www.logitech.com

WINGMAN FORCE FEEDBACK: this gaming mouse is literally 'sensational'. It crunches on sand, skates on snow and slides on pools of oil.

329

voice recorders

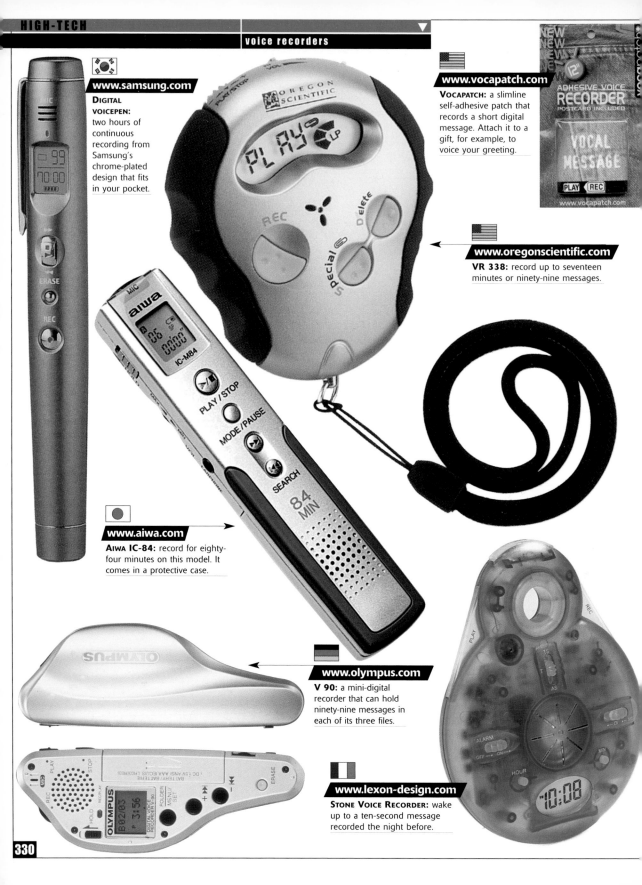

www.samsung.com

DIGITAL VOICEPEN: two hours of continuous recording from Samsung's chrome-plated design that fits in your pocket.

www.vocapatch.com

VOCAPATCH: a slimline self-adhesive patch that records a short digital message. Attach it to a gift, for example, to voice your greeting.

www.oregonscientific.com

VR 338: record up to seventeen minutes or ninety-nine messages.

www.aiwa.com

AIWA IC-84: record for eighty-four minutes on this model. It comes in a protective case.

www.olympus.com

V 90: a mini-digital recorder that can hold ninety-nine messages in each of its three files.

www.lexon-design.com

STONE VOICE RECORDER: wake up to a ten-second message recorded the night before.

electronic books and pens

www.cpen.com

C-PEN 800 C: this portable scanner pen can read, translate and memorise messages. It's also a dictionary and address book.

www.ebook-gemstar.com

E-BOOK RCA-GEMSTAR: colourful digital reading in portrait or landscape format. The way we will read in the future.

www.gocode.com

INFOPEN: a futuristic scanner pen that can detect miniscule web or email addresses as barcodes in printed text and access the relevant websites. It links paper to the Internet.

www.cytale.com

CYBOOK: with this touch screen e-book, in colour, equipped with a 15,000-page memory, you can enjoy your own portable library.

www.anoto.com

STYLO ANOTO: a digital pen that has joined the wireless revolution.

www.atfolio.net

@FOLIO: bookworms on the move can read downloaded text on a sensitive button-free liquid crystal screen. Turn the pages using the wheel.

www.ibm.fr

ELECTRONIC NEWSPAPER: download your favourite daily and read sixteen pages of electronic newsprint.

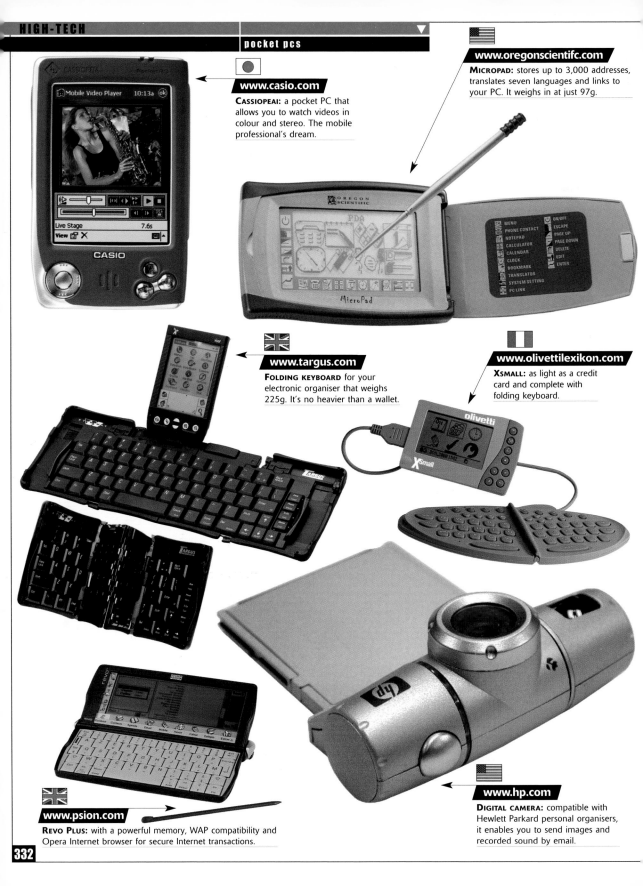

www.oregonscientifc.com

MICROPAD: stores up to 3,000 addresses, translates seven languages and links to your PC. It weighs in at just 97g.

www.casio.com

CASSIOPEAI: a pocket PC that allows you to watch videos in colour and stereo. The mobile professional's dream.

www.targus.com

FOLDING KEYBOARD for your electronic organiser that weighs 225g. It's no heavier than a wallet.

www.olivettilexikon.com

XSMALL: as light as a credit card and complete with folding keyboard.

www.psion.com

REVO PLUS: with a powerful memory, WAP compatibility and Opera Internet browser for secure Internet transactions.

www.hp.com

DIGITAL CAMERA: compatible with Hewlett Parkard personal organisers, it enables you to send images and recorded sound by email.

🇬🇧 **www.electrotextiles.com**

ELEKTEX: the first keyboard made of fabric, washable and flexible. Still at prototype stage.

🇺🇸 **www.hp.com**

JORNADA 540: a pocket PC with WAP, fax and (soon) Bluetooth technology.

🇺🇸 **www.palm.com**

PALM M505: the new Palm boosts a screen with 65,000 colours and a Dragonball processor (33MHz)

🇺🇸 **www.compaq.com**

iPACK POCKET: the lightest pocket PC with this type of screen (with 4,096 colours).

🇩🇰 **www.ericsson.com**

THIRD GENERATION: Ericsson's prototype allows a glimpse of the design and technology to come.

www.trium.com

TRIUM'S CONCEPT PHONE:
a prototype bracelet phone
that combines elegance
with technology.

www.motorola.com

**MOTOROLA ACCOMPLI
008:** compatible with
WAP and GPRS
technology, this phone lets
you call, email, access the
Internet and translate. It's
a virtual office for those
who don't need one.

www.motorola.com

WATCHPHONE FROM MOTOROLA:
a prototype WAP-compatible
phone that can be worn like a
watch. It can be linked to your
PC and has radio Internet
access and Bluetooth headset.

www.motorola.com

**TIMEPORT 280 FROM
MOTOROLA:** combines
email and web access,
fax, SMS, VoiceNotes
and PC synchronisation.

www.sony.com

SONY MZ5: record
music without a PC
connection, using a
CD player.

www.ericsson.com

ERICSSON R380-S: access
PDA, email, PC and WAP
technology on a touch
screen. It weighs only 164g.

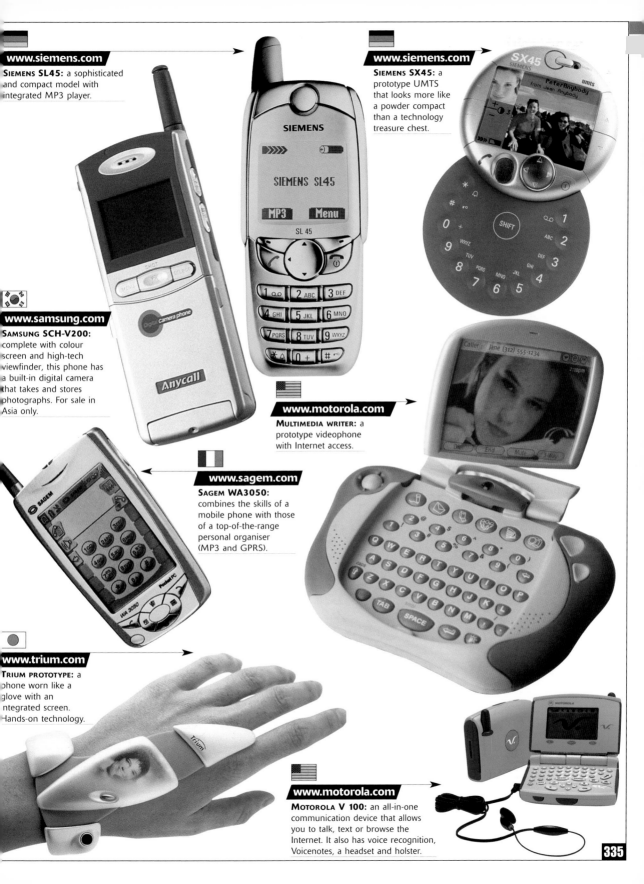

www.siemens.com
Siemens SL45: a sophisticated and compact model with integrated MP3 player.

www.siemens.com
Siemens SX45: a prototype UMTS that looks more like a powder compact than a technology treasure chest.

www.samsung.com
Samsung SCH-V200: complete with colour screen and high-tech viewfinder, this phone has a built-in digital camera that takes and stores photographs. For sale in Asia only.

www.motorola.com
Multimedia writer: a prototype videophone with Internet access.

www.sagem.com
Sagem WA3050: combines the skills of a mobile phone with those of a top-of-the-range personal organiser (MP3 and GPRS).

www.trium.com
Trium prototype: a phone worn like a glove with an integrated screen. Hands-on technology.

www.motorola.com
Motorola V 100: an all-in-one communication device that allows you to talk, text or browse the Internet. It also has voice recognition, Voicenotes, a headset and holster.

www.rf3now.com

ANTI-RADIATION EARPIECE: filters the allegedly damaging waves emitted by mobiles.

www.samsung.com

SAMSUNG'S WATCHPHONE: is it a watch or a high-tech wristphone? Both.

www.samsung.com

SAMSUNG SCH-M220: a TV phone with a TFT colour screen. Available only in Asia.

www.younggeneration.de

SOLAR-POWERED CHARGER: for travellers and outdoor enthusiasts wanting to charge their phones, personal PCs or GPS systems, the natural way.

www.trium.com

TRIUM COSMO: equipped with a large screen and multiple functions, this curvaceous design is also a WAP phone.

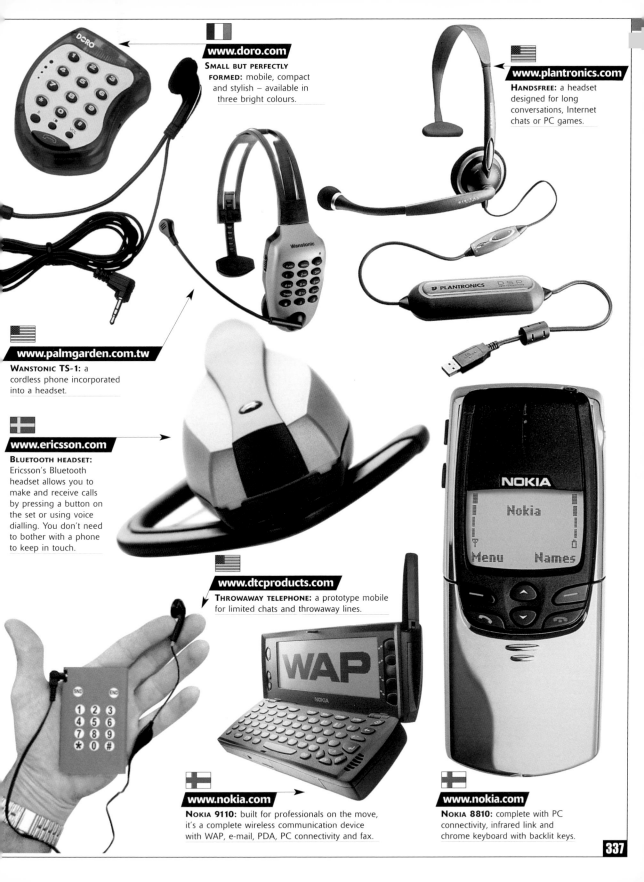

www.doro.com

SMALL BUT PERFECTLY FORMED: mobile, compact and stylish – available in three bright colours.

www.plantronics.com

HANDSFREE: a headset designed for long conversations, Internet chats or PC games.

www.palmgarden.com.tw

WANSTONIC TS-1: a cordless phone incorporated into a headset.

www.ericsson.com

BLUETOOTH HEADSET: Ericsson's Bluetooth headset allows you to make and receive calls by pressing a button on the set or using voice dialling. You don't need to bother with a phone to keep in touch.

www.dtcproducts.com

THROWAWAY TELEPHONE: a prototype mobile for limited chats and throwaway lines.

www.nokia.com

NOKIA 9110: built for professionals on the move, it's a complete wireless communication device with WAP, e-mail, PDA, PC connectivity and fax.

www.nokia.com

NOKIA 8810: complete with PC connectivity, infrared link and chrome keyboard with backlit keys.

337

www.nwbphones.com

MINI 2800: a small circular phone with handset for hands-free, high-quality communication.

www.classicphone.com

EIFFEL TOWER: a working replica of Ericsson's 1892 model.

www.thomson.fr

OLA: Philippe Starck designed this telephone as an extension of your own arm.

www.philips.com

MAGIC 2 DECT: the first cordless telephone/ answering machine/fax, complete with detachable scanner. It can send emails to your computer without a connection.

TELEPHONE

www.hammacher.com

RED TELEPHONE BOX: not only can you make waterproof calls, you can also take a shower.

www.continentaledison.com

LOOKEA 500: the first colour viewphone for the general public. Connect it to a TV to enlarge the caller's picture or to a video recorder to transmit recorded images.

www.spyzone.com

TRUTH PHONE: this phone is used by espionage officers to detect lies through the stress levels of the speaker's voice.

www.ericsson.com

ERICSSON PROTOTYPE: a visually appealing model unveiled by Ericsson.

www.adl-systeme.com

SYS 315: a new generation fax machine that incorporates a touch screen for sending (and correcting) messages.

www.asia-sources.com.hk

MOUSE PHONE: just lift the cover and you've got a hands-free phone.

www.bang-olufsen.com

BEOCOM 2: a cordless phone made of a stylish single piece of aluminium that makes you want to carry on talking forever.

www.conairphone.com

TELEPHONE RADIO ALARM: equipped with a memory capable of storing the details of sixty-four people, it displays their name when they call.

http//:retro.digt.ru

RETRO RUSSIAN: a copy of a wall phone owned by the last Russian Czar, Nicholas II. Made of wood and copper, it often features in film sets.

MULTI-NAVIGATOR: the first portable navigator to combine GPS technology with an integrated electronic compass, altimeter and weather-forecasting barometer.

www.simrad.se

HD 52: a water-resistant portable GPS that sends a distress signal at the press of a button.

www.magellangps.com

COLOR TRAK: Magellan invented the portable GPS and have now come up with a high-resolution colour screen.

www.lowrance.com

IFINDER provides information on roads, oceans and shores and can be linked to your PC.

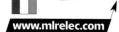

www.mlrelec.com

SP24XC: provides twelve parallel channels, 1,000 points to build your own electronic charts and thirty-six hours of continual use.

www.garmin.com

ETREX LEGEND: water-resistant, small and compact, this GPS has side-mounted function keys.

www.casio.com

PROTREK SATELLITE NAVI: Casio's GPS watch is compact, light (84g) and water resistant to fifty metres. It's also PC-compatible.

walkie-talkies

www.lexon-design.com

OLYMPIC: available in three colours, this stylish model has sixty-nine channels and thirty-nine speakers on each of them.

www.cobraelec.com

FRS 115: a walkie-talkie with fourteen channels that's also a stereo FM radio.

www.nwbphones.com

NEW BELL PHONES 99151: a digital model that works up to a distance of 3km.

www.rldrake.com

MINITALK 99: a robust transceiver, equipped with a power-saving mode for idle periods.

www.midlandradio.com

SPEAKEASY 75509: automatically voice-activated, this model has a power range of 3km and can eliminate irritating noises.

www.icomamerica.com

IC-R3: this walkie-talkie is also a mini television set.

www.nike.com

PSC COMMUNICATE: a pair of compact family walkie-talkies that share a charger.

www.audiovox.com

FRS 1438: an excellent walkie-talkie that's sturdy, sporty, stylish and safety conscious.

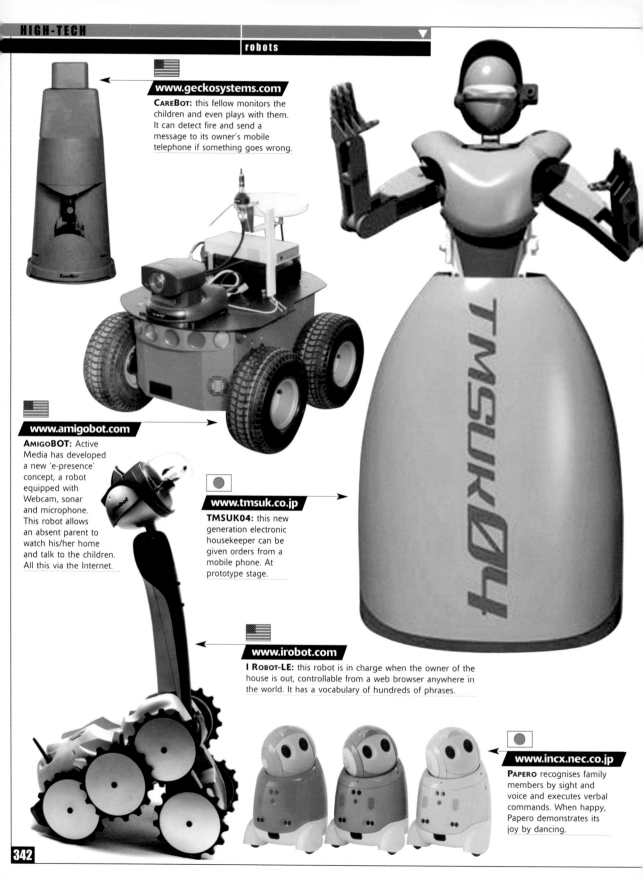

CareBot: this fellow monitors the children and even plays with them. It can detect fire and send a message to its owner's mobile telephone if something goes wrong.

AmigoBOT: Active Media has developed a new 'e-presence' concept, a robot equipped with Webcam, sonar and microphone. This robot allows an absent parent to watch his/her home and talk to the children. All this via the Internet.

TMSUK04: this new generation electronic housekeeper can be given orders from a mobile phone. At prototype stage.

I Robot-LE: this robot is in charge when the owner of the house is out, controllable from a web browser anywhere in the world. It has a vocabulary of hundreds of phrases.

Papero recognises family members by sight and voice and executes verbal commands. When happy, Papero demonstrates its joy by dancing.

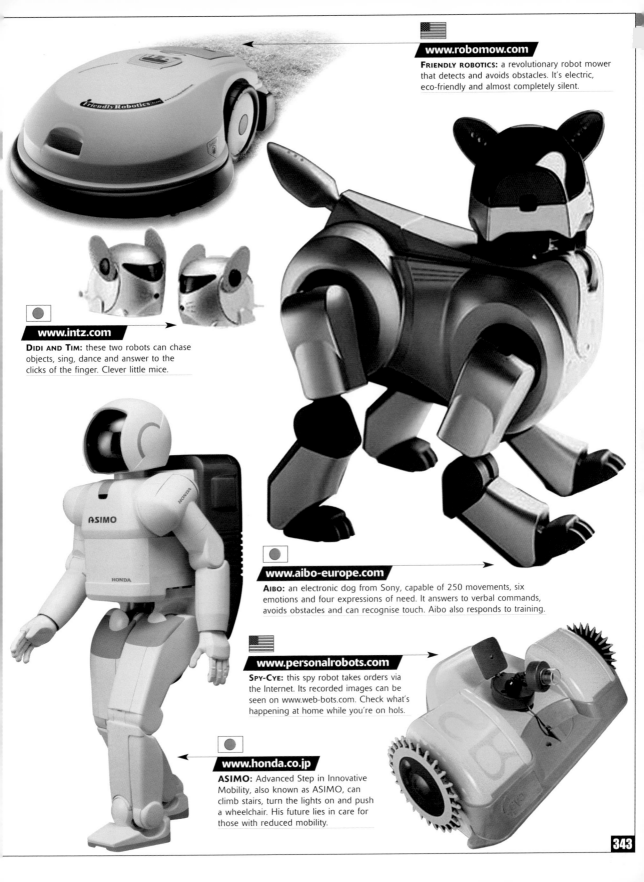

www.robomow.com

FRIENDLY ROBOTICS: a revolutionary robot mower that detects and avoids obstacles. It's electric, eco-friendly and almost completely silent.

www.intz.com

DIDI AND TIM: these two robots can chase objects, sing, dance and answer to the clicks of the finger. Clever little mice.

www.aibo-europe.com

AIBO: an electronic dog from Sony, capable of 250 movements, six emotions and four expressions of need. It answers to verbal commands, avoids obstacles and can recognise touch. Aibo also responds to training.

www.personalrobots.com

SPY-CYE: this spy robot takes orders via the Internet. Its recorded images can be seen on www.web-bots.com. Check what's happening at home while you're on hols.

www.honda.co.jp

ASIMO: Advanced Step in Innovative Mobility, also known as ASIMO, can climb stairs, turn the lights on and push a wheelchair. His future lies in care for those with reduced mobility.

sports & leisure

sporting activities
water sports
wind sports
mountain sports
urban sports
archery
golf

transport
balloons, planes & helicopters
cars
unclassifiable vehicles
motorbikes & scooters
bicycles
scooters

holidays & hobbies
artistic pursuits
children's games
pets
outdoor hobbies
games for young and old
garden
camping & hiking
weather & optics
holidays

  ❶

www.apreamare.it

APREAMARE 9 CABINATO: a cabin cruiser that combines speed, comfort and style.

❷

www.riva.com

AQUARIVA: a traditional boat produced in the oldest boatyard in the world. That doesn't stop it doing over 42 knots!

 ❸

www.interpc.fr/cazavant

CAZAVANT: this reproduction fifties fishing boat, complete with pine decking, is equipped with high-tech materials. It has a polyester hull and is specially adapted for shallow waters.

 ❹

www.classic-boats.com

TOFINOU: based on a design from the thirties, this seven-metre sailing dinghy has teak decking and mahogany fittings.

 ❺

www.accf.fr

CORMORAN 4,50: it looks like a turn-of-the-century dinghy but conceals the latest boat design. Perfect for pleasure sailing and regattas.

 ❻

www.stagnol.com

SEA BIRD: built according to the designs drawn up in 1889 by the great naval architect Fife, the Sea Bird is an elegant solid mahogany boat.

www.dufour-yachts.com

GIB'SEA 43: Dufour's well-designed family yacht is powerful and stylish.

www.chantier-pinta.com

JNP 12: a 12m boat with a partially retractable keel that allows it to sail in shallow coves and in rivers.

www.catamaran-outremer.com

OUTREMER 50 LIGHT: a streamlined catamaran for comfortable sailing in all conditions.

www.beneteau.com

OCÉANIS CLIPPER 473: Bénéteau's new model is both speedy and comfortable.

www.cnb.fr

CHÂTEAU BRANAIRE: CNB is a naval shipyard that produces custom-built boats (20–32m in length), in aluminium or composite materials.

www.defline-yachts.com

DEFLINE 19: under six metres in length, this boat is designed for offshore racing. It has a unique double keel system that enhances its performance.

www.yapluka.fr

YAPLUKA 53: custom-built, this aluminium catamaran is solid, stable and comfortable.

 ❶

www.windride.com

WINDRIDER RAVE: the first hydrofoil trimaran designed for fast recreational sailing, the Rave gives seasoned sailors an extraordinary carpet ride. Once you've mastered the foot-steering, you'll be flying above the water.

 ❷

www.petter-quality-yachts.com

PETTER 55: powerful and easy to handle, this large catamaran moves with high speed due to its rotating carbon fibre wingmast.

 ❸

www.hobiecat.com

HOBIE CAT 16: the classic all-round catamaran, designed in 1969, is perfect for beginners and seasoned sailors alike.

 ❹

www.lasersailing.com

FUN BOAT: this catamaran, cast in one piece, is ready to sail in seconds. Perfect for beginners and exceptionally stable, it can take three people.

 ❺

www.navalforce3.com

CHALLENGE 37: a high-performance trimaran, equipped with a practical folding system that allows it to convert to a singe-hull. Perfect for arriving in port.

 ❻

www.catana.com

CATANA 582: this luxury yacht combines easy manoeuvrability and stylish comfort. Relax in an air-conditioned environment, furnished in leather and mahogany.

6

1 www.francisdesign.com

KATANA: a French-designed yacht equipped with the latest technology.

2 www.rodriguezgroup.com

MANGUSTA 108 OPEN: a giant powerboat, 33m in length and with a top speed of 60 knots.

3 www.pershing.it

88 SILVER: this silver beauty achieves a speed of 40 knots.

4 www.ferretti-yacht.com

FERRETTI 68: made by the renowned Italian company, this boat is a powerful thoroughbred.

5 www.sunseeker.com

MANHATTAN 84: equipped with two jacuzzis, three cabins and one suite, this 26m yacht is furnished in maple burr and cherry wood.

6 www.kingcat.com

KINGCAT M270: this powerful luxury catamaran has five rooms, a bar and a jacuzzi. It boasts 200 square metres of living space.

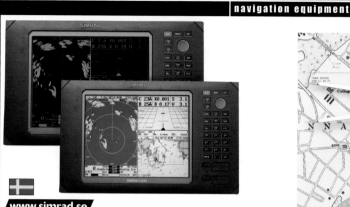

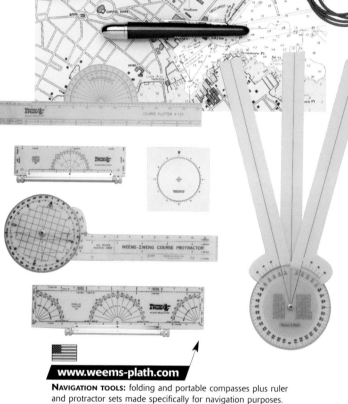

www.simrad.se

SIMRAD CA50: radar, GPS, chart plotter and echo sounder, equipped with a colour screen with special technology for bright sunlight viewing.

www.geonav.it

GEONAV: connect this mini system in your car or boat and you've got a GPS set, chart plotter, compass and clock. Splash-proof and shock absorbent, it's ideal for power boats, sail boats and dinghies.

www.weems-plath.com

NAVIGATION TOOLS: folding and portable compasses plus ruler and protractor sets made specifically for navigation purposes.

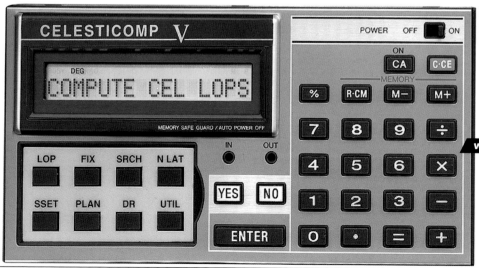

www.celesticomp.com

CELESTICOMP V: a complete and compact on-board computer that's easy to use and opens up celestial navigation to all sailing enthusiasts.

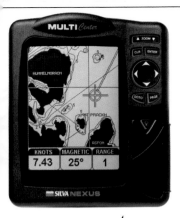

www.tacktick.com

RACE MASTER: a tactical race compass that's waterproof, the TO4O is solar-powered and therefore independent. A 'must have' for sailors keen to win.

www.silva.se

MULTI CENTER: monitor boat data and wind shifts, edit waypoints and use as a graphical navigator. The Multi Center also has an auto-pilot setting. Don't leave port without it.

www.icomamerica.com

RADIO IC-MLV: the world's smallest waterproof handheld marine radio.

www.casio.com

MONTRE SPF 40: an all-encompassing marine watch, equipped with compass, barometer, thermometer, graphic tidal map display and count down option. Wear your world on your wrist.

www.cassens-plath.de

SEXTANT HORIZON ULTRA: this is the world's most popular sextant, complete with full view horizon mirror, double prism level and calculator compartment.

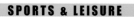

www.yamaha-motor.com

WAVE RUNNER XLT 1200: the most powerful jet ski on the market.

www.denbol.nl

GEMINI: the only double tube with a separate chamber for your feet. It can accommodate three people.

www.sevylor.com

JET BEB: enjoy a comfortable ride with its ergonomic handles and nylon cover.

www.solowatersports.com

SOLO SKI BOAT: the skier is also the driver, thanks to the remote control system in the handle. Go it alone.

www.seadoo.com

XP: named 'Watercraft of the Century' by the watercraft world. Feel at one with the water in this high-performance machine.

www.watergames.com

AQUANAUT: a sub aqua water ski for underwater tows.

www.seadoo.com

LRV: this model is big enough for four people and all their luggage.

www.hosports.com

ASX CARBON: a powerful new monoski for accomplished skiers wanting to do tight turns.

www.kawasaki.com

750 SXI PRO: combines speed, precision and acceleration and is suitable for recreational riding and competitive racing.

www.airchair.com

AIRCHAIR: a cross between a water ski and a flying carpet. Sit down, fasten your seat belt and take off.

www.kawasaki.com

ULTRA 150: powered by a 1,176cm³ engine, this is one of the fastest two-seater jet skis around.

357

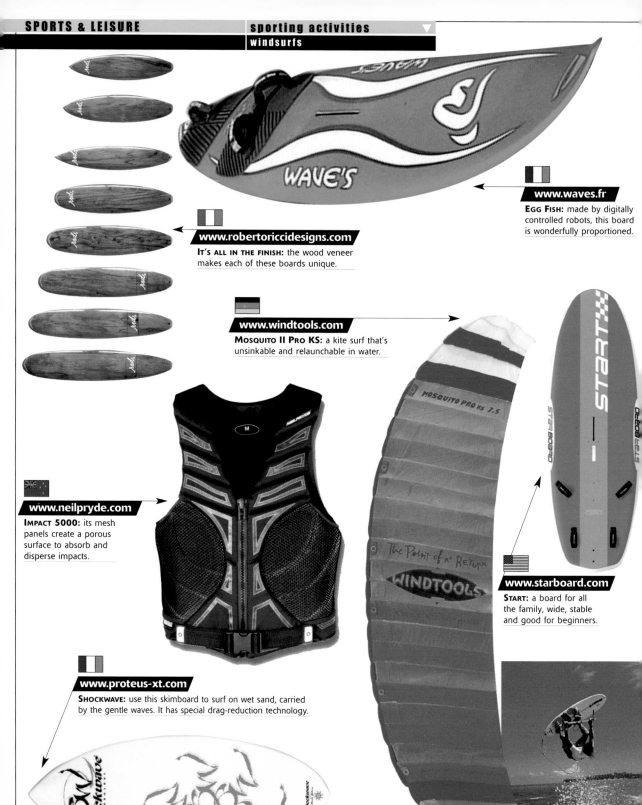

www.waves.fr

EGG FISH: made by digitally controlled robots, this board is wonderfully proportioned.

www.robertoriccidesigns.com

IT'S ALL IN THE FINISH: the wood veneer makes each of these boards unique.

www.windtools.com

MOSQUITO II PRO KS: a kite surf that's unsinkable and relaunchable in water.

www.neilpryde.com

IMPACT 5000: its mesh panels create a porous surface to absorb and disperse impacts.

www.starboard.com

START: a board for all the family, wide, stable and good for beginners.

www.proteus-xt.com

SHOCKWAVE: use this skimboard to surf on wet sand, carried by the gentle waves. It has special drag-reduction technology.

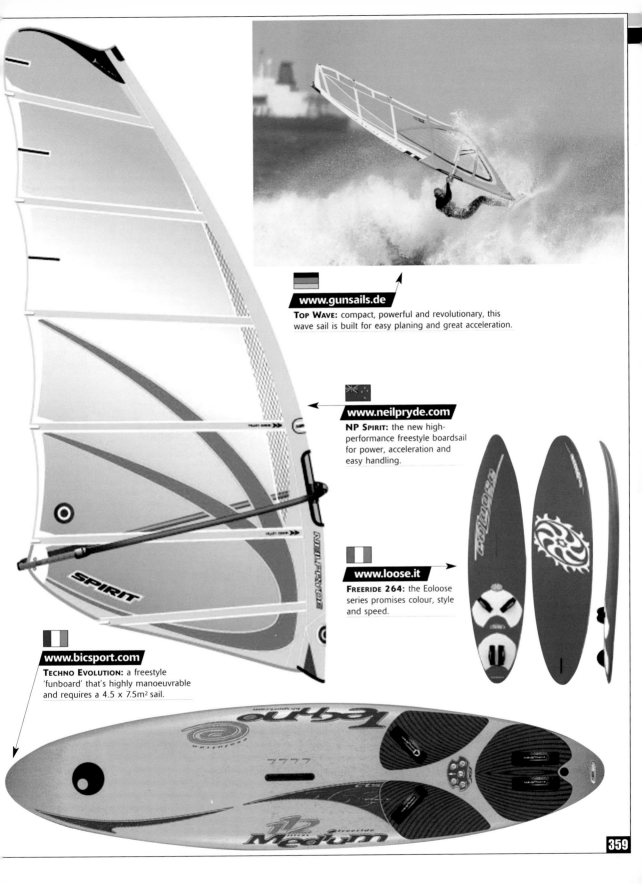

www.gunsails.de

TOP WAVE: compact, powerful and revolutionary, this wave sail is built for easy planing and great acceleration.

www.neilpryde.com

NP SPIRIT: the new high-performance freestyle boardsail for power, acceleration and easy handling.

www.loose.it

FREERIDE 264: the Eoloose series promises colour, style and speed.

www.bicsport.com

TECHNO EVOLUTION: a freestyle 'funboard' that's highly manoeuvrable and requires a 4.5 x 7.5m² sail.

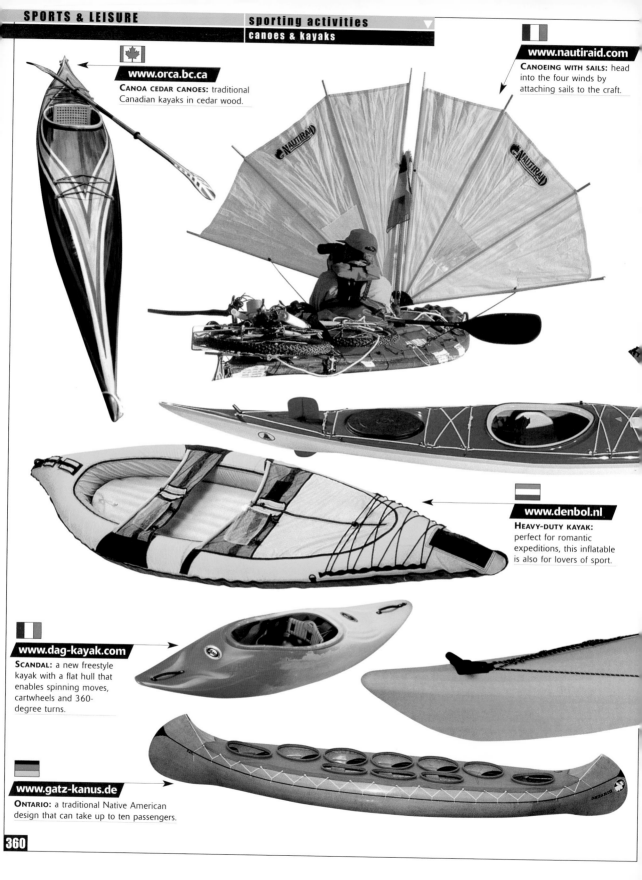

www.orca.bc.ca

CANOA CEDAR CANOES: traditional Canadian kayaks in cedar wood.

www.nautiraid.com

CANOEING WITH SAILS: head into the four winds by attaching sails to the craft.

www.denbol.nl

HEAVY-DUTY KAYAK: perfect for romantic expeditions, this inflatable is also for lovers of sport.

www.dag-kayak.com

SCANDAL: a new freestyle kayak with a flat hull that enables spinning moves, cartwheels and 360-degree turns.

www.gatz-kanus.de

ONTARIO: a traditional Native American design that can take up to ten passengers.

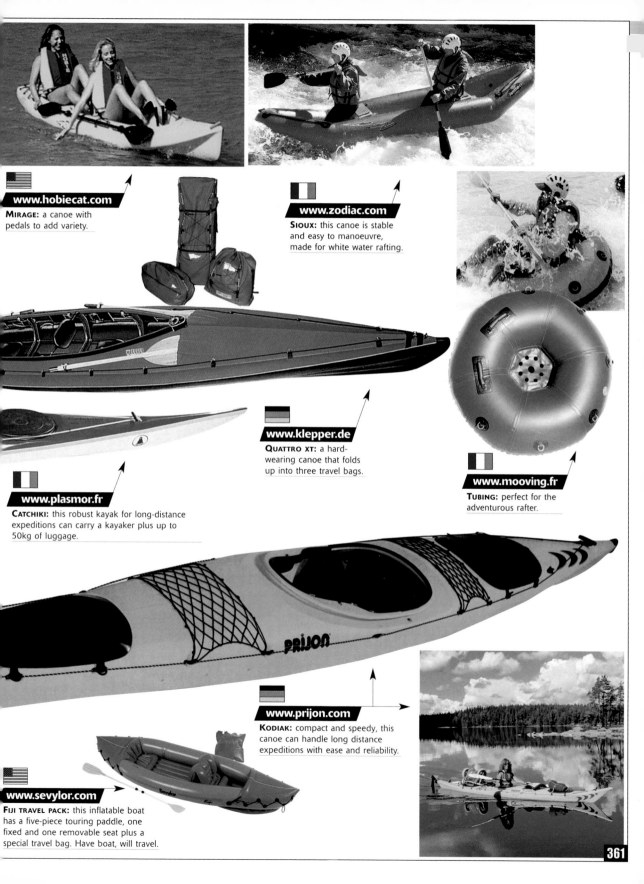

www.hobiecat.com

MIRAGE: a canoe with pedals to add variety.

www.zodiac.com

SIOUX: this canoe is stable and easy to manoeuvre, made for white water rafting.

www.klepper.de

QUATTRO XT: a hard-wearing canoe that folds up into three travel bags.

www.plasmor.fr

CATCHIKI: this robust kayak for long-distance expeditions can carry a kayaker plus up to 50kg of luggage.

www.mooving.fr

TUBING: perfect for the adventurous rafter.

www.prijon.com

KODIAK: compact and speedy, this canoe can handle long distance expeditions with ease and reliability.

www.sevylor.com

FIJI TRAVEL PACK: this inflatable boat has a five-piece touring paddle, one fixed and one removable seat plus a special travel bag. Have boat, will travel.

www.bionicdolphin.com

BIONIC DOLPHIN: as graceful, agile and rapid as a real dolphin, this submarine is made to order and can do acrobatic moves.

www.watergames.com

YELLOW SUBMARINE: half boat, half submarine – perfect for above and below the water.

www.sportsub.com

SPORTSUB III: the gem in the collection, this sub can hold three people and is equipped with the latest technology and panoramic viewing facilities.

www.submersiblesubmarines.com

NEWT SUIT: a thruster-propelled diving suit, equipped with articulated joints, thruster and metal claws.

www.ussubs.com

TRITON 650: the latest design from US Submarines is a two-passenger submersible with surface stability and excellent visibility.

www.submersiblesubmarines.com

YS 1000: a compact three-person submersible with spacious and comfortable viewing.

www.bellaqua.com

BOB: Breathing Observation Bubble, Bob, is an underwater scooter that allows you to enjoy an underwater experience for up to forty minutes without mask or regulator.

www.ussubs.com

DISCOVERY 1000: a small luxury submarine for two, four or six passengers, with panoramic viewing and hydraulic efficiency.

www.seahornet.com.au

LASER SPEARGUN: perfect aim for lovers of underwater fishing.

www.oceanicusa.com

PRO EAR 2000: designed by divers and doctors to overcome ear problems, including difficulties with equalising.

www.scubapro-uwatec.com

TUBA FLIP: fold this snorkel away in the pocket of your jacket or in your luggage.

www.xios.ch

EYE SEA: divers can now find their boats using a revolutionary navigation system and a transmitter submerged a few metres below the vessel.

www.mares.it

MARES HUB: this integrated diving vest is produced by the famous Italian manufacturer and combines safety with comfort.

www.sea-quest.com

PRO UNLIMITED: a reinforced harness that adjusts itself automatically to the shape of your lower back for comfort and safety.

www.suunto.com

STINGER WATCH: this dive computer, housed within a robust watch case, has an exceptional memory and can download messages on to a PC.

www.aqualung.com

SEAL MASK: this model forms part of the AquaSphere range and combines the field of vision of a diving mask with the lightness and aerodynamic performance of swimming goggles.

www.forcefin.com

ACCELERATOR: enjoy extra underwater acceleration using this fin, propelled by exclusive design technology.

www.hydrooptix.com

MAX MASK: allows panoramic 140-degree vision thanks to an invisible lens that reproduces what your eye sees above water.

www.oceanicusa.com

ZETA: this servo-assisted regulator replicates natural breathing (or nearly).

www.cressi-sub.it

CRESSI-SUB BOTTLES: ensure safety and ease of use. Breathe easy.

www.aropec.com

TITANIUM BLADES: useful for tricky underwater moments.

www.seaandsea.com

MX-5 CAMERA: simple, speedy and wide-angled, this waterproof camera was designed for those wanting to capture underwater moments.

www.hammacher.com

DIVING MOBILE: an electric motor that can last for an hour underwater. It was designed for snorkelling and diving with breathing apparatus.

www.beuchat.fr

CARBON PRO FINS: PRE-PREG technology (using a composite of glass and impregnated carbon) has made these fins favourites with the experts.

www.skatewing.de

SKATEWING: sail along on roller skates or skis, as if on water.

www.metamorfosi.com

CONAR: an innovative safety parachute for hang-gliding and paragliding. A patented shock-absorbent fabric cone in the apex allows it to unfold more quickly.

www.landyachting.com

SENSATIONAL LAND YACHT: the flagship land yacht, made by the world's leading manufacturer, Seagull, to celebrate fifteen years of business. It's made of fine wooden strips. Equally elegant but more affordable designs are also available.

SEAGULL
tel 97 400 600

www.landyachting.com

www.freesky.de

SKYRAY: for lovers of free fall and equipped with rigid wings, the Skyray is the result of three years of research. Worn on your back, under the parachute, it makes you feel you're flying like a bird.

www.flexifoil.com

BUGGY: sit on it as if on a deckchair and sail across the sand at the speed of wind – with the help of a traction kite.

www.solsports.com.br

SOL: a Brazilian specialist in aerial sports equipment with a worldwide distribution brings you this paragliding harness.

www.demetz.com

BANDIT: these glasses were designed specifically for parachutists.

www.apcoaviation.com

BAGHEERA: named after the panther that protected Mowgli in Kipling's novel, this is a high-performance paraglider in which you feel totally secure.

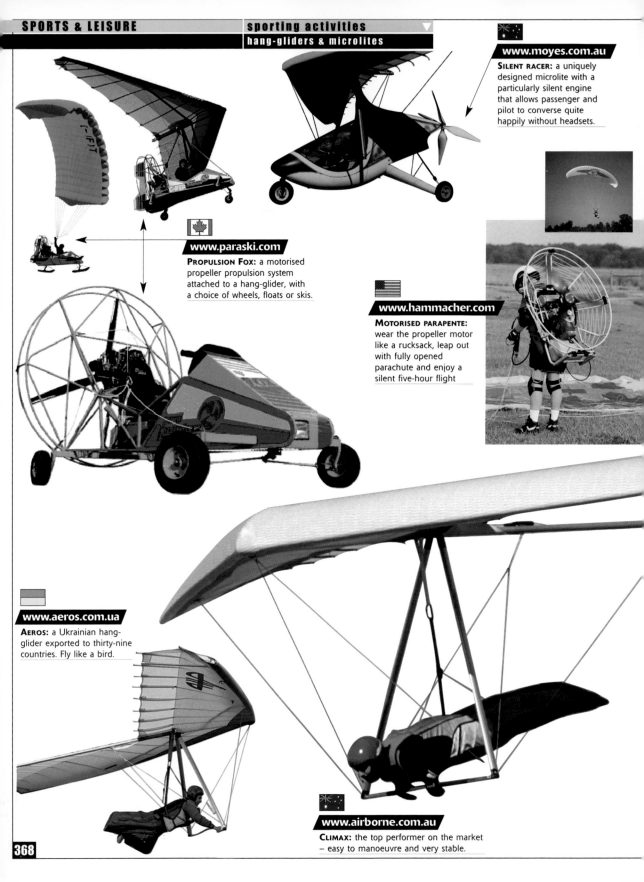

www.moyes.com.au

SILENT RACER: a uniquely designed microlite with a particularly silent engine that allows passenger and pilot to converse quite happily without headsets.

www.paraski.com

PROPULSION FOX: a motorised propeller propulsion system attached to a hang-glider, with a choice of wheels, floats or skis.

www.hammacher.com

MOTORISED PARAPENTE: wear the propeller motor like a rucksack, leap out with fully opened parachute and enjoy a silent five-hour flight

www.aeros.com.ua

AEROS: a Ukrainian hang-glider exported to thirty-nine countries. Fly like a bird.

www.airborne.com.au

CLIMAX: the top performer on the market – easy to manoeuvre and very stable.

COSMOS makes hang-gliders for all conditions and holds world records for speed, altitude and distance without refuelling. The Cosmos is the only twin-seater civilian craft made entirely of composite materials and equipped with retractable landing gear. Other models are also on the cards, equipped with floats and skis.

www.boreal-club.com

THE QUANTUM SHOE has a reinforced heel and new super-grip rubber technology.

www.gabel.net

WALKING STICK: a telescopic stick with attached compass that can also be used as a camera 'monopod'.

www.petzl.com

ZYPER-Y: a revolutionary system of energy absorption that divides the intensity of the shock in three in the event of a fall.

www.natureetdecouvertes.com

ARROKA GOURD: sewn by hand in calfskin, this gourd is lined with latex and comes originally from the Pyrenees.

www.avalung.com

AVALUNG: survival kit equipped with breathing tube in the event of an avalanche. Breathe in through the snow-covered jacket and exhale into a different zone.

www.makhila.com

LE MAKHILA: these walking shoes are hand-worked in the Basque country.

www.bcaccess.com

TRACKER DTS: the Digital Transceiving System has a dual receiving antenna that captures and interprets the signal and then visually displays the distance and direction to the victim.

www.timex.com

GRIP CLIP: the intrepid Lara Croft sports this watch, the latest in designer wear for climbers.

www.millet.fr

AIR PACK: in the event of an avalanche, the climber releases the ABS and in a matter of seconds two inflated pouches prevent him/ her from being buried or suffocated.

www.kong.it

FROG: a new connector takes over the role of traditional carabiners with its automatic clamping.

www.asolo.com

MTF 700 BOOTS: equipped with indestructible soles, shock-absorbant heels, easy fasteners and plastic injection for extra waterproofing. Beat that…

www.blackdiamondequipment.com

CAMALOT NUT: a very reliable friend to anchor in the rock rifts.

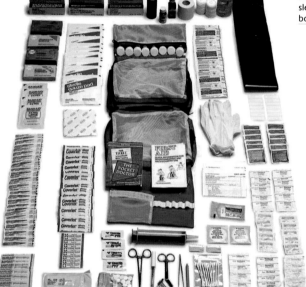

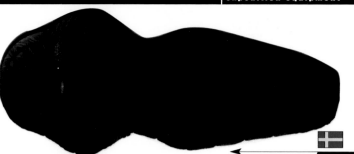

www.fjallraven.se

MAGNUM SILHOUETTE: this sleeping bag hugs your body in low temperatures.

www.orgear.com

SNOQUALMIE SOMBRERO: the famous Mexican hat has turned into protective headgear with fur ear muffs to keep both wind and snow at bay.

www.ccrane.com

EXPEDITION: this torch is extremely powerful and is army issue in the US.

www.orgear.com

EXPEDITION KIT: all the medical equipment you could need on a Himalayan-style expedition, safely contained in a case.

www.stormwhistles.com

STORMWHISTLE: the US Navy use this survival whistle, even underwater.

www.phdesigns.co.uk

MINIMUS: winner of a British Design Council award, this sleeping bag is amazingly light and compact.

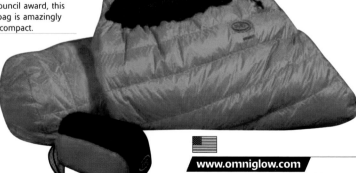

www.omniglow.com

OMNIGLOW: glow-in-the-dark sticks are useful for emergency illumination outdoors.

www.ajungilak.no

VARMESKO: indoor boots to keep your feet nicely toasted in the mountains.

www.keela.co.uk

KEELA: this small Scottish manufacturer uses the latest fabric design technology in its outdoor clothes.

www.hammacher.com

HEAT GLOVE: rechargeable electric warmth for frozen hands (for five hours).

www.macpac.co.nz

HUBBLE: an expedition tent from New Zealand that withstands even the most merciless conditions.

www.ferrino.it

HIGH LAB TENT: tested in the field, this three-person tent is perfect for high-altitude expeditions. It has a flame-resistant, breathable and waterproof inner tent, shock-corded Duraluminium poles and adjustable snow flap.

❶
www.rossignol.com

PROLINE SNOWBOARDS are made of three materials. Microcell dampens the vibrations, wood adds pep and punch and Isocore brings extra lightness and response.

❷
www.alpinasports.com

MADSHUS COLLECTION: Thor and Odin are the kings of telemarking.

❸
www.k2skis.com

LUNA: a range of K2 boards for the fairer sex.

❹
www.k2skis.com

SKY BOARD FATTY PRO: short skis for beginners keen to experience excitement and for lovers of acrobatic skiing.

❺
www.scottusa.com

VOLTAGE: total freedom for freeride fans.

❻
www.rossignol.com

POWER PULSION: the first short ski with an integral plate that directs the power to the tips.

❼
www.cebe.com

MARK: comfortable leather glasses that are popular with snowboarders and bikers.

❽
www.fischerski.com

SL FIBRE CROWN: perfect for intermediate skiers wanting to execute controlled downhill turns.

1
www.dynastar.com

TEAM CONCEPT: imaginative children's skis designed by a top name in ski design.

2
www.voelkl.com

P40, FUNCARVER AND VERTIGO: for racing, carving and freeriding.

3
www.salomonsports.com

SB 10: this is the skiboard for the real professionals who want to challenge the slopes and themselves.

4
www.red-corp.com

BULLET TOOL: a compact and practical tool to adjust the screws on boards and skis with a quick movement of the hand.

5
www.head.com

CYBER CROSS LIGHT: an all-purpose women's ski, equipped with a super light foam core.

6
www.salomonsports.com

FAST BACK: new graphics for freeriders who like to carve fresh snow.

7
www.tecnica.fr

INNOTEC R ULTRAFIT: ski boots that combine flexibility in the bindings with excellent calf support.

8
www.rossignol.com

SOFT SHOE: at last, the combination of rigid plastic and supple design means real comfort.

www.roces.com

CVR2W: this skate is fitted with the Tri Fit System and has a plastic frame, supple interior flexible shell and 'memory' buckle.

www.blauwerk.de

SIDEWALKER CRUISER: part scooter, part bicycle and designed for the snow.

www.vizamotors.com

VENOM SCOOTER: a motorised scooter equipped with a front wheel in summer and a ski in winter.

www.snowbike.com

BRENTER SNOWBIKE: invented in 1949 when it was known as Sit Ski, this is the real snow bike.

www.snobikes.ca

HIBRYD: is it a bike, a ski or a scooter?

www.redlinesnowmobiles.com

954 REVOLUTION: a powerful and eco-friendly snowmobile, this model is the coolest thing on the mountain.

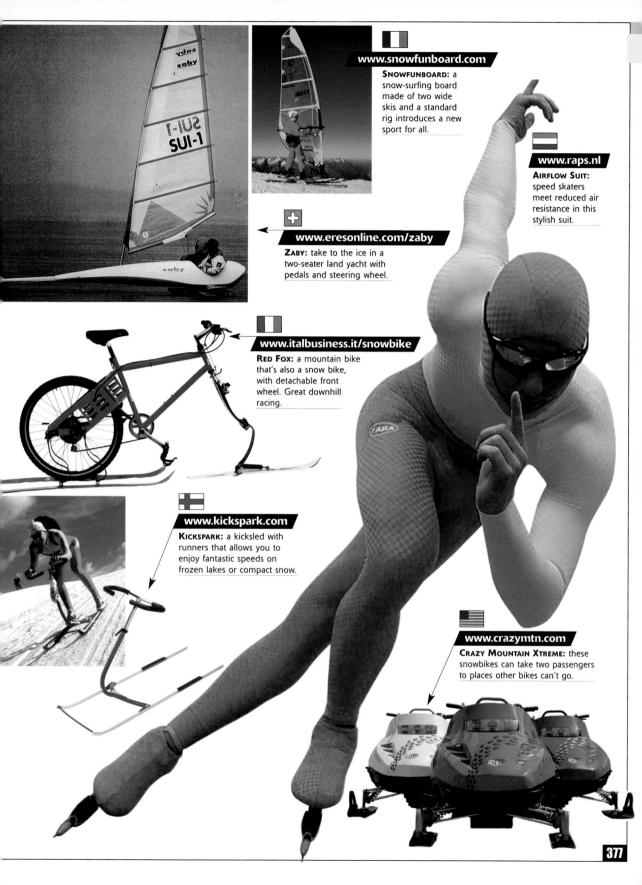

www.snowfunboard.com

SNOWFUNBOARD: a snow-surfing board made of two wide skis and a standard rig introduces a new sport for all.

www.raps.nl

AIRFLOW SUIT: speed skaters meet reduced air resistance in this stylish suit.

www.eresonline.com/zaby

ZABY: take to the ice in a two-seater land yacht with pedals and steering wheel.

www.italbusiness.it/snowbike

RED FOX: a mountain bike that's also a snow bike, with detachable front wheel. Great downhill racing.

www.kickspark.com

KICKSPARK: a kicksled with runners that allows you to enjoy fantastic speeds on frozen lakes or compact snow.

www.crazymtn.com

CRAZY MOUNTAIN XTREME: these snowbikes can take two passengers to places other bikes can't go.

www.morpho.tm.fr

MIGUET: designed for children, these snowshoes are impregnated with the scent of apple so that they can be found more easily.

www.tsl-snowshoes.com

TSL 217: a high-performance snowshoe, particularly on hard snow.

www.yubashoes.com

T-REX: these snowshoes leave frightening prints in the snow.

www.oleysled.com

TRADITIONAL: an authentic wooden toboggan with basket and seat back.

www.grivel.com

VIOLINO: one of the few snowshoes that adapt to boots with crampons.

www.hammacher.com

SLEIGH RIDES IN THE SNOW: Justin Carriage's models are so authentic that they often feature in films.

www.yupiskishoes.com

YUPI: enjoy speed, climbing power and fun with these gliding snowshoes.

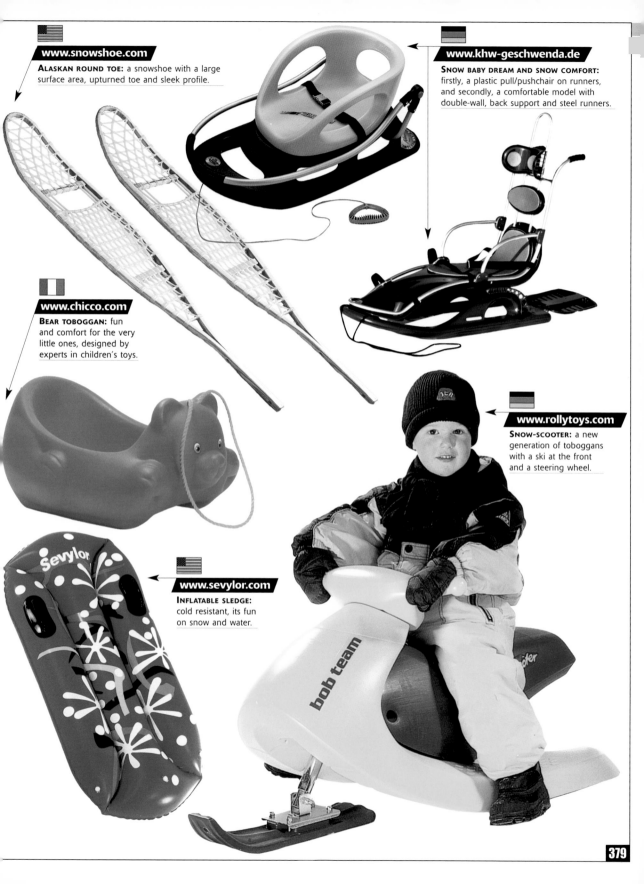

www.snowshoe.com

ALASKAN ROUND TOE: a snowshoe with a large surface area, upturned toe and sleek profile.

www.khw-geschwenda.de

SNOW BABY DREAM AND SNOW COMFORT: firstly, a plastic pull/pushchair on runners, and secondly, a comfortable model with double-wall, back support and steel runners.

www.chicco.com

BEAR TOBOGGAN: fun and comfort for the very little ones, designed by experts in children's toys.

www.rollytoys.com

SNOW-SCOOTER: a new generation of toboggans with a ski at the front and a steering wheel.

www.sevylor.com

INFLATABLE SLEDGE: cold resistant, its fun on snow and water.

www.concept2.com

ROWING MACHINE: recognised as one of the most reliable models, it has an onboard computer that tests Olympic rowers.

www.panattasport.it

KIDS SYSTEM: designed for children and equipped with a computer screen that advises on how to sit properly.

www.vasatrainer.com

VASATRAINER: train at home or outdoors, working on muscles used by cyclists, joggers or surfers.

www.striale.com

ELECTRONIC MINISTEPPER: for working those thighs, buttocks and calf muscles.

www.oemmeb.it

ENERGYSKI: a ski simulator that works all the muscles and can be regulated according to weight.

www.striale.com

POWER STATION 3000: a multi-task exercise bench for intensive body building.

www.somethy.fr

DREAM PADDLES: developed for top swimmers, these flippers calculate calorie and power usage.

www.teuco.it

FITNESS CORNER: an exercise equipment cubicle attached to a shower. Work out, turn the corner and relax your muscles.

www.lifefitness.com.fr

LIFECYCLE BIKE: an exercise bike developed by a fitness machine specialist, complete with twenty intensity levels, a heart rate monitor and computerised progress check.

www.carefitness.com

VOYAGER SYSTEM: an exercise bike programme for a virtual ride in the country. The four gears allow you to choose between flat roads and hills.

www.hammacher.com

CALORIE-COUNTER HULA HOOP: updated from the fifties, this model provides electronic music and vocal encouragement.

www.polar.fi

SMARTEDGE: a multi-purpose watch that monitors your heart rate and calorie usage.

www.hypno.it

MAIA 2001: just click the wheels off and you're ready to walk.

www.streetflyers.com

INVISIBLE: these shoes become in-line skates by releasing the two retractable wheels. The ingenious design was inspired by the landing gear system in airplanes.

www.roces.com

SIR ISACC SAS: equipped with an anti-shock foot-bed and large wheels, this is the skate for off-road adventures.

www.tecnica.it

FIBER RACE: carbon-fibre shell, Aerotec aluminium frame, five wheels and leather upper. Get set, go!

www.missionrh.com

PROTOTEAM: inspired by hockey skates, this model has a very solid composite fibre shoe and blends comfort with performance.

www.zapworld.com

FRONT-WHEEL DRIVE: pulled along as if by a mower, you can enjoy speeds of up to 24km/h with this Power Ski.

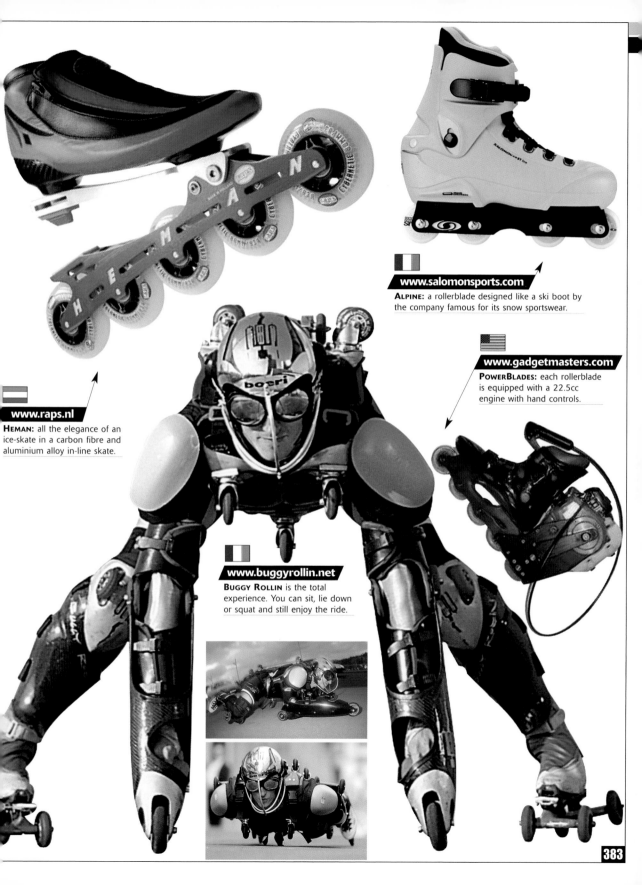

www.salomonsports.com
ALPINE: a rollerblade designed like a ski boot by the company famous for its snow sportswear.

www.gadgetmasters.com
POWERBLADES: each rollerblade is equipped with a 22.5cc engine with hand controls.

www.raps.nl
HEMAN: all the elegance of an ice-skate in a carbon fibre and aluminium alloy in-line skate.

www.buggyrollin.net
BUGGY ROLLIN is the total experience. You can sit, lie down or squat and still enjoy the ride.

383

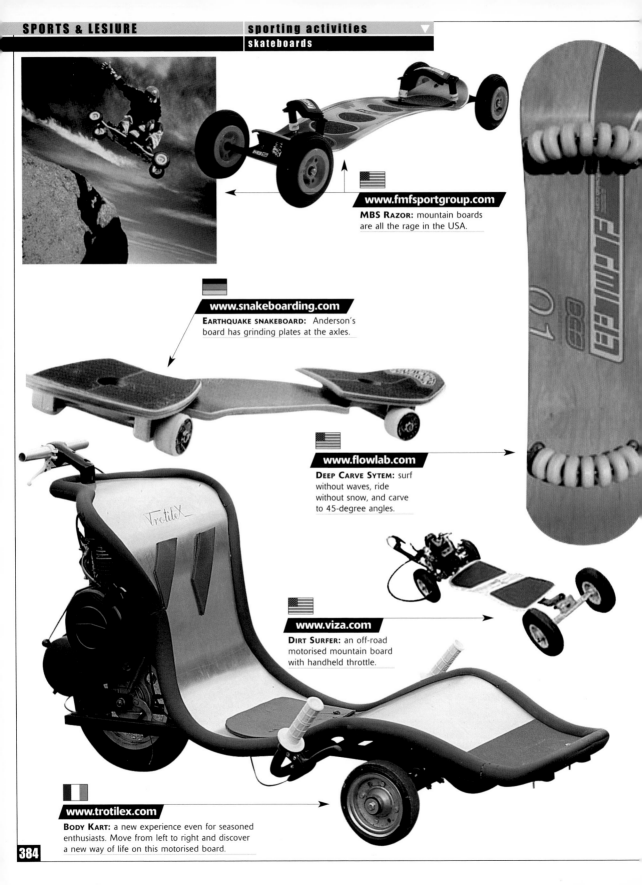

www.fmfsportgroup.com

MBS Razor: mountain boards are all the rage in the USA.

www.snakeboarding.com

Earthquake snakeboard: Anderson's board has grinding plates at the axles.

www.flowlab.com

Deep Carve Sytem: surf without waves, ride without snow, and carve to 45-degree angles.

www.viza.com

Dirt Surfer: an off-road motorised mountain board with handheld throttle.

www.trotilex.com

Body Kart: a new experience even for seasoned enthusiasts. Move from left to right and discover a new way of life on this motorised board.

www.grassboard.com

FREERIDER: this board can cope with any surface, including grass, pebbles and uneven terrain.

www.freebord.com

COMBI: equipped with four side wheels and two central ones, Freebord's Alpha model moves like a snowboard.

www.k2sports.net

CARVEBOARD: just add the Power Stick shaft and you've got yourself a scooter.

www.loko.co.uk

EXCEL FREE STYLE: this board can take up to 90kg in weight and delivers a new suspension sensation with its different wheel design.

www.ep-x.com

MAXIMUM COMFORT IN ALL CONDITIONS: enjoy a smooth ride whatever the terrain.

www.futurehorizons.net

HOVERBOARD: a hovercraft in the shape of a skateboard, this is a real flying carpet. It was part of the special effects in the film Back To The Future.

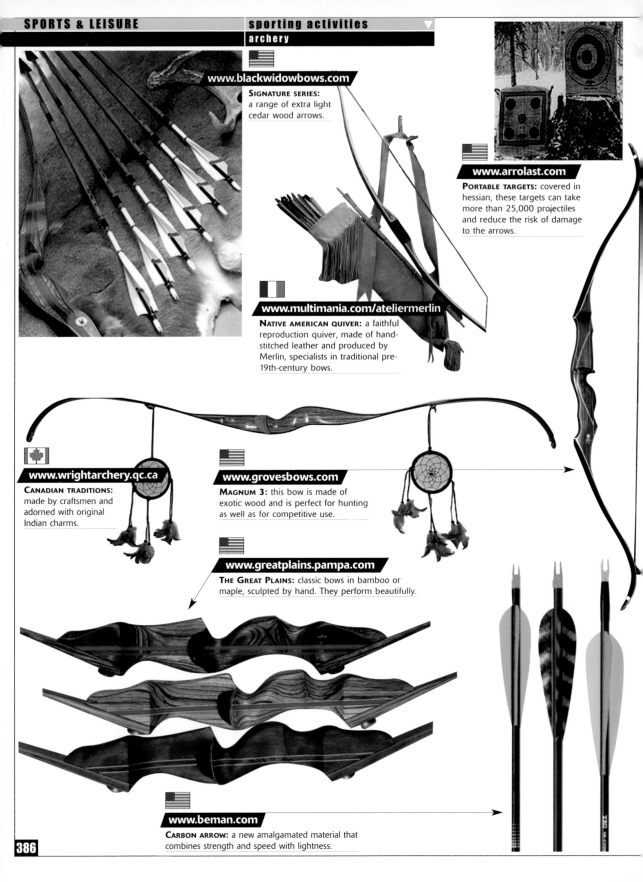

www.blackwidowbows.com

SIGNATURE SERIES: a range of extra light cedar wood arrows.

www.arrolast.com

PORTABLE TARGETS: covered in hessian, these targets can take more than 25,000 projectiles and reduce the risk of damage to the arrows.

www.multimania.com/ateliermerlin

NATIVE AMERICAN QUIVER: a faithful reproduction quiver, made of hand-stitched leather and produced by Merlin, specialists in traditional pre-19th-century bows.

www.wrightarchery.qc.ca

CANADIAN TRADITIONS: made by craftsmen and adorned with original Indian charms.

www.grovesbows.com

MAGNUM 3: this bow is made of exotic wood and is perfect for hunting as well as for competitive use.

www.greatplains.pampa.com

THE GREAT PLAINS: classic bows in bamboo or maple, sculpted by hand. They perform beautifully.

www.beman.com

CARBON ARROW: a new amalgamated material that combines strength and speed with lightness.

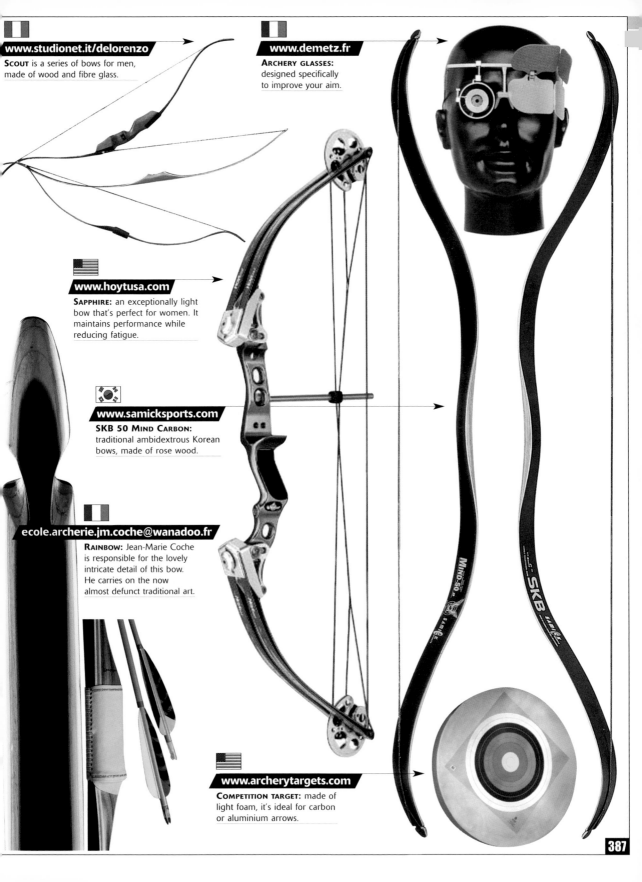

www.studionet.it/delorenzo
Scout is a series of bows for men, made of wood and fibre glass.

www.demetz.fr
Archery glasses: designed specifically to improve your aim.

www.hoytusa.com
Sapphire: an exceptionally light bow that's perfect for women. It maintains performance while reducing fatigue.

www.samicksports.com
SKB 50 Mind Carbon: traditional ambidextrous Korean bows, made of rose wood.

ecole.archerie.jm.coche@wanadoo.fr
Rainbow: Jean-Marie Coche is responsible for the lovely intricate detail of this bow. He carries on the now almost defunct traditional art.

www.archerytargets.com
Competition target: made of light foam, it's ideal for carbon or aluminium arrows.

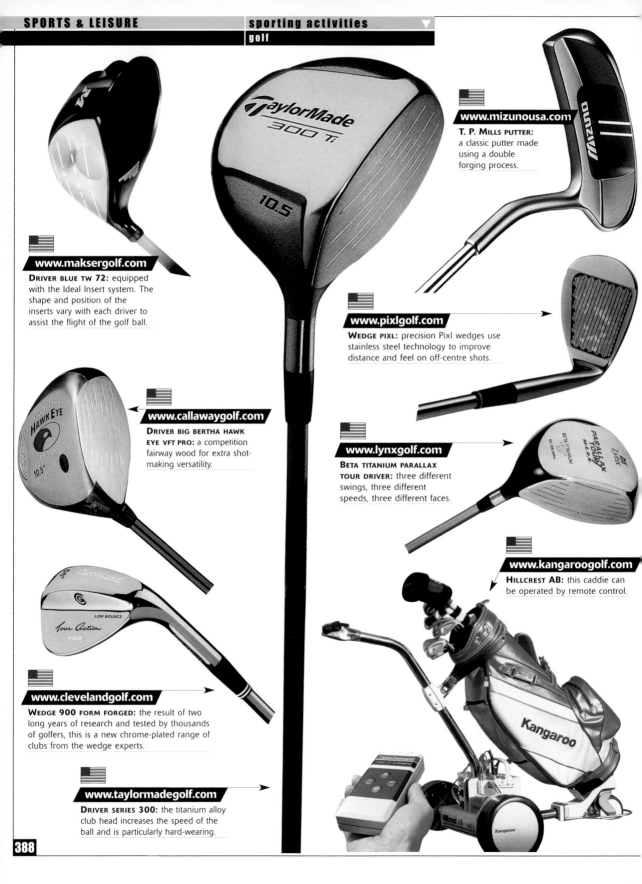

T. P. MILLS PUTTER: a classic putter made using a double forging process.

DRIVER BLUE TW 72: equipped with the Ideal Insert system. The shape and position of the inserts vary with each driver to assist the flight of the golf ball.

WEDGE PIXL: precision Pixl wedges use stainless steel technology to improve distance and feel on off-centre shots.

DRIVER BIG BERTHA HAWK EYE VFT PRO: a competition fairway wood for extra shot-making versatility.

BETA TITANIUM PARALLAX TOUR DRIVER: three different swings, three different speeds, three different faces.

HILLCREST AB: this caddie can be operated by remote control.

WEDGE 900 FORM FORGED: the result of two long years of research and tested by thousands of golfers, this is a new chrome-plated range of clubs from the wedge experts.

DRIVER SERIES 300: the titanium alloy club head increases the speed of the ball and is particularly hard-wearing.

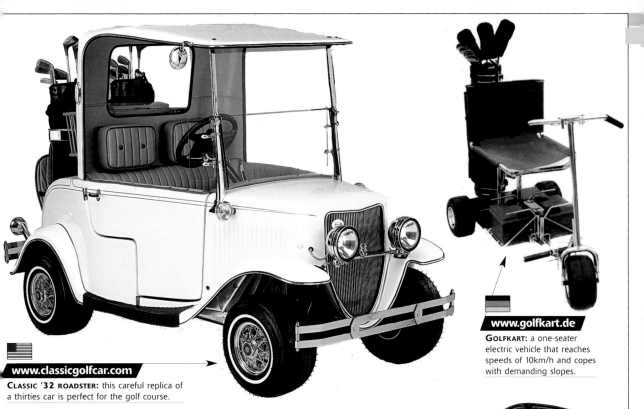

www.prospective-concepts.ch

STINGRAY AND KANGAROO: a team of designers have produced two aerial concepts for Festo.

www.dg-flugzeugbau.de

PLANEUR DG-1000: the new two-seater from DG with excellent performance and elegance.

www.zeppelin-nt.com

ZEPPELIN NT: founded in 1908 by Count Zeppelin, the most famous manufacturer of airships is preparing a new twelve-seater version of the New Technology Zeppelin. Could the future of luxury tourism be international airship travel?

www.aeriane.com

SWIFT: a foot-launchable sailplane. Once aloft, the pilot sits in a hammock and enjoys speeds of over 35km/h.

www.us-lta.com

LIGHTER-THAN-AIR (LTA): used mostly for publicity purposes, this airship can be fitted with Skymax, an image projector that transforms it into a huge flying screen.

www.hammacher.com

ONE-PERSON HELIUM BALLOON: eight times smaller than a hot-air balloon, this environmentally friendly design can lift a passenger several hundred metres, reviving a sport popular at the beginning of the 20th century.

www.cameronballoons.co.uk

HOT-AIR BY DESIGN: the world leader in hot-air balloons, Cameron manufactures traditional designs as well as a wide range of other models, made to order.

www.milleniumairship.com

SKY FREIGHTER: incredible but true – an amphibious airship, capable of transporting 300 tonnes of cargo at a speed of 85 knots.

www.lange-flugzeugbau.de

ANTARES: an electric motorglider with a high-performance, almost silent, propulsion system.

www.skytec-engineering.de

VELAIR: human-powered flight at last! Take off through pedal power and then glide at an average speed of 30km/h.

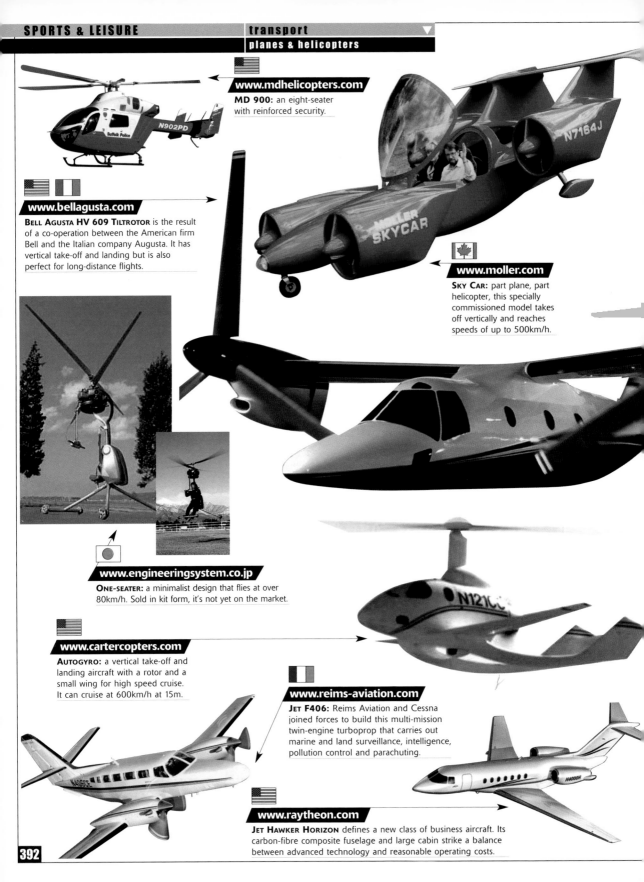

www.mdhelicopters.com

MD 900: an eight-seater with reinforced security.

www.bellagusta.com

BELL AGUSTA HV 609 TILTROTOR is the result of a co-operation between the American firm Bell and the Italian company Augusta. It has vertical take-off and landing but is also perfect for long-distance flights.

www.moller.com

SKY CAR: part plane, part helicopter, this specially commissioned model takes off vertically and reaches speeds of up to 500km/h.

www.engineeringsystem.co.jp

ONE-SEATER: a minimalist design that flies at over 80km/h. Sold in kit form, it's not yet on the market.

www.cartercopters.com

AUTOGYRO: a vertical take-off and landing aircraft with a rotor and a small wing for high speed cruise. It can cruise at 600km/h at 15m.

www.reims-aviation.com

JET F406: Reims Aviation and Cessna joined forces to build this multi-mission twin-engine turboprop that carries out marine and land surveillance, intelligence, pollution control and parachuting.

www.raytheon.com

JET HAWKER HORIZON defines a new class of business aircraft. Its carbon-fibre composite fuselage and large cabin strike a balance between advanced technology and reasonable operating costs.

www.flyproducts.com

AUTOGYRO: designed by a former military helicopter pilot, Swirl is a rear engine propulsion single-seater weighing 135kg with a top horizontal speed of 130km/h.

www.robinsonhelicopter.com

ROBINSON R22: the most famous helicopter in the world, this model has reached sales of over three million in sixty countries.

www.aerospace.bombardier.com

GLOBAL EXPRESS delivers a new category in business aircraft as a result of an alliance between global aerospace leaders. It has a spacious cabin large enough for an office, meeting room and bedroom, with additional space for the cabin crew. It can transport up to fifteen passengers 11,112km (without landing) at a speed of 1,100km/h.

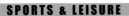 **www.acclimo.com**

LIMOUSINE LINCOLN 120: a car for the stars, this is the American dream, luxurious and oversized.

www.ferrari.com

MODENA 360: one of the most prestigious cars and a symbol of Italian style.

www.chrysler.com

PT CUISER: simultaneously retro and modern, a bold hybrid design by young Bryan Nesbitt.

www.matra.com

M72: a new two-seater open-top design.

www.bmw.com

MINI COOPER: the British car that took the world by storm in 1959 still remains a favourite forty years later.

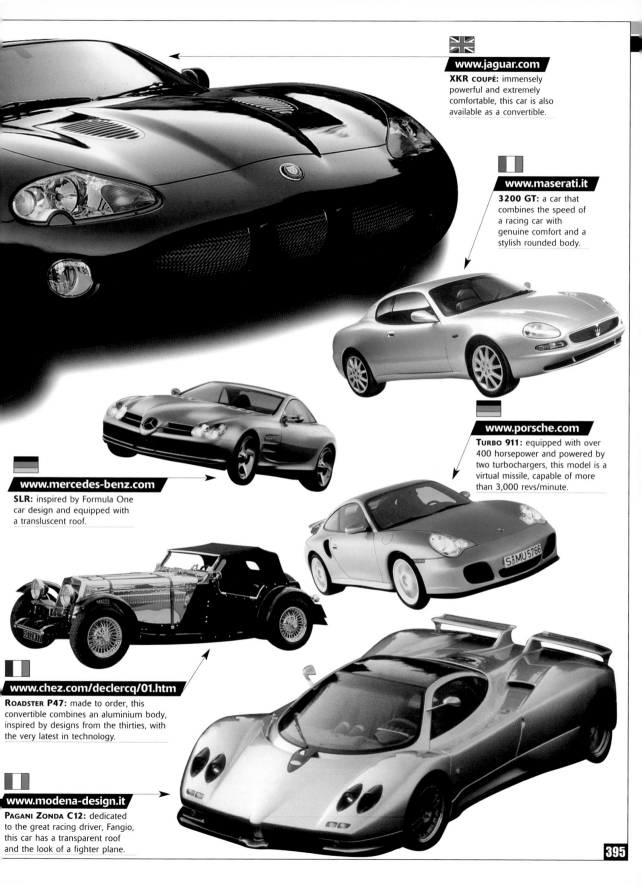

www.jaguar.com

XKR COUPÉ: immensely powerful and extremely comfortable, this car is also available as a convertible.

www.maserati.it

3200 GT: a car that combines the speed of a racing car with genuine comfort and a stylish rounded body.

www.porsche.com

TURBO 911: equipped with over 400 horsepower and powered by two turbochargers, this model is a virtual missile, capable of more than 3,000 revs/minute.

www.mercedes-benz.com

SLR: inspired by Formula One car design and equipped with a transluscent roof.

www.chez.com/declercq/01.htm

ROADSTER P47: made to order, this convertible combines an aluminium body, inspired by designs from the thirties, with the very latest in technology.

www.modena-design.it

PAGANI ZONDA C12: dedicated to the great racing driver, Fangio, this car has a transparent roof and the look of a fighter plane.

www.ferrari.com

FERRARI 550 BANCHETTA PININFARINA: 12-cylinder elegance and presence, Italian style.

www.bmw.com

Z8 FROM BMW: with a 5-litre, 32-valve VS engine, it's capable of zero to 100 in 4.7 seconds.

www.mercedes-benz.com

ROADSTER SLK 320 FROM MERCEDES: convert from a hard top coupé to an open top cabriolet in seconds. Just press a button.

www.chrysler.com

STRATUS CONVERTIBLE: complete with spacious interior, a sound system worthy of a concert hall and speed control for long distance comfort.

www.opel.com

OPEL SPEEDSTER: futuristic design, powerful acceleration and great roadholding.

www.rolls-royce.co.uk

ROLLS-ROYCE CORNICHE: continuing a long tradition of exclusive British cars.

www.audi.com

AUDI TT: a car equipped with sporty appeal combined with extraordinary elegance and exceptional acceleration.

www.toyota.com

ROADSTER MR FROM TOYOTA: an original design, with the engine at the front. This car has a remarkable power-to-weight ratio.

www.smart.com

SMART CABRIO: an original design with an electronic Tritop fabric soft top.

www.jaguar.co.uk

JAGUAR F-TYPE: a sports car with sensual lines and wonderful sophistication. Available in 2003. Start saving now.

Corniche

www.tatooo.com

TATOO.COM FROM RINSPEED: old meets new in this car, inspired by designs from the fifties but manufactured in the Internet era.

www.mercedes.com

SLA VISION FROM MERCEDES: a small roadster with a retro interior and bold body design.

www.nissandriven.com

CYPACT CONCEPT FROM NISSAN: 'cyber' meets 'compact' in this eco-friendly sports coupé, with its new NEO Di injection engine.

www.honda.com

SPOCKET FROM HONDA: at the press of a button the rear seats disappear, the roof retracts and the coupé becomes a convertible.

www.peugeot.com

607 FÉLINE FROM PEUGEOT: complete with a unique sliding bubble roof that resists heat and water.

www.peugeot.com

KART UP: a small roadster with a half-sized steering wheel and a forward-leaning roof, and **E-DOLL**, an electric three-seater vehicle, with the driver's seat in the middle. Silent progress ensured.

www.citroen.com

**MULTIFUNCTION FROM
CITROËN:** convertible,
pick-up and sedan –
all in one.

www.bugatti-cars.de

VEYRON FROM BUGATTI is
named after Pierre Veyron,
champion at Le Mans in 1939.

www.peugeot.com

VROOMSTER: like a
motorbike with its
handlebar steering wheel
and back-seat passenger.

www.volkswagen.com

DUNE FROM VOLKSWAGEN: the New
Beetle has a suspension that adapts
to the road conditions but will it still
have the vase on the dashboard?

www.bombardier-atv.com

QUAD DS 650: the first quad produced by the manufacturer of snow-bikes and jetskis. It's already breaking all the records.

www.argoatv.com

ARGO CONQUEST: an amphibious vehicle with eight-wheel drive that can cope with any surface imaginable.

www.honda.com

FOURTRAX RANCHER: a four-wheel drive with automatic speeds and electric start, built for hard work.

www.hummer.com

HUMMER: a monster four-wheel drive vehicle that is every man's fantasy – risk-free adventure, freedom, comfort and safety in all conditions. Launched by Arnold Schwarzenegger, it has already captured the imagination of Beverly Hills.

www.yamaha-motor.com

QUAD 660 RAPTOR: aggressive design combined with snake-like agility in a fiercely powerful four-wheel drive vehicle.

www.ibex4x4.co.uk

IBEX: John Foers designed this four-wheel drive vehicle for intensive use. Sold as a kit or already assembled.

www.timdutton.com

COMMANDER: a competent amphibious car with four-wheel drive.

www.scorpionvehicles.com

SCORPION MKIII: used by the army and by extreme sports fanatics. Irresistible, it resists nothing.

www.kasea.com

ADVENTURE BUGGY: an all-terrain buggy with fully automatic electric start and excellent suspension. It can climb 45-degree slopes with ease.

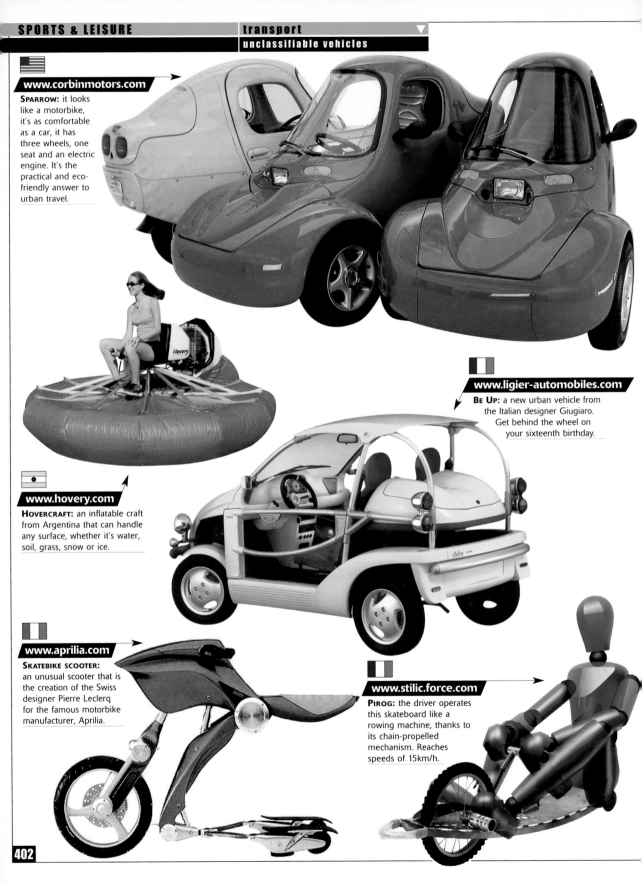

www.corbinmotors.com

SPARROW: it looks like a motorbike, it's as comfortable as a car, it has three wheels, one seat and an electric engine. It's the practical and eco-friendly answer to urban travel.

www.hovery.com

HOVERCRAFT: an inflatable craft from Argentina that can handle any surface, whether it's water, soil, grass, snow or ice.

www.aprilia.com

SKATEBIKE SCOOTER: an unusual scooter that is the creation of the Swiss designer Pierre Leclerq for the famous motorbike manufacturer, Aprilia.

www.ligier-automobiles.com

BE UP: a new urban vehicle from the Italian designer Giugiaro. Get behind the wheel on your sixteenth birthday.

www.stilic.force.com

PIROG: the driver operates this skateboard like a rowing machine, thanks to its chain-propelled mechanism. Reaches speeds of 15km/h.

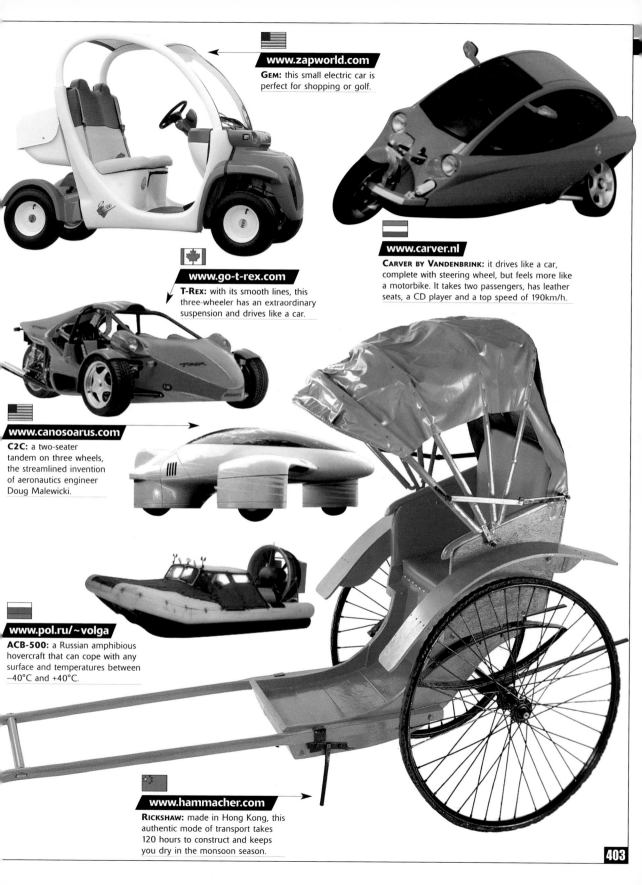

www.zapworld.com

GEM: this small electric car is perfect for shopping or golf.

www.carver.nl

CARVER BY VANDENBRINK: it drives like a car, complete with steering wheel, but feels more like a motorbike. It takes two passengers, has leather seats, a CD player and a top speed of 190km/h.

www.go-t-rex.com

T-REX: with its smooth lines, this three-wheeler has an extraordinary suspension and drives like a car.

www.canosoarus.com

C2C: a two-seater tandem on three wheels, the streamlined invention of aeronautics engineer Doug Malewicki.

www.pol.ru/~volga

ACB-500: a Russian amphibious hovercraft that can cope with any surface and temperatures between −40°C and +40°C.

www.hammacher.com

RICKSHAW: made in Hong Kong, this authentic mode of transport takes 120 hours to construct and keeps you dry in the monsoon season.

403

www.roulottes.nl

AUTHENTIC CARAVANS: horse-drawn wooden caravans that are so attractive they are often allowed in areas in which other camping vehicles are prohibited.

www.hoening.com

TWIN: a double eight-seater tandem for four 'pedal-pushers' and four young passengers.

www.nihola.com

NIHOLA: a tricycle built for three – two at the front, one at the back.

www.surreybikes.com

DELFINO: a pedal-powered vehicle for a large family. It takes up to nine adults with two small children in front.

www.citroen.fr

OSMOSE: offering a compromise between pedestrians and drivers, this vehicle has three seats at the front and and one at the back for anyone wanting to hop aboard. The digital screen displays its destination.

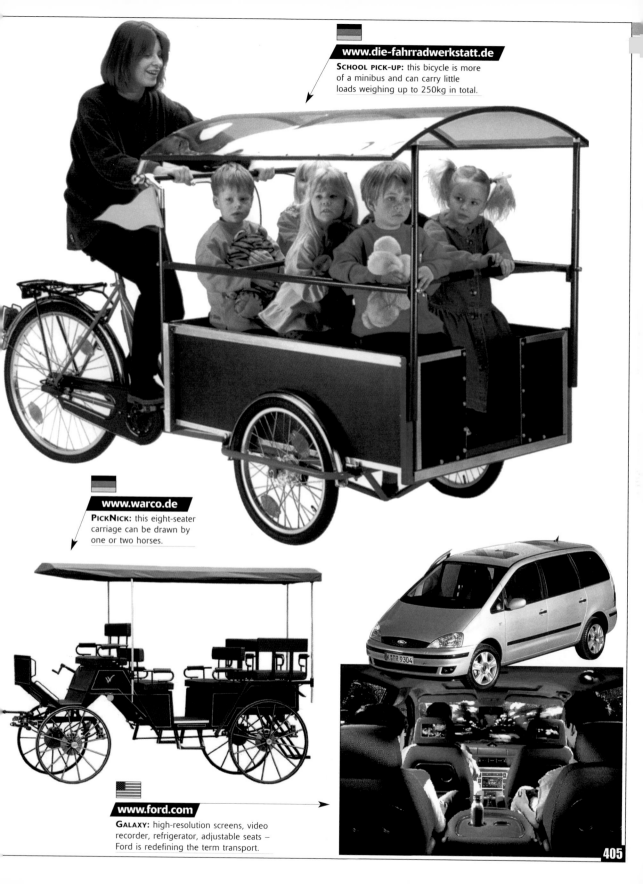

www.die-fahrradwerkstatt.de

SCHOOL PICK-UP: this bicycle is more of a minibus and can carry little loads weighing up to 250kg in total.

www.warco.de

PICKNICK: this eight-seater carriage can be drawn by one or two horses.

www.ford.com

GALAXY: high-resolution screens, video recorder, refrigerator, adjustable seats – Ford is redefining the term transport.

www.cagiva.it

CAGIVA NAVIGATOR: equipped with a Suzuki engine, this machine is a powerful beast (96 horsepower with 8,400 revs/minute) with a solid chassis and telescopic hydraulic fork.

www.yamaha-motor.com

YAMAHA FRJ 1300, a top of the range bike with 1,300cc electronic fuel injection engine, adjustable rear suspension and catalytic converter.

www.bmw.com

BMW K 1200 LT: a big engine touring bike with third-generation integral ABS. This is a very special machine in the luxury touring class.

www.triumph.co.uk

TRIUMPH SPEED TRIPLE: muscular and made for action, this three-cylinder machine has twin headlights, black finish and attitude.

www.ducati.com

DUCATI MONSTER 600: this is Ducati's smallest cylinder machine (51 horsepower). What it lacks in power it makes up for in sensation and style.

www.aprilia.com

APRILIA MOTO 6.5: the result of Philippe Starck's imagination and Aprilia's technology, this single cylinder bike is remarkable.

www.side-bike.com

ZEUS: a homogeneous vehicle with integral chassis, Peugeot engine and passenger pod. Combines style, safety and comfort on the road.

www.triketec.de

TDI GREEN MILLENNIUM: you need a driving licence to enjoy this tricycle with its 1,600cc injection engine, 48 horsepower and economic yet powerful performance.

www.agusta.it

AGUSTA MV F4: created by Massimo Tamburini, this motorbike is considered to be one of the most beautiful machines on the market.

www.honda.com

HONDA CBR 900 RR FIREBLADE: the most powerful of the 900cc machines on the market, not forgetting comfort and safety, of course.

www.harley-davidson.com

HARLEY-DAVIDSON HERITAGE SOFTAIL CLASSIC: a classic and distinctive motorbike, as powerful as it is magnificent, boasting a Twin Cam 88 MC engine.

www.piaggio.com

VESPA PX 125-200: the new version of the famous 1946 model of which over 15 million have been sold.

www.peugeot.com

SPEED X RACE: this latest version of the Speedflight 2 model is one of two new Peugeot designs. The other is the Louxor.

cargobike.com

www.cargobike.com

TREKKER: a Peugeot scooter that can carry 80kg and 160 litres. It owes its remarkable stability to its low centre of gravity.

www.benelli.com

ADIVA: this scooter has a folding roof that can be erected and dismantled within ten seconds, using just one hand.

www.italjet.com

FORMULA 125 LC: the only twin-cylinder scooter, complete with centre hub steering, differentiated tyres and dual disk brakes.

www.yamaha-motor.com

XP500 T Max: comes complete with an advanced scooter engine, capable of powerful acceleration and effortless speed.

www.suzuki.com

UX 50: combines the latest technology with hot off the press design.

www.bmw.com

C1 is a new concept in urban transport. It's the first two-wheeler with real protection.

www.aprilia.com

Habana: the comfortable seat and hydraulic twin shock absorbers guarantee a smooth ride.

www.porsche.com

FS EVOLUTION: a bicycle designed for high performance and maximum safety on difficult terrain.

www.swiss-flyer.com

FLYER: an electric bike with an engine that stops at a speed of 24km/h.

www.bmw.com

MOUNTAIN BIKE Q6.S: a mountain bike with shock-absorbing suspension.

www.conferencebike.com

CONFERENCE BIKE: designed by Eric Staller for seven simultaneous cyclists. So where will Snow White sit?

www.zapworld.com

ELECTRIC MOTOR KIT: install on any bike for easier pedalling.

www.windcheetah.co.uk

WINDCHEETAH: tomorrow's mountain bike, ergonomic and speedy.

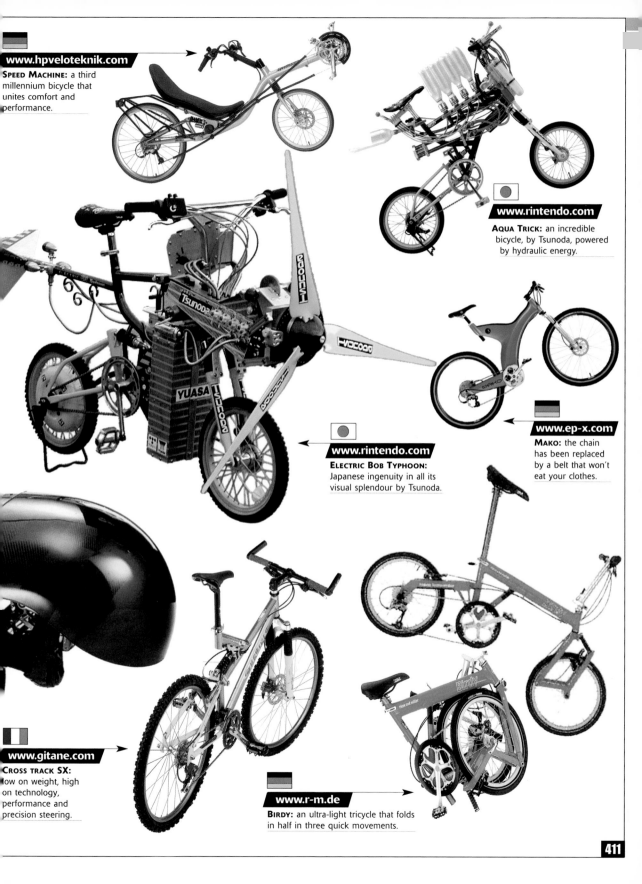

www.hpveloteknik.com

SPEED MACHINE: a third millennium bicycle that unites comfort and performance.

www.rintendo.com

AQUA TRICK: an incredible bicycle, by Tsunoda, powered by hydraulic energy.

www.rintendo.com

ELECTRIC BOB TYPHOON: Japanese ingenuity in all its visual splendour by Tsunoda.

www.ep-x.com

MAKO: the chain has been replaced by a belt that won't eat your clothes.

www.gitane.com

CROSS TRACK SX: low on weight, high on technology, performance and precision steering.

www.r-m.de

BIRDY: an ultra-light tricycle that folds in half in three quick movements.

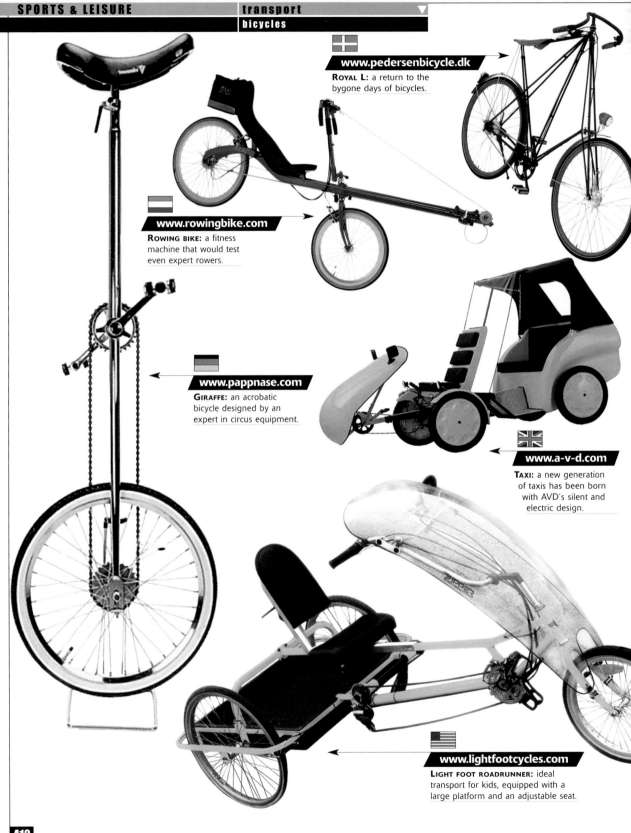

www.pedersenbicycle.dk

ROYAL L: a return to the bygone days of bicycles.

www.rowingbike.com

ROWING BIKE: a fitness machine that would test even expert rowers.

www.pappnase.com

GIRAFFE: an acrobatic bicycle designed by an expert in circus equipment.

www.a-v-d.com

TAXI: a new generation of taxis has been born with AVD's silent and electric design.

www.lightfootcycles.com

LIGHT FOOT ROADRUNNER: ideal transport for kids, equipped with a large platform and an adjustable seat.

www.toxy.de

QUANTUM: semi-reclined pedalling in a streamlined machine.

www.tu-bicycle.co.jp

ROBIN: a mini-bike that dismantles completely.

www.koolstop.com

HIGH BICYCLE: inspired by an early 20th-century design, executed by J. Mesicek.

www.diblasi.it

FOLDING TRICYCLE: fold the seat, handlebars and pedals for easy transport.

www.r-m.de

EQUINOX: a bike for cyclists and walkers, complete with a seat back.

www.hase-spezialraeder.de
Lepus: practical, comfortable,
collapsible – perfect.

www.ligfiets.net/j-en-s
Quest: an aerodynamic machine that
combines speed with comfort.

www.karbonkinetics.com
Mako: the emphasis is on comfort
rather than speed with this machine.

www.cyclesmaximus.com
Trishaw: the practical way
to take the whole family out.

www.hpveloteknik.com
Streamer: hi-tech,
stylish and robust
transport for all weathers.

www.christianiabikes.com
Light-split: people and luggage
come first in this rickshaw at the
forefront of transport.

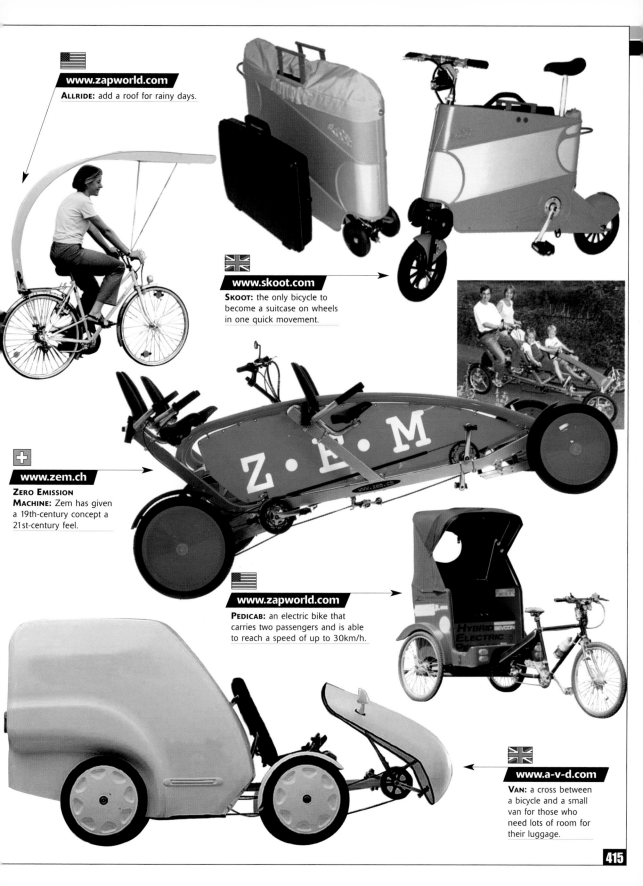

ALLRIDE: add a roof for rainy days.

SKOOT: the only bicycle to become a suitcase on wheels in one quick movement.

ZERO EMISSION MACHINE: Zem has given a 19th-century concept a 21st-century feel.

PEDICAB: an electric bike that carries two passengers and is able to reach a speed of up to 30km/h.

VAN: a cross between a bicycle and a small van for those who need lots of room for their luggage.

www.badsey.com

EMX CRUISER: Bill Badsey launched the first electric scooter in 1991. This is the new collapsible version.

www.comebike.com

USE BIKE: easy to use with a large ergonomic handle and all-purpose wheels.

www.trotilex.com

TROTILEX: complete with a Solex motor and capable of 30km/h on the road.

www.sabbah.fr

ELECTRIC, comfortable and collapsible transport.

www.tboard.com

LIGHT AND SPEEDY: collapsible scooter with an engine at the rear.

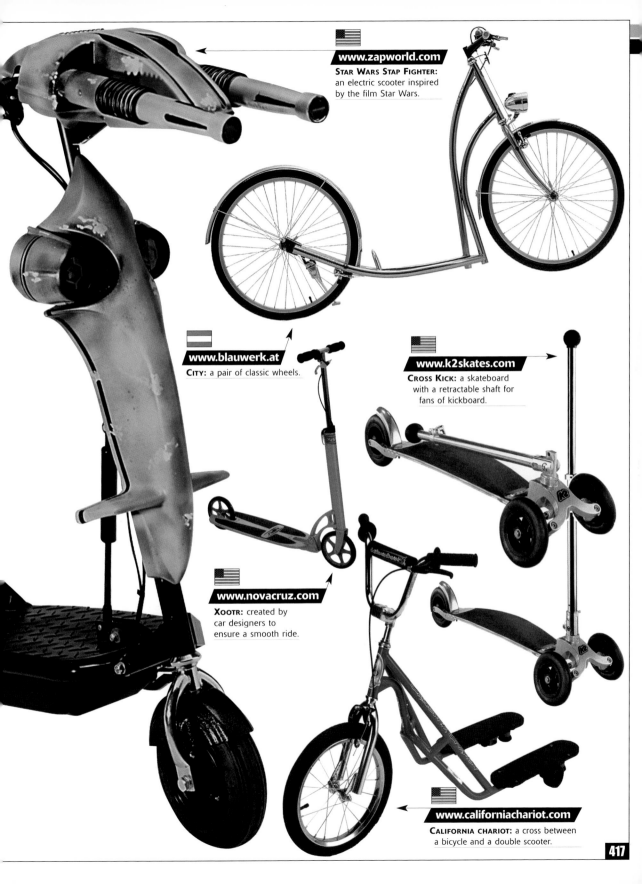

www.zapworld.com
STAR WARS STAP FIGHTER: an electric scooter inspired by the film Star Wars.

www.blauwerk.at
CITY: a pair of classic wheels.

www.k2skates.com
CROSS KICK: a skateboard with a retractable shaft for fans of kickboard.

www.novacruz.com
XOOTR: created by car designers to ensure a smooth ride.

www.californiachariot.com
CALIFORNIA CHARIOT: a cross between a bicycle and a double scooter.

www.lefranc-bourgeois.com

LIMITED EDITION: a Louise Philippe-style piece of furniture that contains all your artistic requirements.

www.talens.com

MANNEQUINS: these adjustable dummies in natural wood make perfect models for aspiring artists.

www.mabef.it

BEECHWOOD FOLDING EASEL: for wandering artists who want to carry all their tools and paints into fields of golden sunflowers.

www.talens.com

PALETTE KNIVES are perfect for quick, expressive and impulsive creations.

www.daler-rowney.co.uk

AQUAFINE: carry your watercolours around in a practical cylinder that unfolds as a palette.

www.max-seuer.com

ISABEY BRUSHES: made entirely by hand in Brittany, traditionally by sailors' wives, who learn their craft for seven years.

www.max-seuer.com

SENNELIER PASTELS & PIGMENTS: have been produced using traditional methods since 1887. Picasso's favourite brand.

www.winsornewton.com

LUXURY CASE: Winsor and Newton have been producing artists' materials of the highest quality since 1832, using 26,000 natural or chemical components.

www.carandache.com

PROFESSIONAL: an elegant wooden box that contains no less that 163 crayons.

www.japanesetools.com

BUNHOU: a tactile Japanese bamboo brush.

www.faber-castell.com

INNOVATION FROM FABER-CASTELL: cedar wood pencils complete with sharpener and eraser.

www.max-seuer.com

RAPHAËL BRUSHES: legendary brushes made by the oldest European manufacturer, founded in 1793.

www.talens.com

PAINTING BY REMBRANDT: oil paints with a big reputation for quality and resistance to light.

www.fine-tools.com

MULTI-FUNCTION PLANE:
a masterpiece of precision
in cast iron, designed by
Clifton according to the
English tradition.

www.hidatool.com

SUMITSUBO: a traditional way of
marking thin and accurate lines,
with a silk line and ink.

www.grobet.com

PRECISION FILES: these tools have
been in production since 1811, when
they were used to make clocks.

www.marpleschisel.com

WOODEN CHISELS: Marples make solid tools
with manganese steel and boxwood.

www.crownhandtools.ltd.uk

SCRAPERS: vital for finishing, these
tools are sold in threes to cater for
different types of wood.

www.dick-gmbh.de

JAPANESE KNIVES, made of steel, are used for scraping, sculpting and engraving wood.

www.gransfors.com

SWEDISH AXES: faultless tools manufactured since 1902 by hand, individually hallmarked and guaranteed for twenty years.

www.pfeiltools.ch

SCULPTING SET: contains twenty wood-carving tools, two Arkansas whetstones and honing oil in a delightful Swiss beechwood box.

www.recordtool.com

PROFESSIONAL VICE: a large woodworking vice that opens up to 38cm.

www.lie-nielsen.com

TRADITIONAL PLANE: inspired by planes from the early 20th century, this tool is handmade by a Maine company.

www.dick-gmbh.de

PRECISION TOOLS: used to make the wonderful Chinese balls-in-balls – five nested spheres.

www.metmusic.com

LUTHIER'S PLANE: specially adapted to work on violins but can also be used on chairs.

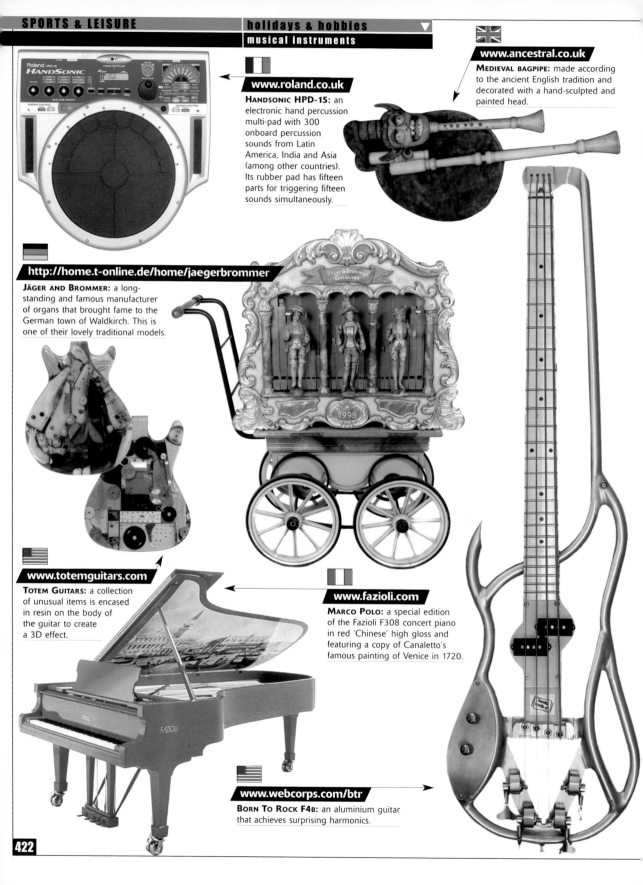

www.roland.co.uk

HANDSONIC HPD-15: an electronic hand percussion multi-pad with 300 onboard percussion sounds from Latin America, India and Asia (among other countries). Its rubber pad has fifteen parts for triggering fifteen sounds simultaneously.

www.ancestral.co.uk

MEDIEVAL BAGPIPE: made according to the ancient English tradition and decorated with a hand-sculpted and painted head.

http://home.t-online.de/home/jaegerbrommer

JÄGER AND BROMMER: a long-standing and famous manufacturer of organs that brought fame to the German town of Waldkirch. This is one of their lovely traditional models.

www.totemguitars.com

TOTEM GUITARS: a collection of unusual items is encased in resin on the body of the guitar to create a 3D effect.

www.fazioli.com

MARCO POLO: a special edition of the Fazioli F308 concert piano in red 'Chinese' high gloss and featuring a copy of Canaletto's famous painting of Venice in 1720.

www.webcorps.com/btr

BORN TO ROCK F4B: an aluminium guitar that achieves surprising harmonics.

www.ninestones.com

DIDGERIDOO: one of the oldest musical instruments in the world, originating from Australia. This ceramic stoneware model is unconventional and forms part of a collection of hand-crafted instruments by Barry Hall. The Burnt Earth series is remarkable.

www.webcorps.com/btr

RESOPHONIC GUITAR: this guitar has metallic resonators that are made by hand in maple wood by Randy Allen.

www.teuffelguitars.com

BIRDFISH: a limited edition guitar that you can make yourself by installing various resonators and interchangeable pickups.

www.snafu.de/~maubrey

ACOUSTIC TUTU: one of the prototype outfits designed for dancers of Die Audio Gruppe. It responds musically to the movements of the performers.

www.denninger-designs.com

PIANO MASON AND HAMLIN: the sculptor George Denninger created this mahogany masterpiece. It was exhibited in the Metropolitan Museum of Art in New York.

www.classicrockinghorses.co.uk

ROCKING HORSE: careful replica of antique wooden originals.

www.nordy.fr

LOOK MUM, NO ROOF: a pedal car for young drivers aged from 4–7.

www.moulinroty.fr

HAMPER AND TOOL BOX: part of the nostalgic collection of yesteryear's toys designed by Moulin Roty.

www.radioflyer.com

WAGON: a classic for years and among the most popular toys in America.

www.roco.co.at

GDR'S IMPERIAL RAILWAY: a minutely faithful reproduction of the trains.

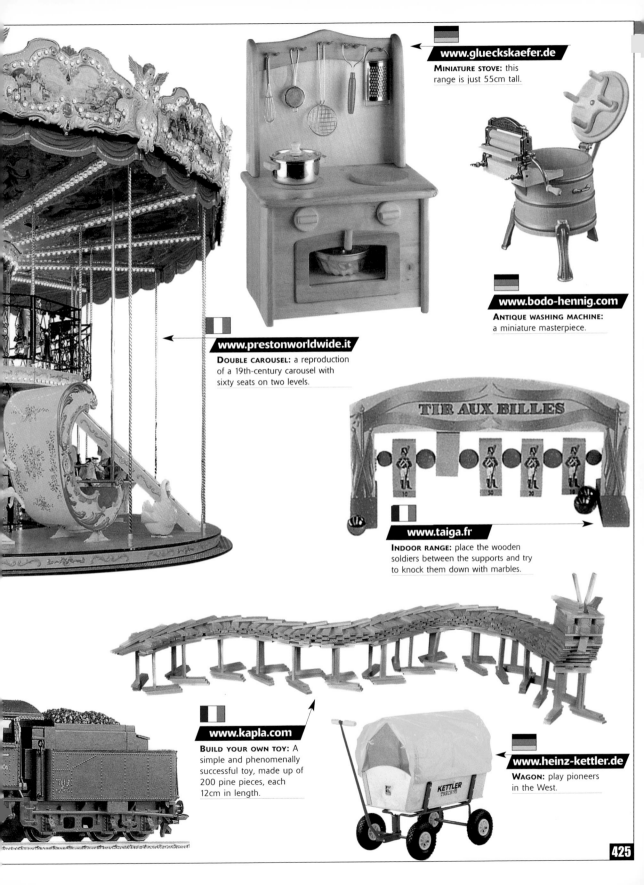

www.glueckskaefer.de

MINIATURE STOVE: this range is just 55cm tall.

www.bodo-hennig.com

ANTIQUE WASHING MACHINE: a miniature masterpiece.

www.prestonworldwide.it

DOUBLE CAROUSEL: a reproduction of a 19th-century carousel with sixty seats on two levels.

TIR AUX BILLES

www.taiga.fr

INDOOR RANGE: place the wooden soldiers between the supports and try to knock them down with marbles.

www.kapla.com

BUILD YOUR OWN TOY: A simple and phenomenally successful toy, made up of 200 pine pieces, each 12cm in length.

www.heinz-kettler.de

WAGON: play pioneers in the West.

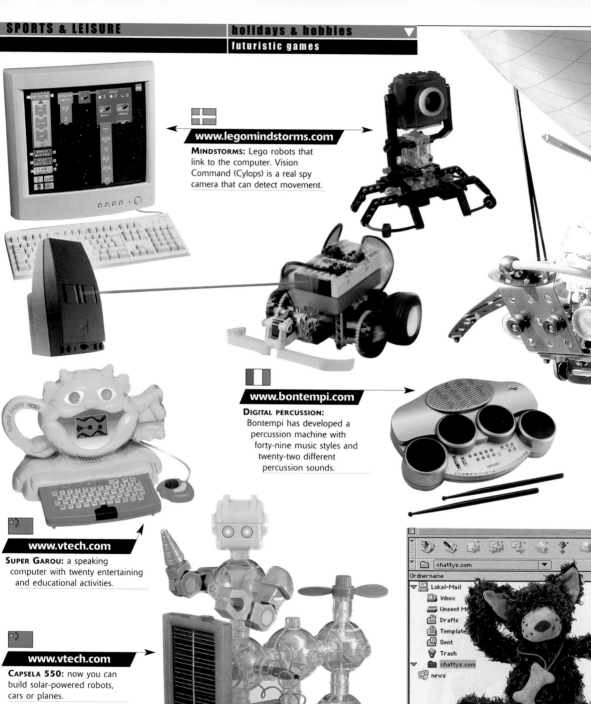

www.legomindstorms.com

MINDSTORMS: Lego robots that link to the computer. Vision Command (Cylops) is a real spy camera that can detect movement.

www.bontempi.com

DIGITAL PERCUSSION: Bontempi has developed a percussion machine with forty-nine music styles and twenty-two different percussion sounds.

www.vtech.com

SUPER GAROU: a speaking computer with twenty entertaining and educational activities.

www.vtech.com

CAPSELA 550: now you can build solar-powered robots, cars or planes.

www.chattys.com

CHATTYS: Sigikid's new concept in soft toys. Visit their website and you'll find each animal has its own email address.

www.meccano.com

AIRSHIP: Meccano's latest creation dedicated to madcap inventors and their ideas.

www.rgmitchell.com

SHUTTLE: children can head for the stars in this machine, complete with rotating motion and space travel sound effects.

www.tomy.com

ROBOT DOG: mummy dog and puppy both obey remote control commands.

UNITED STATES

USA

50 CENTS A RIDE

www.tigertoys.com

VIRTUAL FISHING ROD: an electronic game that means you can catch six sorts of fish without going near a river.

www.glamorous.co.jp

DUCKING CHAIR: you'll never watch telly alone again.

www.tangletoys.com
TANGLE: endless stress-free fun in search of the impossible circle.

www.playsam.com
PLAYSAM: beautiful wooden toys designed by a talented duo.

www.remington.fr
DUCK'N DRY: have fun drying the children's hair.

www.bodo-hennig.com
HOW WE USED TO LIVE: a 19th-century house, complete with electricity.

www.haring.com
TOYS BY KEITH HARING raise funds for people with Aids.

www.groupe-berchet.com

THE MOULINEX BERCHET COLLECTION: two large brand names have joined forces to create a collection of fully functioning household appliances for children, based on those used by their parents. Stylish and safe education for all.

www.oregonscientific.com

SPACE CONSOLE: it looks like a CD player but it's also a radio and electronic game player.

www.selecta-spielzeug.de

MODERN LIVING: a contemporary house with functional furniture. Just add another floor when the family decides to expand.

www.momastore.com

DESIGNER LIVING: New York's Museum of Modern Art sells this miniature house, complete with contemporary furniture, sliding partitions and abstract art. Hands off, parents.

www.heinz-kettler.de

SAFARI: this go-kart has a generous ergonomic seat, large wheels and a hand-controlled brake.

www.rollytoys.com

MERCEDES: a dream convertible, with pedals that's more convincing than the real thing.

www.kokua.de

LIKEaBIKE: a chain-free bike for cyclists over two years old.

www.turbokarting.be

SULKY: part rocking-horse, part go-kart, part bicycle.

www.chicco.com

CABRIO: the first electric open-car top from Chicco, complete with accelerator and pedal brake.

www.groupe-berchet.com

FREESTER FROM TOYS-TOYS: the first car with a heat engine, capable of 20km/h. It takes petrol and is for young drivers over six.

www.injusa.com

REPSOL: an electronic motorbike for 3–9-year-olds, capable of 6km/h.

www.groupe-berchet.com

SCOOT ROLLER: Charton's scooter converts easily into a three-wheeler.

www.playsam.com

ROADSTER: one of the wooden cars made to order by Ulf Hanses and Björn Dahlström.

www.rollytoys.com

RALLYE UNIMOG: a four-wheel drive vehicle with pedals, complete with gear lever, brakes and tools.

www.boxtown.com

HOUSE IN A BOX: made of
cardboard, this house is easy
to assemble, already decorated
and very good value.

www.lapetitemaison.com

LA PETITE MAISON: a French-style house with
real floor, electricity and air conditioning.

www.barbarabutler.com

BARBARA BUTLER specialises in
designing wooden playhouses
in startling colours and interesting
themes, including a fort, lighthouse,
boat and palace.

• **HILLSIDE HAMLET TREE FORT**

• **TREETOP BUNGALOW**

• **CALISTOGA**

• **CANYON PERCH**

www.cardboardcastles.co.uk

DIY Tudor: a folding cardboard cottage that you can build and paint yourself.

www.treecamp.com

Milland Forest Crafts: assembled in two days, these treehouses are made to order and have waterproofed roofs. Outdoor style and safety.

www.play-houses.com

Historic houses: choose from a Tudor Cottage, Regency Gothic or Queen Anne house for your children. Inspired by historic designs, they are faithful reproductions in wood.

www.katelynskastles.com

Katelyn's castle: one of many designs made to order, using salvaged material collected over twenty-five years by Katelyn.

www.customplayhouses.com

Victorian Ashlynn: a fully furnished home, complete with covered verandah and interior mezzanine floor.

• **Tudor Cottage**

• **Regency Gothic**

• **Queen Anne**

433

www.doggeneration.com

OH MY DOG! the first perfume for our canine companions. They certainly have the nose for it.

www.mawa-design.de

BIRDY: a seed frame that captures Nature in action.

www.wedgwood.com

CAT CHIC: a ceramic cat bowl designed by none other than Nick Munro.

www.unclemilton.com

AQUARIUM WITH PERISCOPE: drop some bait in at the end of a rod and look through the lens for a completely dry underwater experience.

www.lapetitemaison.com

IN THE DOG HOUSE: a kennel in the style of his master's home.

www.designf.co.jp

DESIGN FOR DOGS: fashion for four-footed folk, in wool, denim and camouflage.

www.quattrozampe.com

FIT FOR A KING: nothing is too good for the princes of the house.

www.atypyk.com

WOOFERANG: a dog-bone-shaped boomerang that always makes its way back to the master (in the dog's mouth).

www.kreo.fr

FUN FOR FELINES: a prototype game for cats by Radi Designers.

www.philipp-plein.com

DOG DAYBED in fur and fake leather.

www.birddiaper.com

TUX WITH TAILS: evening wear for parrots, designed by the experts.

www.multimania.com/gabuzo

ARTISTIC ANTICS: watch the activity in the anthill. The ants are contained by the chalk circle at the top.

www.jungletalk.com

HIDE A TREAT: tuck your bird's favourite food inside and watch him try to get to it.

www.mondes-interieurs.com

WROUGHT-IRON CAGES in distressed gold.

435

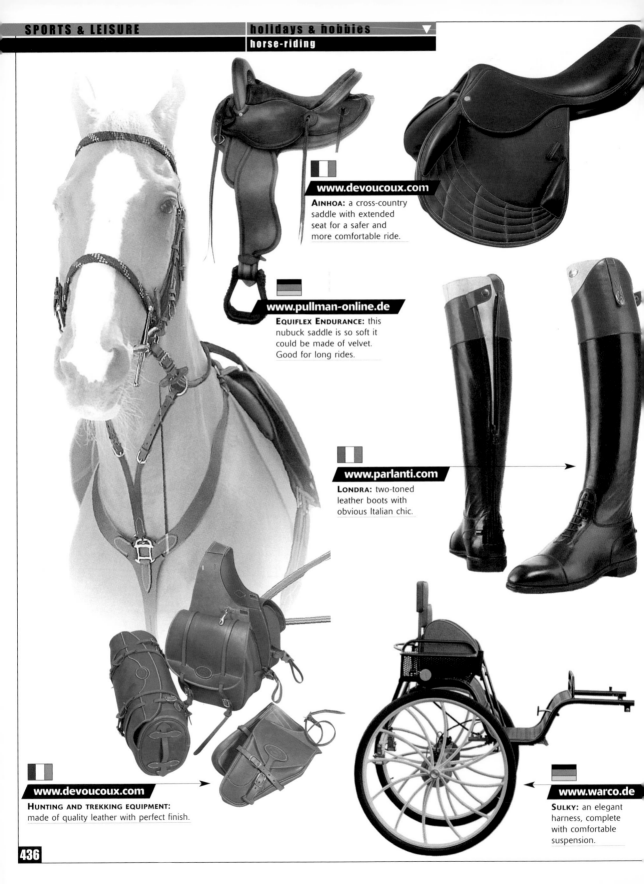

www.devoucoux.com

AINHOA: a cross-country saddle with extended seat for a safer and more comfortable ride.

www.pullman-online.de

EQUIFLEX ENDURANCE: this nubuck saddle is so soft it could be made of velvet. Good for long rides.

www.parlanti.com

LONDRA: two-toned leather boots with obvious Italian chic.

www.devoucoux.com

HUNTING AND TREKKING EQUIPMENT: made of quality leather with perfect finish.

www.warco.de

SULKY: an elegant harness, complete with comfortable suspension.

www.ariat.com

LEATHER LEGGINGS, with elastic straps to ensure a perfect fit.

www.equiport.co.uk

EQUIPORT RIDING HAT: the very British model in black velvet.

www.selles-g-mercier.com

SAUVETERRE: equipped with short girth straps, this saddle keeps your legs in a natural position using front and back knee rolls.

www.doublejsaddlery.com

HEXCEL PERFORMER PRO: their exclusive technology gives these shoes extra comfort and grip.

www.musto.co.uk

RIDING COAT: you can adjust the sleeves, remove the hood and protect yourself from the wet and wind. It's made with two layers of Gore-Tex and is even machine washable!

www.oldwestantiques.com

COWBOY SPURS: following in the footsteps of the buffalo head spurs designed by August Buermann.

www.doublejsaddlery.com

RUSTY CONCHO: a saddle made of dyed leather and decorated with a pattern of oak leaves.

437

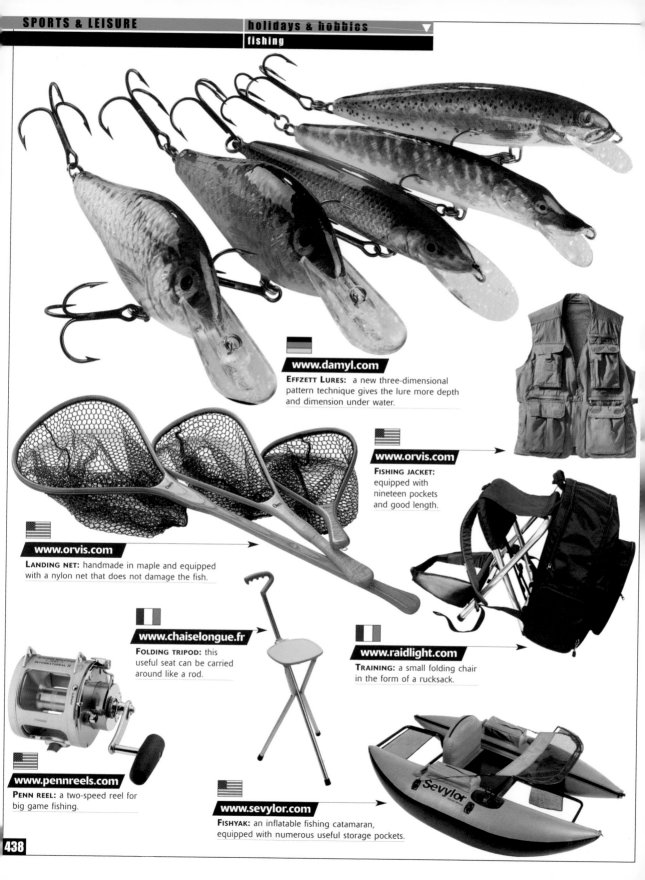

www.damyl.com

EFFZETT LURES: a new three-dimensional pattern technique gives the lure more depth and dimension under water.

www.orvis.com

FISHING JACKET: equipped with nineteen pockets and good length.

www.orvis.com

LANDING NET: handmade in maple and equipped with a nylon net that does not damage the fish.

www.chaiselongue.fr

FOLDING TRIPOD: this useful seat can be carried around like a rod.

www.raidlight.com

TRAINING: a small folding chair in the form of a rucksack.

www.pennreels.com

PENN REEL: a two-speed reel for big game fishing.

www.sevylor.com

FISHYAK: an inflatable fishing catamaran, equipped with numerous useful storage pockets.

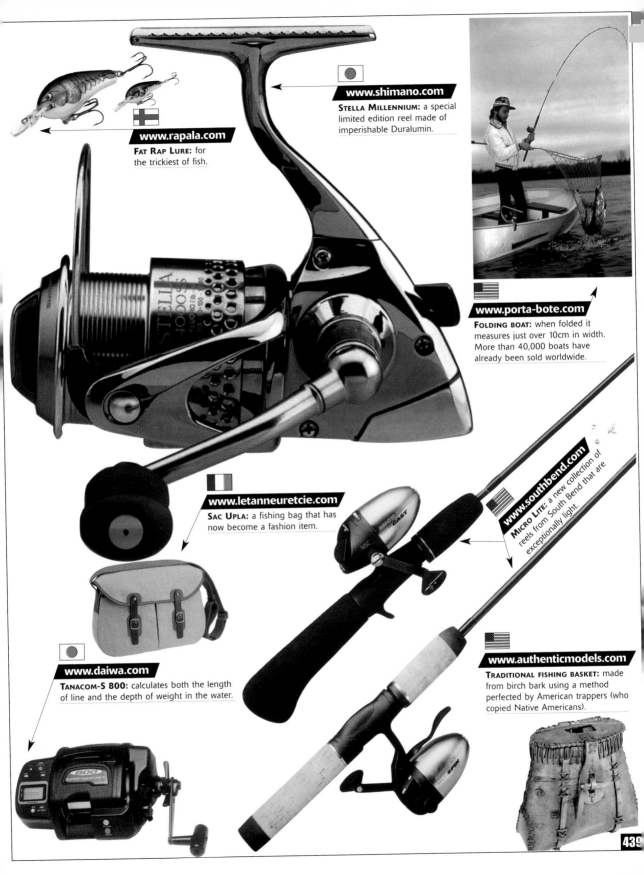

www.shimano.com

STELLA MILLENNIUM: a special limited edition reel made of imperishable Duralumin.

www.rapala.com

FAT RAP LURE: for the trickiest of fish.

www.porta-bote.com

FOLDING BOAT: when folded it measures just over 10cm in width. More than 40,000 boats have already been sold worldwide.

www.letanneuretcie.com

SAC UPLA: a fishing bag that has now become a fashion item.

www.southbend.com

MICRO LITE: a new collection of reels from South Bend that are exceptionally light.

www.daiwa.com

TANACOM-S 800: calculates both the length of line and the depth of weight in the water.

www.authenticmodels.com

TRADITIONAL FISHING BASKET: made from birch bark using a method perfected by American trappers (who copied Native Americans).

THE ART OF MAKING YOUR OWN FLIES is an ancient one. It involves assembling wool, feathers and hair around a hook in order to create lures as attractive as real insects. The flies shown here are made using these materials.

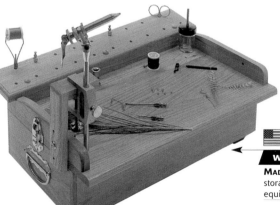

 www.petitjean.com

MP-VICE: a multi-purpose vice for hooks between 8/0 and 32 in size. All components fit into the pedestal base.

 www.orvis.com

MADISON CASE: for both storage and assembly, equipped with a vice support.

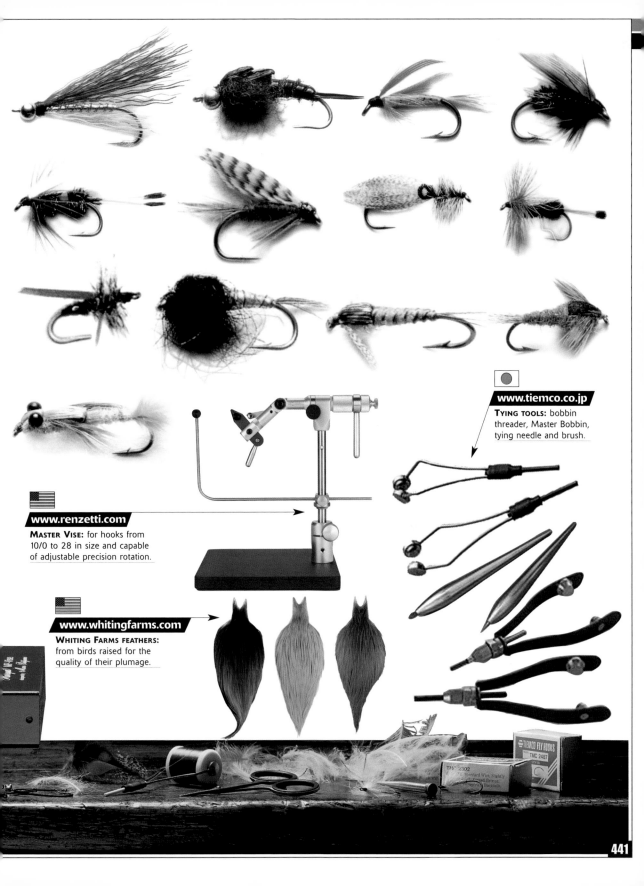

www.silvercreekindustries.com

COMMANDEAR: amplify even the smallest of sounds using this headset. You can hear an animal walking on dry leaves at a distance of 100m.

www.remingtontreestands.com

CLASSIC CLIMBER: climb up a tree, attach the perch to the trunk and wait, hidden in the foliage and comfortable on a padded seat.

www.beretta.it

WATERFOWL JACKET: a reversible camouflage jacket in which to keep warm and dry while watching for waterfowl.

www.speer-bullets.com

NITREX BULLETS: perfection in ammunition.

www.bonner-tech.com

GAME DETECTOR: detects and illuminates even the slightest change in temperature through infrared technology.

www.rocimport.com

AMMUNITION BOX: now recycled as a stylish container.

www.uslproducts.com

CAMOUFLAGE TENT: having been loaded on to a four-wheel vehicle, it then covers it entirely when erected.

www.lebeau-courally.com

SAFARI: this prestigious knife is engraved with the seal of the acclaimed Lebeau-Courally company.

www.kettner.com

BUSH-LINE KNIVES: solid and sharp hunting blades, perfectly crafted.

www.jackite.com

FLIGHT NOT FRIGHT: these high fliers are so effective that hunters use them as decoys.

www.lechameau.com

FONTENOY BOOTS: water-resistant lined leather boots for long walks in the country.

www.levysleathers.com

CARTRIDGE BELTS AND STRAPS: perfectly made in saddler's leather on the outside and soft leather on the inside.

www.kettner.com

PERCH ON PIRSCH: made of oak and leather, this stick cum seat weighs only 800g and is perfectly stable.

www.barbour.com

DEERSTALKER, SHERLOCK AND COTSWORLD: undeniably British, eternally classic.

443

www.verney-carron.com

SUPER 911 PLUME: a limited edition model engraved in gold to commemorate the 190th anniversary of Verney-Carron. It's both elegant and robust.

www.perazzi.com

EXTRA GOLD: a 28mm ornate shotgun, decorated with hunting scenes picked out in gold.

www.lebeau-courally.com

AMBASSADOR: this powerful 9.3mm express rifle is coated with platinum and elaborately inlaid with three-coloured gold foliage and game scenes on blackened steel. A work of art.

www.armureriejeannot.com

GRANGER: the result of many hours of dedicated work, each Granger gun is unique.

DRILLING PLUS 20 THERMO STABIL: this gun is 'universal' in that it can fire different calibres. It has dual-mechanism manual loading and ensures precision and flexibility.

B25 SPECIAL: Browning's famous shotgun is shown here in its 20mm version.

WEATHERBY 460 WBY MAG

MARK V LAZERMARK: perfect for elephant hunting with its 460mm cartridges.

SO 6 EESS: Beretta's great classic now has enamel highlights – in ruby red, emerald green or sapphire blue.

K95 RIFLE: light and exceptionally precise, this single shot rifle with telescopic sight is safe and easy to handle.

BIG BORE LEVEL ACTION RIFFLE 444: reminiscent of the era of Buffalo Bill, this gun is produced by one of the largest American firearms manufacturers.

THE MADAM, used for waterfowl.

www.primos.com

PRIMOS: have specialised in hunting calls for twenty-five years. They believe in reproducing rather than imitating the sounds of the wild. 'Speak the language' is their motto.

DUCK CALL

CALL ROPE

ELK CALL

ELK ANTLERS, just rub together.

www.larkinam.com

SAMBA: A Brazilian whistle in rosewood, first used as a bird call and then as an instrument.

http://pages.infinit.net/ccfa

MOCKINGBIRD: a famous bird call in copper and silver birch.

BUCK EXPERT: one of the most innovative manufacturers of hunting equipment in North America, this Canadian company has also founded a study centre for wild animals.

TURKEY CALL

GOOSE CALL

SQUIRREL CALL

WAPITI CALL

BEAR CALL

HAYDEL make quality game calls that work in all conditions.

LUXURY GOOSE CALLS

SQUIRREL CALL: adjustable, it reproduces the bark of the Bushytail or the cry of a Grey Squirrel.

ELK CALL

QUIRREL WHISTLE, with rope.

TURKEY HEN CALL: rub one against the other.

www.thundertiger.com

SUPER DECATHLON 40: a seaplane from Thundertiger, experts in radio-controlled engines.

www.aerophile.com

AEROPHILE 380: this helium balloon is anchored to a towline and can lift two people to a height of eighty metres.

www.eyefo.com

EYE-FO: this Frisbee carries a message that can be seen in the dark. Choose and change your flying greeting.

www.hammacher.com

TRAMPOLINE: for safe high jinks.

www.mayhemuk.com

LIE DETECTOR: the levels of stress are detected in the speaker's voice and light up the monitor. Watch my lips…

www.hammacher.com

BUBBLE RACERS: sold in pairs, these gently inflated giant spheres are great for all sorts of games.

www.avivasports.com

HYDRO BRONC: an inflatable sphere that tackles rapids or walks on water. Just move around inside the chamber and you're off.

www.draganfly.com

BIG BROTHER: an inflatable, helium-filled flying saucer. Radio-controlled and equipped with a micro video camera and transmitter, it's an 'eye in the sky'.

www.draganfly.com

DRAGANFLYER II: a radio-controlled helicopter with four propellers and an exposed electric motor.

www.kangoojumps.ch

KANGOO JUMPS: rebound exercise shoes that are not only fun but good for you – they reduce the impact by 60 per cent.

www.zorb.com

ZORB: this inflatable sphere is three metres in diameter and contains either one or two harnesses. Absorbs shocks but emits enjoyment.

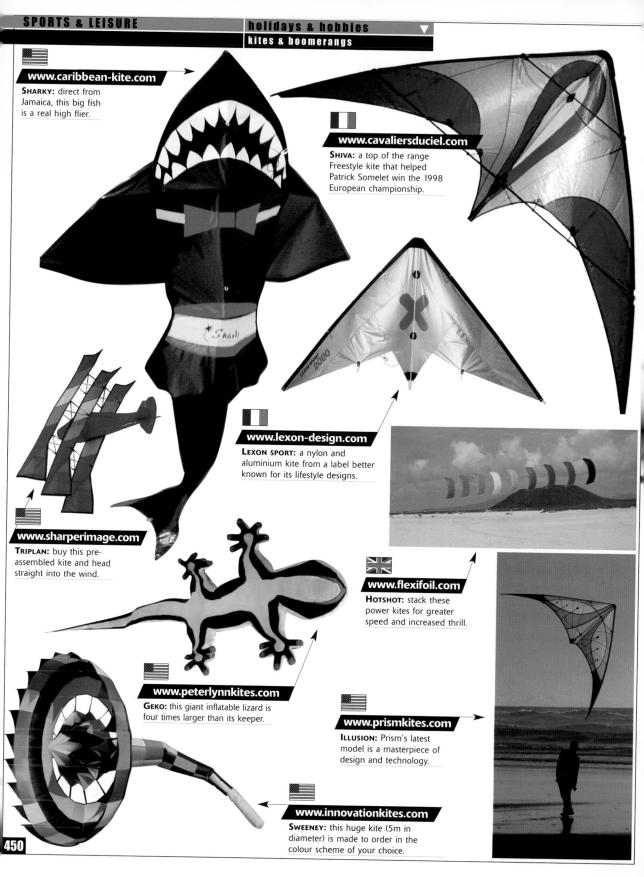

www.caribbean-kite.com

SHARKY: direct from Jamaica, this big fish is a real high flier.

www.cavaliersduciel.com

SHIVA: a top of the range Freestyle kite that helped Patrick Somelet win the 1998 European championship.

www.lexon-design.com

LEXON SPORT: a nylon and aluminium kite from a label better known for its lifestyle designs.

www.sharperimage.com

TRIPLAN: buy this pre-assembled kite and head straight into the wind.

www.peterlynnkites.com

GEKO: this giant inflatable lizard is four times larger than its keeper.

www.flexifoil.com

HOTSHOT: stack these power kites for greater speed and increased thrill.

www.prismkites.com

ILLUSION: Prism's latest model is a masterpiece of design and technology.

www.innovationkites.com

SWEENEY: this huge kite (5m in diameter) is made to order in the colour scheme of your choice.

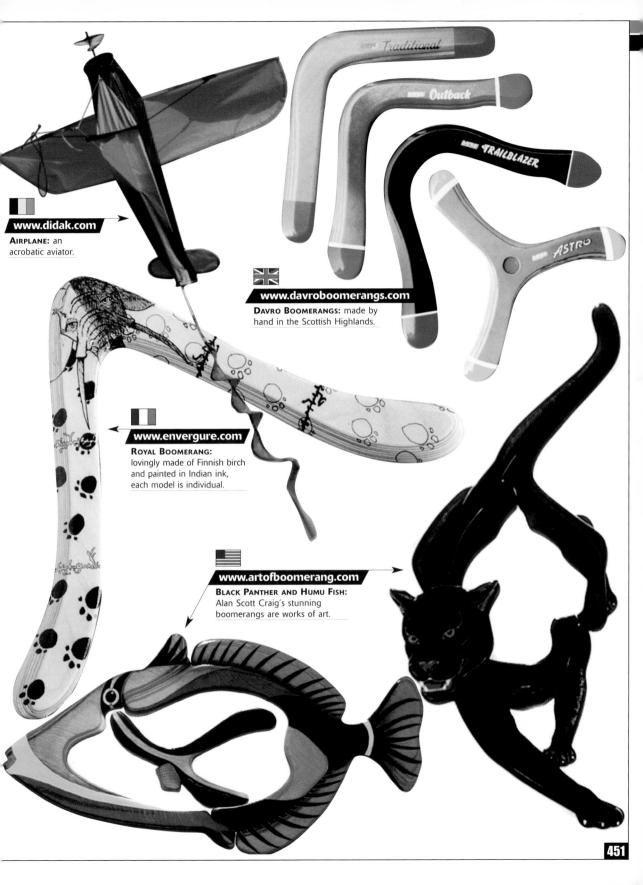

www.didak.com

AIRPLANE: an acrobatic aviator.

Traditional

Outback

TRAILBLAZER

ASTRO

www.davroboomerangs.com

DAVRO BOOMERANGS: made by hand in the Scottish Highlands.

www.envergure.com

ROYAL BOOMERANG: lovingly made of Finnish birch and painted in Indian ink, each model is individual.

www.artofboomerang.com

BLACK PANTHER AND HUMU FISH: Alan Scott Craig's stunning boomerangs are works of art.

451

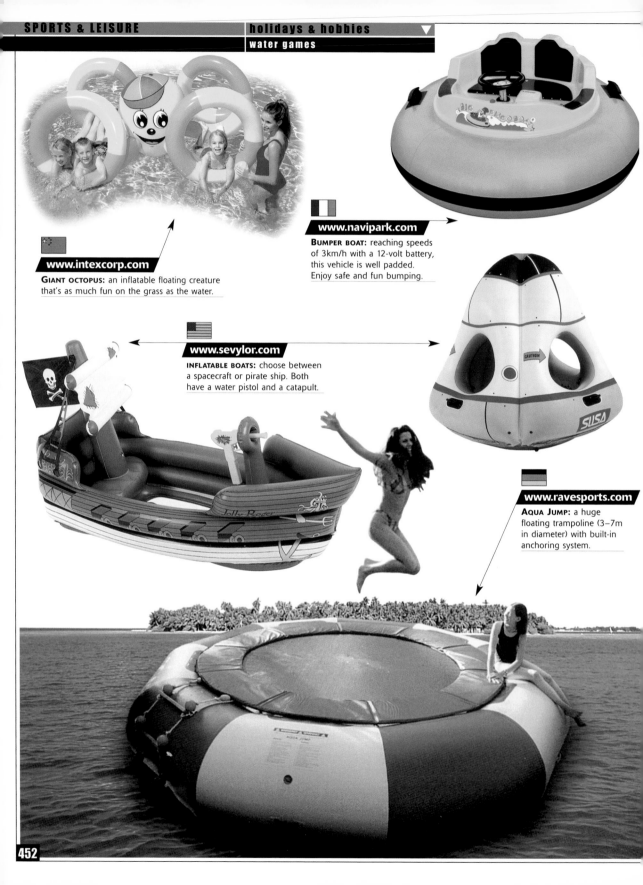

www.intexcorp.com

GIANT OCTOPUS: an inflatable floating creature that's as much fun on the grass as the water.

www.navipark.com

BUMPER BOAT: reaching speeds of 3km/h with a 12-volt battery, this vehicle is well padded. Enjoy safe and fun bumping.

www.sevylor.com

INFLATABLE BOATS: choose between a spacecraft or pirate ship. Both have a water pistol and a catapult.

www.ravesports.com

AQUA JUMP: a huge floating trampoline (3–7m in diameter) with built-in anchoring system.

452

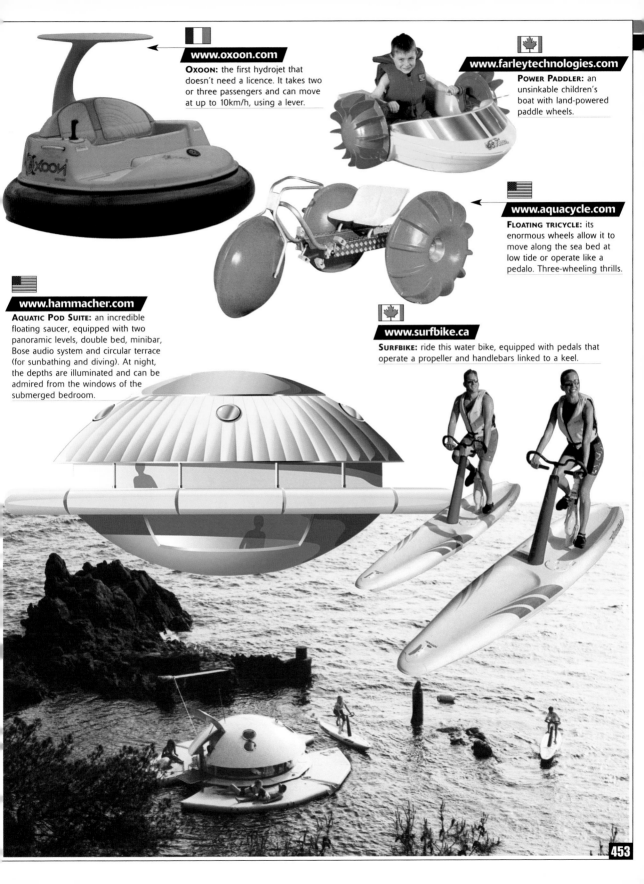

www.oxoon.com

OXOON: the first hydrojet that doesn't need a licence. It takes two or three passengers and can move at up to 10km/h, using a lever.

www.farleytechnologies.com

POWER PADDLER: an unsinkable children's boat with land-powered paddle wheels.

www.aquacycle.com

FLOATING TRICYCLE: its enormous wheels allow it to move along the sea bed at low tide or operate like a pedalo. Three-wheeling thrills.

www.hammacher.com

AQUATIC POD SUITE: an incredible floating saucer, equipped with two panoramic levels, double bed, minibar, Bose audio system and circular terrace (for sunbathing and diving). At night, the depths are illuminated and can be admired from the windows of the submerged bedroom.

www.surfbike.ca

SURFBIKE: ride this water bike, equipped with pedals that operate a propeller and handlebars linked to a keel.

www.alton-greenhouses.co.uk

MINI GREENHOUSE: an octagonal and compact structure that is perfect for smaller gardens. Designed by Alton, experts in the field since 1921.

www.dick-gmbh.de

MADE BY HAND: traditional Japanese tools, including a bamboo fan rake, planing hoe and cuttlefish-type hoe, from the German firm, Dick.

www.smithandhawken.com

GARDEN WORKBENCH: complete with a grill on which to hang tools, a drawer and an easily removable copper bowl. Re-pot with ease.

www.vivaiocorazza.com

CARALLUMA HESPERIDUM: one of the many beauties from Vivaia Corazza, a specialist in unusual plants from all over the world.

www.trade-winds.be

SHOW'R: a garden shower in summer or a boot cleaner in winter, it can be moved around easily on its platform on wheels.

www.barbadine.com

ARISTOLOCHIA RINGENS: just one of the tropical flowers from Réunion Island sold by Barbadine.

www.haws.co.uk

WATER ART: attach these copper sculptures to your pipe and enjoy an aquatic display.

www.le-potager.com

SURPRISINGLY GOOD: red corn, purple potatoes, cherry-coloured cucumber? Available as seeds or fully grown in a basket.

www.natureetdecouvertes.com

GARDEN SINK: a galvanised steel table with a tap and sink, inspired by an early 20th century model.

www.trade-winds.be

REEL BEAUTY: an elegant garden hose reel, at last.

www.chaiselongue.fr

ELEPHANT WATERING CANS: introduce the children to the delights of gardening.

www.tohubohu.fr

METAL AND RATTAN: the only watering can with a pompon.

www.hesperiden.de

TALL STORY: a watering can that holds up to seven litres. Also available in green.

www.haws.co.uk

GREEN FINGERTIPS: a traditional design in a very natural colour.

www.koziol.de

ELISE: a recyclable plastic watering can, available in nine colours.

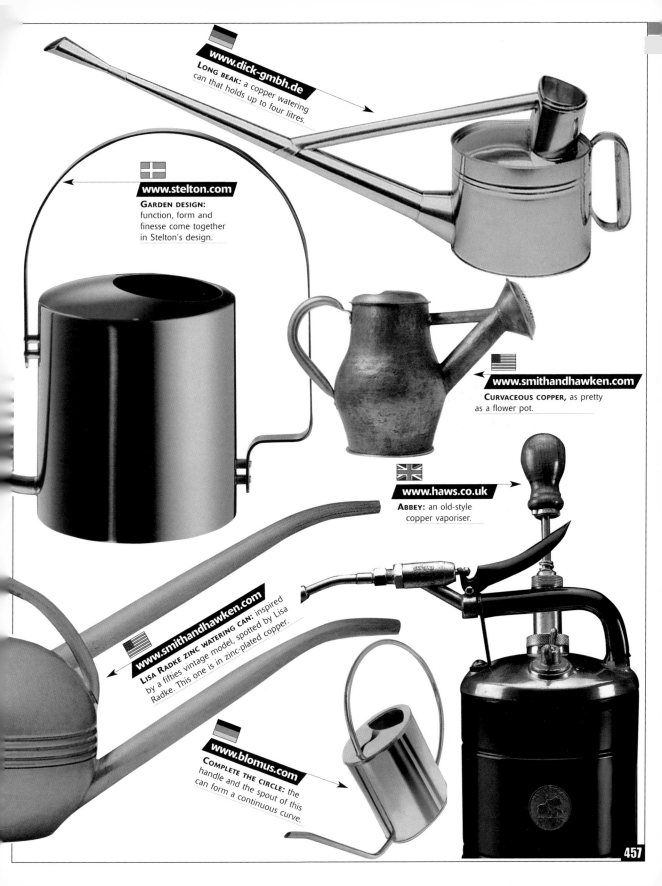

www.dick-gmbh.de

LONG BEAK: a copper watering can that holds up to four litres.

www.stelton.com

GARDEN DESIGN: function, form and finesse come together in Stelton's design.

www.smithandhawken.com

CURVACEOUS COPPER, as pretty as a flower pot.

www.haws.co.uk

ABBEY: an old-style copper vaporiser.

www.smithandhawken.com

LISA RADKE ZINC WATERING CAN: inspired by a fifties vintage model, spotted by Lisa Radke. This one is in zinc-plated copper.

www.blomus.com

COMPLETE THE CIRCLE: the handle and the spout of this can form a continuous curve.

www.conmoto.com

GARDEN CREATURES: light up your garden at night by placing candles behind these little characters.

www.hesperiden.de

GARDEN GNOMES: for kitsch rather than kitchen gardens.

www.smithandhawken.com

STEP UPON A TERRAPIN: a new cast-iron path design for muddy areas.

www.lassco.co.uk

WEATHER VANE: a collection of copper birds and animals that point the way.

www.david-goode.com

THE FERRYMAN: an impish ferryman by David Goode, the master of bronze sculptures.

www.fairweathersculpture.com

SPOUTING SCULPTURE: this bronze gargoyle behaving badly in a barrel makes an interesting water fountain.

www.trade-winds.be

PLANT-A-DRAGON: a cast-iron border that protects trees and shrubs.

www.douches-de-jardins.com

ROBINSON: stay naturally clean using a garden shower in bamboo and brass.

www.authenticsmodels.com

SEA HORSE: a painted wooden sign held aloft on a wrought-iron support.

www.topiaryinc.com

TOPIARY: ivy-coloured structures in the shape of a monkey or a Loch Ness monster. Just water regularly.

www.venini.it

TROMPE-L'ŒIL: Chinese lanterns, made of glass, provide safe and festive outdoor lighting.

www.cinna.fr

HARLEQUIN: an oil lamp in blown Pyrex glass.

www.natureetdecouvertes.com

ELECTRIC GARLAND: Chinese lantern look-alikes in rice paper make lovely lamps.

www.stoneforest.com

KASUGA: this granite lantern was sculpted by hand, according to Japanese tradition.

www.gardena.fr

POOL LIGHTS: these glass bowls appear to float on the surface of the water.

www.leonardo.de

DIEGO: plant these coloured glass lights in the soil for outdoor evening fun.

www.tectona.fr

OIL LAMPS: blown-glass lighting.

www.britelyt.com

PETROMAX: the famous traditional gas lamp design has been much copied over the years. It's still a bestseller.

www.unopiu.it

VENEXIA: a suspended glass lamp made according to the ancient mouth-blown technique known as 'Balloton'.

www.talisman-trading.co.uk

MOROCCAN LAMP: made of metal and coloured glass, this model plays with light, colour and shadows.

www.ligne-roset.tm.fr

ZEBULON: an oil lamp in aluminium and Pyrex.

www.moonlight.outdoorlighting.de

MOONLIGHT: large luminous spheres that you can place on the lawn or near your pool to provide unusual illumination.

46

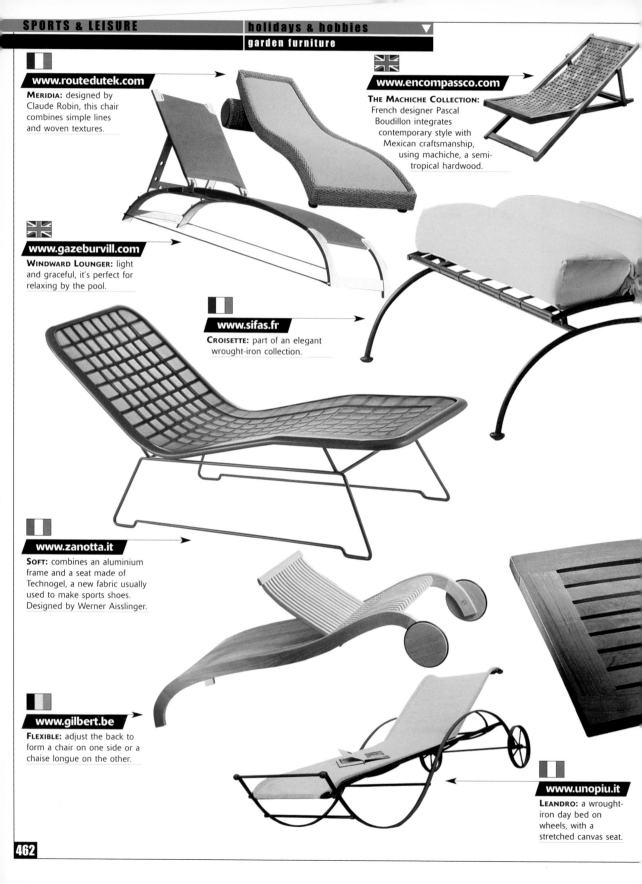

www.routedutek.com

MERIDIA: designed by Claude Robin, this chair combines simple lines and woven textures.

www.encompassco.com

THE MACHICHE COLLECTION: French designer Pascal Boudillon integrates contemporary style with Mexican craftsmanship, using machiche, a semi-tropical hardwood.

www.gazeburvill.com

WINDWARD LOUNGER: light and graceful, it's perfect for relaxing by the pool.

www.sifas.fr

CROISETTE: part of an elegant wrought-iron collection.

www.zanotta.it

SOFT: combines an aluminium frame and a seat made of Technogel, a new fabric usually used to make sports shoes. Designed by Werner Aisslinger.

www.gilbert.be

FLEXIBLE: adjust the back to form a chair on one side or a chaise longue on the other.

www.unopiu.it

LEANDRO: a wrought-iron day bed on wheels, with a stretched canvas seat.

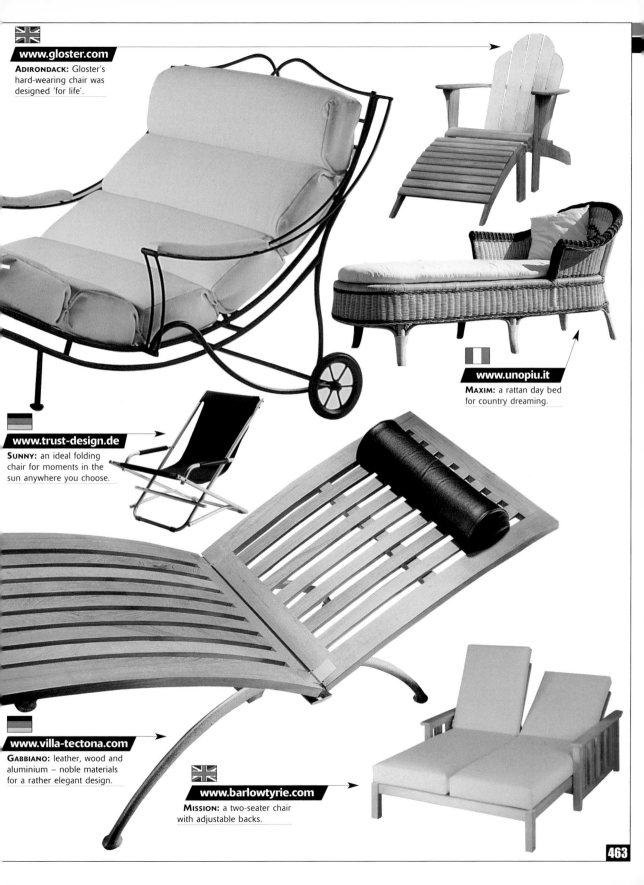

www.gloster.com

ADIRONDACK: Gloster's hard-wearing chair was designed 'for life'.

www.unopiu.it

MAXIM: a rattan day bed for country dreaming.

www.trust-design.de

SUNNY: an ideal folding chair for moments in the sun anywhere you choose.

www.villa-tectona.com

GABBIANO: leather, wood and aluminium – noble materials for a rather elegant design.

www.barlowtyrie.com

MISSION: a two-seater chair with adjustable backs.

463

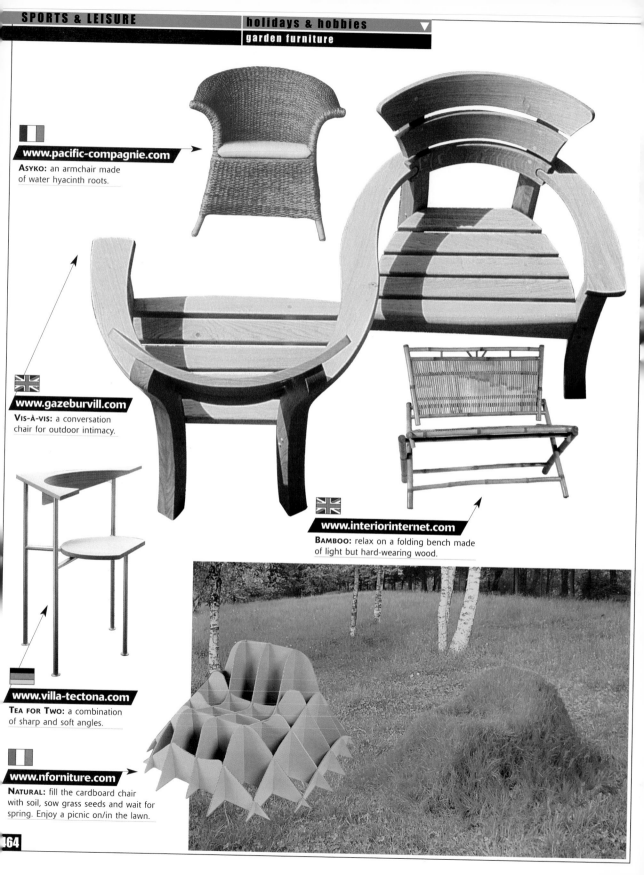

www.pacific-compagnie.com

Asyko: an armchair made of water hyacinth roots.

www.gazeburvill.com

Vis-à-vis: a conversation chair for outdoor intimacy.

www.interiorinternet.com

Bamboo: relax on a folding bench made of light but hard-wearing wood.

www.villa-tectona.com

Tea for Two: a combination of sharp and soft angles.

www.nforniture.com

Natural: fill the cardboard chair with soil, sow grass seeds and wait for spring. Enjoy a picnic on/in the lawn.

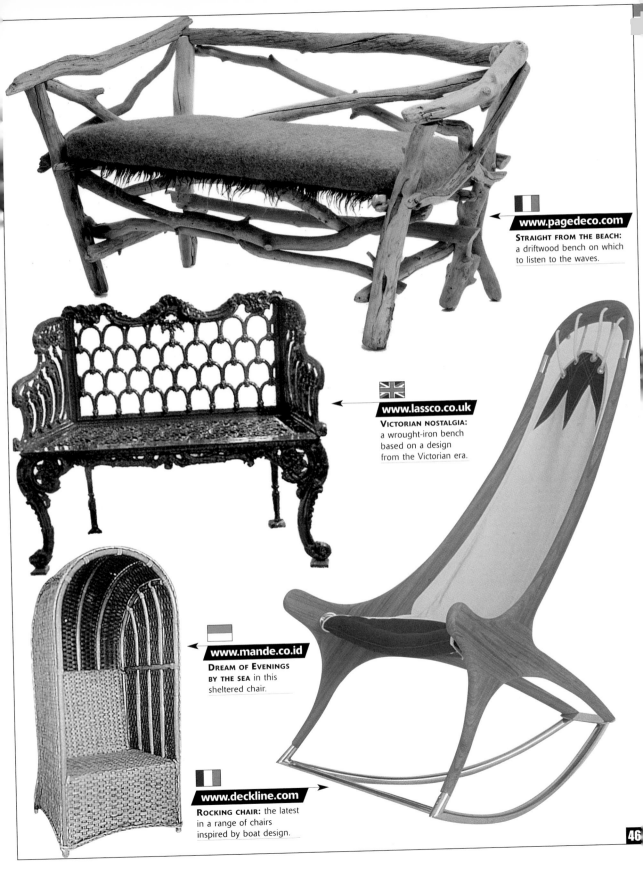

www.pagedeco.com

STRAIGHT FROM THE BEACH: a driftwood bench on which to listen to the waves.

www.lassco.co.uk

VICTORIAN NOSTALGIA: a wrought-iron bench based on a design from the Victorian era.

www.mande.co.id

DREAM OF EVENINGS BY THE SEA in this sheltered chair.

www.deckline.com

ROCKING CHAIR: the latest in a range of chairs inspired by boat design.

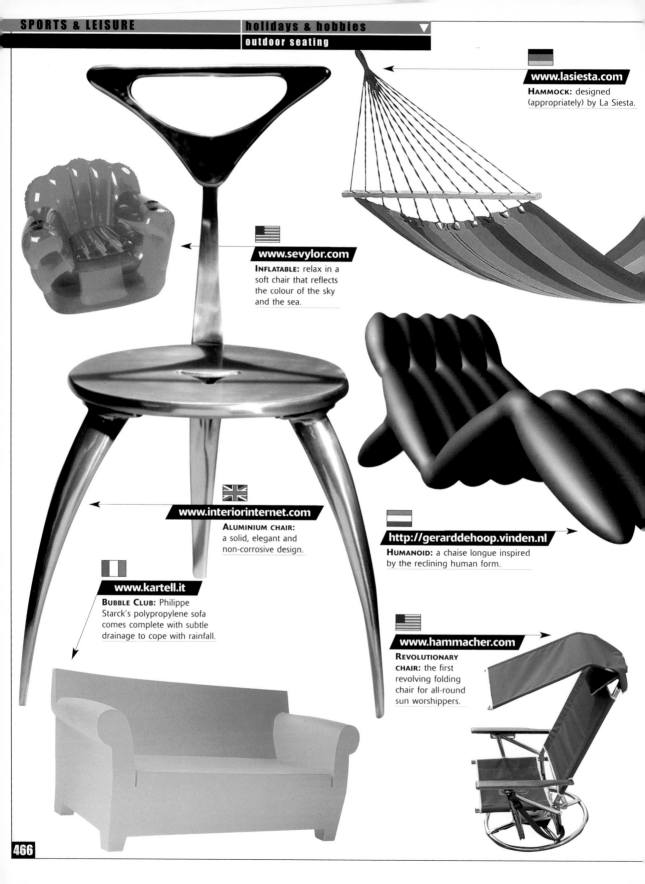

www.lasiesta.com

HAMMOCK: designed (appropriately) by La Siesta.

www.sevylor.com

INFLATABLE: relax in a soft chair that reflects the colour of the sky and the sea.

www.interiorinternet.com

ALUMINIUM CHAIR: a solid, elegant and non-corrosive design.

http://gerarddehoop.vinden.nl

HUMANOID: a chaise longue inspired by the reclining human form.

www.kartell.it

BUBBLE CLUB: Philippe Starck's polypropylene sofa comes complete with subtle drainage to cope with rainfall.

www.hammacher.com

REVOLUTIONARY CHAIR: the first revolving folding chair for all-round sun worshippers.

www.airchair.ch

AIRCHAIR: more comfortable than a hammock, this relaxing seat needs only one point of fixation. Lounge in limbo.

www.interiorinternet.com

SUNLOUNGER: this fibre-glass chaise longue has its own canopy.

www.marc-newson.com

ORGONE CHAIR: designed by Marc Newson, originally in metal, this chair is now sold in plastic version.

www.kartell.it

GNOMES: garden gnomes make useful indoor and outdoor stools or tables. Hand-painted in plastic, these models were originally commissioned from Philippe Starck for the St Martin's Lane Hotel in London.

www.nipooria.com

NIPOORI: when open it's a barbecue, but when closed it's a tandoori oven in which to prepare Indian cuisine.

www.kamado.com

KAMADO: all the advantages of an electric barbecue inside a traditional ceramic oven.

www.conmoto.com

MONO: a versatile design with an easily removable grill over a table equipped with candle holders. Stylish, practical and atmospheric.

www.heibi-metall.de

SOLINO: a suspended grill that is also a stylish piece of garden sculpture.

www.ferraboli.it

MORENO: just the right size for barbecued kebabs.

www.ferraboli.it

CAPANNA: this outdoor cooker is light and easy to manage.

www.conmoto.com

GRILL WOK: now you can enjoy the delights of wok cooking, even in your garden.

www.muji.co.jp

FIELD COOKER: boils, heats, smokes, grills, fries and cooks – all outside. You just provide the food, it will do the rest.

www.conmoto.com

MATTEN GRILL: created by Günter Matten, a specialist in oven design, as this stylish piece of equipment displays so effectively.

www.viceversashop.com

BARBECUE EASY: a spherical design that moves around the garden easily.

www.iguanauk.co.uk

MORDELLO: a traditional Mexican oven, based on a 16th-century design.

www.weber.com

WEBER: the luxury version of the classic American barbecue design, complete with attached table.

469

www.unopiu.it

PING-PONG PARTY: take a table-tennis table and an octagonal one, both collapsible, join together and invite twenty friends over.

www.picnicatascot.com

LUXURY PICNIC: the perfect rucksack for a gourmet picnic.

www.tefal.fr

SEAFOOD FONDU: the compartment at the top keeps the food warm while six diners enjoy their own bowls with handles for the broth.

www.peartreehouse.com

DRINKDECK: made to measure, high-altitude aperitifs, thanks to this treehouse designer.

www.streetrodproductions.com

BEVERAGE KART: a small vehicle with refrigerated bar at its rear.

www.unopiu.it

ALADDIN: an enormous wrought-iron pavilion based on a 19th-century Tuscan design. This model is draped in Indian fabric.

http://chez.com/agnespetit

TUSSIL AND CATYLI: two papier-mâché tablemats in the shape of leaves. Designed by Agnès Petit and sold with transparent plates.

www.moulinex.fr

MEXICAN DINNER: six hotplates for the tortillas, six warming areas for the tacos and a cooking pot in the middle. Tuck in.

www.barbecook.com

INFRÀ: keep perfectly warm outside with this infrared terrace heater. Efficient and stylish outdoor warmth for chilly nights.

http://obelix.dorea.co.za/tnt

BushDozer: a safari tent made to order in South Africa and adapted to fit four-wheel drive vehicles and trailers.

www.growtech.com.hk

Anti-mosquito watch: it emits a soft sound similar to that of the dragonfly to keep the mozzies away.

www.coleman.com

Portable hearth: easy to dismantle and carry, the fire is an efficient and safe way to keep warm outdoors.

www.lanternnet.com

Radio Lantern: the famous Dietz lamp has been on the market since 1840. This model is equipped with a generator operated by the heat of the flame and is capable of producing the power needed to make a radio work.

www.stearnsinc.com

Pharao: a light weight inflatable mattress with a multi-chamber design that prevents you rolling off.

www.gsioutdoors.com

Coffee in the wild: a stylish percolator and one-cup espresso machine for those who can't live without their real coffee.

www.hennessyhammock.com

HENNESSY HAMMOCK: both bed and shelter, this light hammock comes with mosquito net and hangs between two trees.

www.pahaque.com

TEPEE: a shower tent that's easy to put up and carry around. No excuse to be dirty!

www.coleman.com

CONVERTIBLE: an inflatable sofa bed for luxury camping under the stars.

www.exdeco.de

CAMPING CONDIMENTS: these salt and pepper shakers light up when twisted. Perfect for picnics after dark.

www.light-my-fire.com

MAYA STICKS: made of 80 per cent resin, these Guatamalan sticks light fires and barbecues the natural way.

www.sunoven.com

SOLAR OVEN: through its system of reflectors, it reaches 200°C and cooks like a traditional oven. No bigger than a suitcase.

www.polyconcept.com

THREE IN ONE: radio, fan and torch.

www.braintan.com

TIPI: made of buffalo leather tanned by hand, oiled, smoked and sewn – according to the old tradition.

www.sogknives.com

TOOLCLIP: a flexible tool for all situations.

www.cascadedesigns.com

PACKTOWL: this is the only towel you need. Its hyper-absorbent and can be packed away immediately after use.

www.salomonsports.com

X-AVENTURE FOOTWEAR: the Advance Chassis Technology absorbs shock and reinforces balance on challenging terrain, even steeply inclined.

www.solarslns.com

AQUA CONE: an ingenious system for making pure water out of undrinkable water, through a process of solar-powered condensation and filtration.

www.lowepro.com

PHOTO TREKKER: the photographer's rucksack.

www.granitegear.com

EXPEDITION DOG PACK: twin rucksacks for dogs. Canine comfort and carriage.

www.elite-it.com

CIOI KERATHERM: a thermos flask with an exclusive insulation system, complete with a thermometer that indicates the internal temperature.

www.orgear.com

Anti-mosquito hat: the stainless steel mesh keeps the insects out without disrupting your view.

www.walrusgear.com

Bug Hut: sleep well under the stars in this anti-mosquito tent.

www.columbia.com

Treeker: undo the zip and your trousers become shorts.

www.camelbak.com

CamelBack: keep well hydrated with this ingenious rucksack.

www.shuttlebike.it

Shuttle-Bike: a simple rucksack for cyclists that contains inflatable tubes for crossing water. Perfect water wheels for all bikes.

www.fjallraven.se

Sydney Cap: keep the sun and rain off your neck with this protective cap.

www.addex-design.com

SURPRISES: a pocket torch with tool box.

www.flexbar.com

BEND-A-LIGHT: a high-intensity flexible lamp that's perfect for those difficult nooks and crannies.

www.streamlight.com

STYLUS 2: a pocket torch in the form of a pen, with a high-intensity diode that lasts 100,000 hours.

www.lewisnclark.com

TRAVEL BOOK LIGHT: hook this small lamp on the page and you can read anywhere, anytime.

www.sapphirelight.co.uk

ASP MIRAGE: this key ring torch emits a soft blue beam with a 180-degree viewing radius visible for 1.5km and available in several colours, including gold.

www.windupradio.com

FREEPLAY: a wind-up flashlight that stores power in a special spring. Wind it up, release the power and let there be light.

www.techass.com

ETERNA LIGHT: emits light visible from a distance of several kilometres for a duration of 700 hours.

STEELMAN. Bend-A-Light Pro

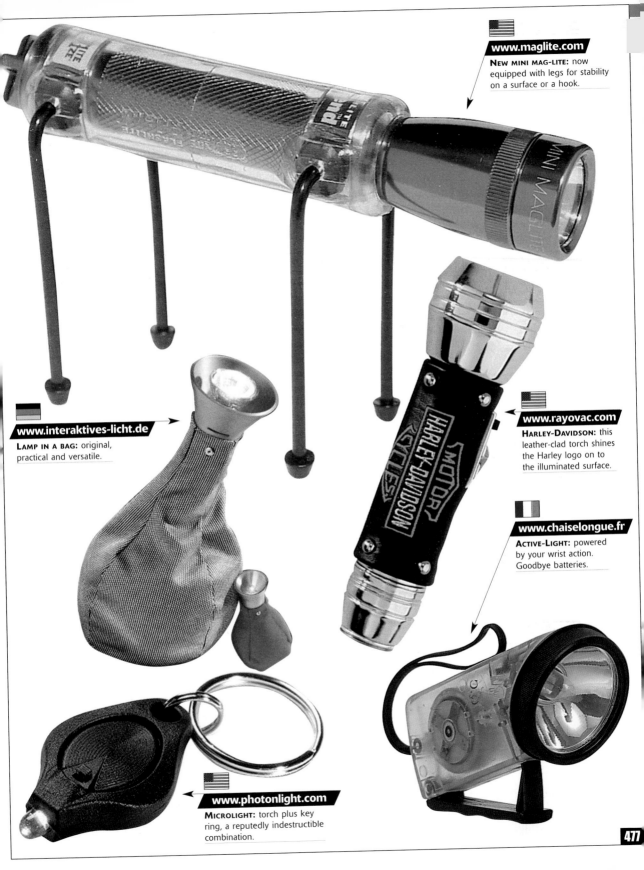

www.maglite.com

NEW MINI MAG-LITE: now equipped with legs for stability on a surface or a hook.

www.interaktives-licht.de

LAMP IN A BAG: original, practical and versatile.

www.rayovac.com

HARLEY-DAVIDSON: this leather-clad torch shines the Harley logo on to the illuminated surface.

www.chaiselongue.fr

ACTIVE-LIGHT: powered by your wrist action. Goodbye batteries.

www.photonlight.com

MICROLIGHT: torch plus key ring, a reputedly indestructible combination.

477

www.victorinox.com

CyberTool 34: a new version of the famous knife, manufactured in Switzerland since 1884. It has thirty-four functions, including a screwdriver for computers.

www.sergeamorusoparis.com

By special appointment: designed by Serge Amoruso, well versed in luxury accessories.

www.cote-a-cote.com

Laguiole: the famous knife used traditionally by shepherds in France's Aveyron region. This is the luxury version.

www.sogknives.com

Sculptura: a folding knife, complete with belt clip.

www.ardi.fr

Kipli: a small knife in polished aluminium that folds out and in again. Small, stylish, safe.

www.knives.net

Ulu: a hand engraved knife used by Alaskan women, on a carbon wood stand.

www.dick-gmbh.de

Damask lapp knives: a rust-proof 'Damascus' steel blade with Nordic silver birch and reindeer horn handle.

www.outdoor-edge.com

COSMO: as beautiful as it is useful, this knife has three blade positions and was designed by Ray Appleton.

www.crkt.com

BEAR CLAW: a light and useful cutting tool, prized by fishermen and independent women.

www.opinel.com

OPINEL: the timeless pocket knife, invented by the mountain dwellers of Savoy over a hundred years ago and still going strong.

www.kershawknives.com

BOA 1580: use just one hand to operate this knife, with its index trigger-assisted opening mechanism.

www.benchmade.com

TK-1: light and easy to carry. Sharp design.

www.leatherman.com

THE WAVE: the next generation of multi-purpose tools with four easy-to-access exterior locking blades, all guaranteed for twenty-five years.

www.pumaknives.de

LIMITED EDITION: a gold-plated steel and ebony knife produced by Puma. Only 230 were made to celebrate the company's 230th anniversary.

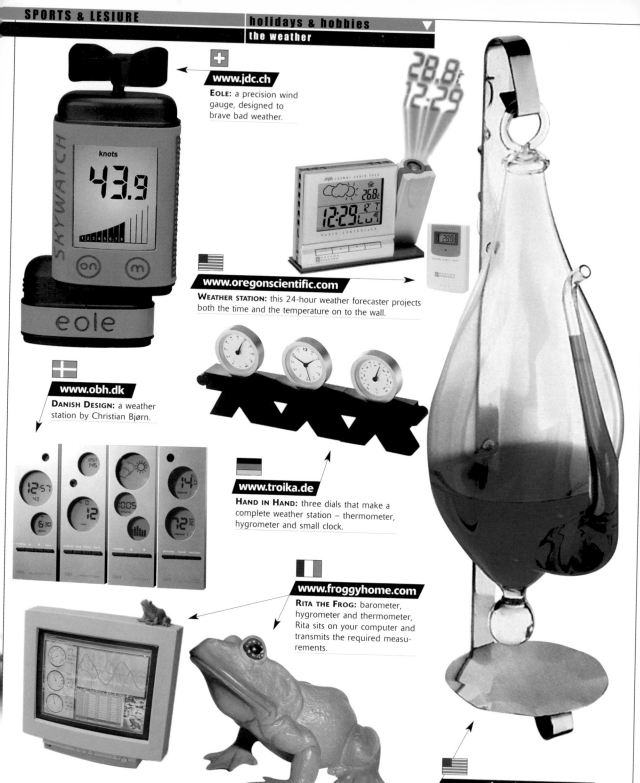

www.jdc.ch

EOLE: a precision wind gauge, designed to brave bad weather.

www.oregonscientific.com

WEATHER STATION: this 24-hour weather forecaster projects both the time and the temperature on to the wall.

www.obh.dk

DANISH DESIGN: a weather station by Christian Bjørn.

www.troika.de

HAND IN HAND: three dials that make a complete weather station – thermometer, hygrometer and small clock.

www.froggyhome.com

RITA THE FROG: barometer, hygrometer and thermometer, Rita sits on your computer and transmits the required measurements.

www.authenticmodels.com

WATER BAROMETER: a replica of a 17th-century model, this machine indicates atmospheric pressure through changes in the volume of coloured water.

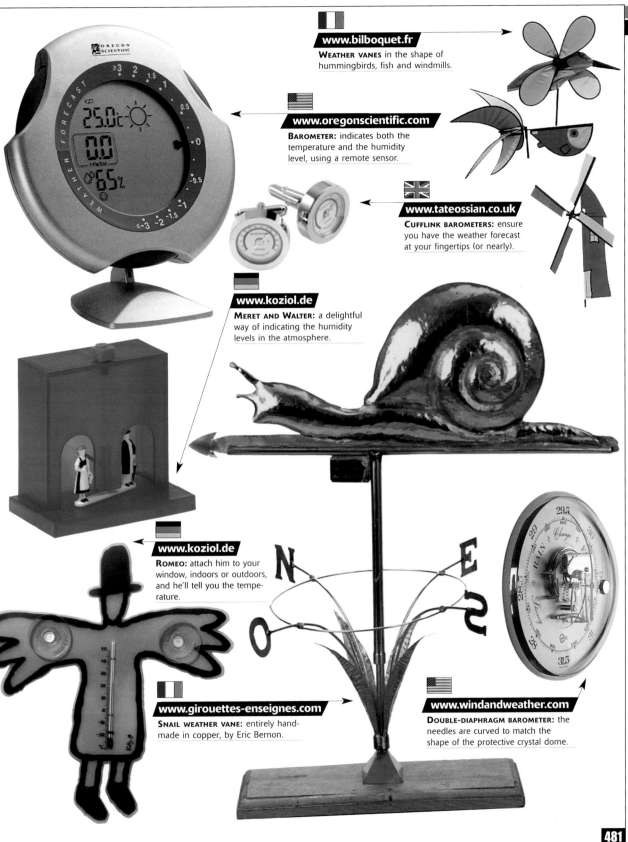

www.bilboquet.fr
WEATHER VANES in the shape of
hummingbirds, fish and windmills.

www.oregonscientific.com
BAROMETER: indicates both the
temperature and the humidity
level, using a remote sensor.

www.tateossian.co.uk
CUFFLINK BAROMETERS: ensure
you have the weather forecast
at your fingertips (or nearly).

www.koziol.de
MERET AND WALTER: a delightful
way of indicating the humidity
levels in the atmosphere.

www.koziol.de
ROMEO: attach him to your
window, indoors or outdoors,
and he'll tell you the temperature.

www.girouettes-enseignes.com
SNAIL WEATHER VANE: entirely handmade in copper, by Eric Bernon.

www.windandweather.com
DOUBLE-DIAPHRAGM BAROMETER: the
needles are curved to match the
shape of the protective crystal dome.

www.zeiss.com

ZEISS DESIGN: a mini-telescope, weighing only 88g, for professional or general use, equipped with a tenfold magnifying power.

www.pentax.com

JUPITER BINOCULARS: compact ergonomic binoculars with Porro-prism design and extra stability.

www.canon.com

5x50 IS: all-weather binoculars, complete with stabiliser.

www.nightowloptics.com

NOGT1 GOGGLES: equipped with an integrated infrared illuminator and extremely close-up focussing range, these glasses are worn like a headband and permit hands-free vision in total darkness.

www.spyzone.com

PREDATOR 6 x: night binoculars with enlarger, infrared technology and a forty-hour charge. You can use it hands free, too.

www.steiner.netzanstalt.de

ADMIRAL GOLD 7 x 50: these binoculars enable you to see even in the most difficult conditions. Water-resistant to 5m and guaranteed to demist in temperatures between −40°C and +80°C, they have an in-built compass with integrated reticle for precise takings of bearings.

www.bushnell.com

NIGHT VISION: 26 x 1020 binoculars allow exceptionally comfortable night vision due to their infrared system and headset.

www.nikon.com

6X15M CF: multi-coated optics make these binoculars powerful and razor-sharp.

www.astronomie-paralux.com

OPERA GLASSES: stylish opera and theatre goers help you see the programme and the actors more clearly.

www.lexon-design.com

LEXON LL67: folding travel binoculars in aluminium.

www.swarovksioptik.com

LASER RF1 RANGE-FINDER: extreme precision, robust design, practical excellence.

www.bird-vu.com

OBSERVATION PLATFORM: this bird feeder has a hidden video camera with microphone that transmits colour images plus sound on to a TV screen.

www.antcorp.com

AMT NIGHT STORM: enjoy water-resistant monocular night vision with in-built infrared illuminator and residual light magnifier.

www.leica.com

TELEVID: watch every detail of nature from dawn to dusk with Leica's monocular.

www.aspsky.org

MINI TELESCOPE: made of copper and capable of 3x magnification, it's as small as a key ring.

www.bushnell.com

VOYAGER SUPER COMPACT: easy to carry with its own strap, this telescope has its own tripod.

www.starlab.com

SUNSPOTTER: track sunspots safely. The light passes through a 62mm lens and is reflected on a white screen via a system of mirrors.

www.medas.fr

PERL MILKY WAY 14 x 100: these luminous binoculars are noted for their lens diameter and are for use on land and in the skies.

www.meade.com

ETX TELESCOPE: the world's biggest seller, its success is due to its small format, flexibility, precision and price.

www.vixen.co.jp

ALTUX: a new heavy-duty equatorial mount designed to load large aperture telescopes, equipped with built-in motors. It's controlled by the computerised Skysensor 2000-PC.

www.parksoptical.com

SUPERIOR SERIES TELESCOPE: a high-performance precision machine designed for professionals and amateurs.

www.jimsmobile.com

NEWTON NGT 18: a new generation of telescopes reserved, until now, for use in observatories. Easy to use, even for novices.

www.celestron.com

NEXTAR 5: compact and easy to use, this telescope has a backlit computer hand control for Go-To tracking with a memory for over 18,000 celestial objects.

www.astrolide-led.com

ASTRONOMY LAMP: a constant red light is emitted by the LED. Remember it takes thirty minutes for your eyes to get used to darkness effectively.

www.edmundscientific.com

STARGLOBE: identify forty-two stars and seventy constellations by aligning time, date and latitude.

www.vixen.co.jp

VIXEN GPE 150-170: a semi-professional telescope with remarkable optical quality. Try a spot of astrophotography.

www.starchair.com

SKY ROVER STAR CHAIR: this chair comes complete with astronomic binoculars. Adjust their position with an electric remote control.

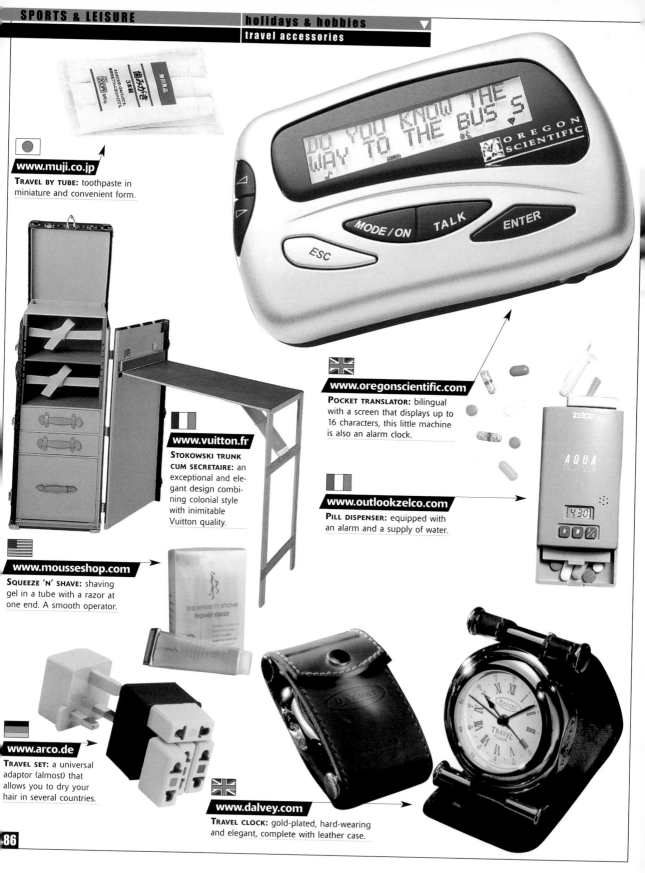

www.muji.co.jp

TRAVEL BY TUBE: toothpaste in miniature and convenient form.

www.vuitton.fr

STOKOWSKI TRUNK CUM SECRETAIRE: an exceptional and elegant design combining colonial style with inimitable Vuitton quality.

www.mousseshop.com

SQUEEZE 'N' SHAVE: shaving gel in a tube with a razor at one end. A smooth operator.

www.arco.de

TRAVEL SET: a universal adaptor (almost) that allows you to dry your hair in several countries.

www.oregonscientific.com

POCKET TRANSLATOR: bilingual with a screen that displays up to 16 characters, this little machine is also an alarm clock.

www.outlookzelco.com

PILL DISPENSER: equipped with an alarm and a supply of water.

www.dalvey.com

TRAVEL CLOCK: gold-plated, hard-wearing and elegant, complete with leather case.

🇬🇧 **www.efx.co.uk**

Lok: an anti-theft lock with extendable cord for secure closure.

➕ **www.ikepod.com**

Manatee: a chronometer that knows what time it is wherever you are. An expert time traveller.

🇬🇧 **www.efx.co.uk**

Shaving kit: razor and aftershave in an aluminium case. Compact chic.

www.silva.se

No distance too far: two instruments, one traditional and one electronic, that calculate map distances in kilometres.

🇺🇸 **www.hammacher.com**

Travel in style: the original bureau was commissioned by a wealthy 19th-century Italian, a keen writer and traveller. Luxury in leather, complete with ten drawers and a seat.

BURJ AL ARAB: this hotel in Dubai is the most luxurious in the world. Its 321m tower was built on an artificial island, 280m from the beach. There are no rooms, but 202 suites instead, each 170m x 780m in size and designed as a duplex, equipped with the latest audio and visual technology. Each one is individual in design. You are met at the airport by a helicopter that lands on top of the tower and are then greeted by the 32m-high waterfalls that adorn the foyer. Choose between four restaurants, one perched in an extension 200m above the sea and the other totally submerged. Enjoy!

www.treehousesofhawaii.com

SANYA NANSHAN TREEHOUSE RESORT: there are four treehouses on Hainan Island, south of China. In one direction all you can see is sea and white sand and in the other a 2,000-hectare park dotted with Buddhist temples and botanic gardens. Definitely at the high end of the market.

www.icehotel.com

THE ICE HOTEL: 3,000 tonnes of ice and 30,000 cubic metres of snow have been used each November for the past ten years to construct this Swedish hotel during the endless night season. The snow beds are covered in reindeer skin, and you'll drink your champagne from glasses sculpted out of ice. The temperature indoors is similar to that of an igloo, −7°C when its −40°C outside. In May the hotel melts back into the river.

www.vladi.de

ISLAND FOR SALE: White Bay Cay in the Bahamas is a 12-hectare private island. Covered in forest, it has two pools in the centre and is fringed by beaches with pure white sand. It's one of the many islands on offer from Vladi, a German real estate company specialising in dream locations for sale.

Index

This index contains the key objects and products that appear in The Dream Catalog. *It does not include specific companies or names of models. General topic headings appear in italics, and page references relevant to these subject areas also appear in italics under individual entries.*

Credits

Please note that the publishers cannot guarantee or be responsible for the availability of all the products featured in *The Dream Catalog*. The Internet is a very fast-moving form of communication, and addresses, like products, can change. Should you have difficulty finding a website, go onto a search engine and type in the name of the label, manufacturer, designer or product and you should be successful. The website addresses included in our selection refer to the manufacturers for the most part, and it is not always possible to buy products on-line from these sites. However, you can usually contact them for a list of outlets. In some cases, we have supplied an email address if the relevant website does not yet exist.

If you are a manufacturer of a dream product not featured in the book, please email us for selection in the next edition.

Product photographs were supplied by the companies themselves, but, in some instances, requests were made for the photographer to be credited:

For Alsi Design, pp.42 & 47: Le Temps des Photos
For Barbara Butler, p.432: Teena Albert
For Buggy Rollin, p.383: Christophe Lebedinsky
For C. Quoi, pp.150, 161, 196, 201: Sylvain Thomas
For Carré Bleu, p.246: Claude Fougeirol
For Heavy Duty, p.81: L J Schneider
For Jack Gomme, p.270: Didier Truffaut
For Lolita Pompadour, p.273: Loïc Guinebault
For MOMA, p.429: Nigel Barker
For Navipark, p.452: Pierre Autef
For Oz Jewel, p.266: Teemu Töyrylä
For Prismkite, p.450: Ron Kramer
For SeaBird, p.347: Nigel Pert
For Shu Uemura, pp.275 & 280: Bertrand Bouet-Willaumez
For Sunseeker, p.352: Sunseeker International

First published in the United Kingdom in 2001 by Cassell & Co.
Produced by COPYRIGHT for Editions Hachette, based on an idea by Pierre Marchand and Hervé Tardy.
English Translation © Cassell & Co. 2001

Translated by Jane Moseley
Proofread by Nikki Sims

Editorial: Raphaele Vidaling (email: vidaling@copyright.fr) with the assistance of Marlene Margui, Charlotte Matyja, Caroline Moreau, Amélie Piron and Émilie Vignon.

The editor would like to thank the following for their help in producing *The Dream Catalog*:
Betty Boyer, Patrick Benoitton, Jean Berton, Camille-Frédérique Blind, Marie Lorrain, Servane Olry, Anne-Laure Oulion-Savelli, Mira Popovic, Emilie Rouffiat, Florence Sortelle, Fabrice Tardy, Valentine Vernaz, Patrice Vogel and Stéphanie Zweifel.

Design Concept: Philippe Marchand
Designed by: Jeanne Pothier, with the assistance of Pierre Gourdé